M000084981

LIFE ON A ROCK

A Bahamas Out-Island Adventure

K. A. Albury

Cover: painting by Guy Paquet

Inside Photos: Author's collection, or as noted.

Copyright © 2008 K. A. Albury
All rights reserved.

ISBN: 1-4392-1006-3
ISBN-13: 9781439210062
Library of Congress Control Number: 2008908145

Visit www.amazon.com to order additional copies.

To

Kitty who encouraged me all the way

and

Peter who had the patience of Job.

For Miller

∽✺∽

THE BEGINNING

With the windows open and the plantation shutters folded back, the night breeze gently caressed me as it passed through the room. In the distant quiet of the night, I could hear the breakers as they rolled onto the beach. As I lay on the cool sheets, I reached for Peter's hand. In his sleep, I gently felt his fingers curve around mine.

Relocating from the city had proved to be traumatic. I always considered myself to be a resilient person, able to adjust to unusual situations and to bounce up to new challenges. Moving should not have been difficult, but it always was.

I was born in Nassau, Bahamas on the third anniversary of the United States' entry into World War II. My mom, a Bahamian, wanted to be with her family when I was born, while my dad, a U.S. Navy Lieutenant Commander, was serving in the Philippines at the time. Since my birth, our family had transferred on several occasions when I was young, and eventually, after sixteen years of living stateside, we returned to Nassau. I knew all about being uprooted.

But, this move to a five hundred-acre island in the middle of Exuma Sound surprised even me. It was in the summer of 1992 when my husband, Peter, and I were ripe to make a major change in our lives. He had not been happy in his job with the Bahamas Government; And, although I loved my own work in the investments field, my company was in the midst of a major acquisition by a large firm in California. When the dust settled, I suspected my position would be redundant. Our two girls, Kelly and Victoria, were grown, so our responsibilities had lightened considerably. Life had become a day-after-day affair. We were in a rut.

I remember the spark in Peter's eyes when he saw the ad in the local paper.

"Hey, look at this," he said that fateful morning over breakfast. He spread the newspaper over the kitchen counter and leaned his six-foot-one frame onto his elbows over the tiny print. "Highborne Cay wants a new couple to manage the island." He glanced out of the window with a far-away look before his eyes returned to the newspaper.

Peter and I always loved the islands. Through the years, we used to look forward to a weekend in our boat with our two kids and to find a beach twenty or thirty miles away where we could anchor for a night or two. We had no fancy boat, no real galley, no dinette, and only two tiny bunks. But we would pack a cooler, a little propane stove and enough food to spend the weekend near one of our favorite spots, Highborne Cay (pronounced 'key' in the islands) which was located in the Central Bahamas.

"Geezus, wouldn't that be a unusual place to work." I said. Once again, I thought about my job that was coming to an end shortly. "So, should we talk about it?"

We knew there was a store, some guest houses and, of course, a marina on the island; But, it was isolated, about a two-hour run across open waters from Nassau.

"Right now, Kate," he paused, looking up, "I'd like to do anything except what I'm doing now." He glanced out the window again. "I know *I* could do a job like that....but, could you?" He turned, waiting for some type of response from me.

"I dunno," I replied, clearing off the breakfast dishes. "It's pretty archaic. Remember when we were there on the boat last Easter holiday? They've only got generators for power, and water's a real luxury. That's like living fifty years ago, Peter." I poured another cup of coffee. "We'd have to leave Nassau—our friends—family. I dunno." I reached over for the scissors, and cut out the ad. Pulling the scotch tape from the kitchen drawer, I stuck the little piece of paper on the frig, typical of me with my excessive organizational skills. (Although that particular trait had landed me some of the top assignments throughout my working career, it often drove Peter crazy.) "But," I added, "it could be interesting....maybe a real challenge."

Over the next several days, every time I went to the frig, the ad was staring me in the face. Could we do it? Were we too soft to take such a job? Were we too pampered, living with all our conveniences?

We batted the idea around for another week. "What have we got to lose by applying?" Peter finally said.

"Yeah," I answered, "but I don't want to commit until we really think this through."

Yet, something in the far reaches of my mind kept nagging at me: Do it while you can! My cancer several years earlier had been a hard fight; by the time the doctors discovered the tumor, the cancer had spread. Through my year of chemotherapy that followed surgery, I learned a very important principle: you must learn to accept life's challenges before you can live life every day to the fullest. Cancer had given me a new perspective.

A few days later, I backed Peter's decision to give Highborne a shot. Remembering the good times of our weekend jaunts was, no doubt, influential in our decision. Peter picked up the phone and made an initial call to the Pennsylvania number listed in the ad. The formal application was created later that evening on our computer after a few glasses of wine and some laughs about how much fun it would be if we could retire to a tropical island and get paid as well.

When we were invited for an interview, I was surprised. When we were hired, I was stunned. Neither Peter nor I had any experience in island management. Now we had to revisit the subject in earnest. We knew our whole comfort zone would be in jeopardy. We would be leaving Nassau where our families' roots ran deep.

When we finally decided to move forward with acceptance, our friends were shocked. "Are you crazy?" asked one of them. "You'll be bored to death there, and you guys don't have a clue about that kind of job!" She was right, of course, and the thought of such a big change was frightening; Yet, it was also strangely refreshing. It would certainly solve Peter's dilemma with his job, and give us both a fresh start at something totally new. Together, we decided to accept.

Our daughters, Kelly and Victoria, were dubious, but they tried to be encouraging. "Nice job, Pa. You gonna hang in the hammock all day?" said Victoria with her usual brightness. Victoria lived in Nassau in an apartment not too far from us. She was through college and had entered the real estate field. She was now on her own.

Kelly, the elder and more savvy of the two, was reserved. She had been living in Florida for the past couple of years and was more worldly than her younger sister. "Are you sure about this, Mum? It's out in the boondocks." (She talked as if we were going into outer space.) "Out there, you have to be a fix-it person. Pa is definitely not that." I had to agree with her. Peter had other talents, but repairing things wasn't one of them.

For many people, a thirty-five mile separation is as easy as commuting to work in the morning. For us, the thirty-five miles by boat over the open ocean would be anything but easy. The girls were right. Now we'd seldom have an opportunity to see them. I glanced at my favorite family photo that rested on the table near the door. We were a close family, and the move would be bittersweet. But the thought of doing such an out-of-the-ordinary job gave us the incentive and the drive to press forward.

Peter was able to leave Nassau a month before me. Rupert and Patsy, the present island managers, were due to finish their tour of duty on October 1st. Peter needed to acclimate himself with the people and procedures of Highborne Cay as soon as possible, so the training process had to begin right away to meet that deadline. His schedule was tight.

It seemed as though he was gone in a flash. He left me with a hug and a kiss to tie up loose ends, and an apology that he wouldn't be there to help me pack for Highborne. In our twenty-five years of marriage, we had seldom been apart.

While Peter familiarized himself in his new line of work, I struggled with the reality of winding things up at my job, at the house, and in my mind. After a full day's work each day, I returned home to the myriad boxes that I labored to pack up, night after night. Sometimes I found myself in tears. Was this all a tragic mistake? Or, was I just letting my emotions get in the way of a new start?

As I sorted through every drawer, every closet, every shelf, I had to make a decision on each item—some for the attic, some for the dump, and others to go with us on our new adventure. There was the big white china horse we had been given as a wedding present over twenty-five years ago; I stroked my fingers gently over its head and neck as I carefully laid it in bubble wrap. An original oil painting we had acquired on our honeymoon in Bermuda had been on our wall since we'd been married; I couldn't leave it behind. I sorted through my favorite kitchen gadgets. How could I live on an island without my favorite potato masher?

However, it wasn't until I saw my little Honda go out the driveway for the last time that I fully realized the gravity of our decision. Packing up was an extremely emotional affair, and I missed Peter terribly.

I reminisced as I sat on the kitchen floor wrapping items. Like me, Peter was a born Bahamian. We had met when were both in our mid-teens. We courted for five years—mere teenagers acting like teenagers. By the time we were twenty, he was asking Dad for my hand in marriage. I remembered that evening well. Peter and Dad had proceeded to get totally inebriated while Dad waited—it seemed like hours—as Peter steeled himself to pop the question. Mom and I had waited patiently in the kitchen. (Mom was patience personified.) When Peter finally asked for my hand, and Dad said yes, everyone was so drunk we almost lost the moment!

Since that fateful day, our love for each other has stood the test of time. Peter has been my confident, my protector, my lover and my best friend. Now, by myself in the house. my loneliness was exacerbated.

But, time moves on. A month later I found myself sitting on bales of hay with a bleating goat as my traveling companion. The *Emmett & Cephas* was an old wooden mailboat that carried everything and anyone to remote places in the Bahamas—the 'out islands' as the locals referred to them. Goat and I rolled around in four-foot swells for most of the day as the old boat chugged along towards its first stop—Highborne Cay—the most northern island in the chain of cays known as the Exumas. When land appeared on the horizon, that's when it really hit me: I was headed to our new home, our new job, and our new life. Little did I know what that meant.

As the *Emmett and Cephas* slowly motored through the Western cut at Highborne, I marveled at my first glimpse of the harbor. It was a picture postcard. A beautiful white sandy beach framed the south side of the marina basin. A few towering casuarina trees lined the beach, their wispy limbs swaying as they were brushed by the gentle trade winds. A hammock was hung between two of these trees, inviting me to stay a while and relax in the shade.

The backdrop for this beach was a long concrete pier which appeared to be used as part of the dock space in the harbor. I could see a large and expensive-looking motor yacht tied there.

As we approached, several men waved from a sturdy four-posted hut at the end of the pier. I waved back, trying to convince myself I wasn't apprehensive. They returned to their labors cleaning some fish at a little built-in table underneath the thatched roof. An empty yellow bucket on a rope indicated there was probably no running water, but fresh sea water was only a bucket's dip away.

Near this thatched hut at the end of the jetty, the water was crystal clear. I could see small sharks, several sting rays and smaller reef fish splashing occasionally at the water's surface in competition for tidbits thrown by the men.

Jutting from the land and running parallel to the concrete jetty was a long wooden pier where several more vessels were securely tied. The *Emmett & Cephas* was headed for a clear space that was obviously reserved for her that day. Several people stood on the pier, waiting for the vessel to dock.

The whole scene was beautiful and serene. This place looked as an old picture postcard of Nassau might have appeared decades ago, except today it was in living color.

Upon arrival I struggled with my luggage over the gunwale of the mailboat, and when I had just about given up the thought of ever actually landing my belongings on the dock, a large calloused hand reached over to grab the suitcase. I looked up to see a big grin on a hefty black man who wore a muscle shirt and shorts, both of which were spotted with oil or grease. He extended his other hand to boost me up over the gunwale and onto the dock.

"M' name's Isaac," he said, smiling.

"I'm Kate," I replied, smiling back. "Thanks for your help. Seems as though I brought everything except my kitchen sink." Isaac chuckled quietly as he picked up the heaviest pieces of my luggage with ease and headed towards the base of the pier.

As the boat's ropes were being cleated, I caught my first glimpse of Peter. As he walked down the dock, tanned and handsome in his green Madras shorts, a tee shirt and a pair of Topsiders, he looked taller than his six-foot-one frame. Seeing him served to reinforce how much I had missed him over the past month.

We had, as the saying goes, a marriage made in heaven. During that time, we had raised both daughters and had been through some tough times including a business crisis and my fight with cancer, but this had only made our marriage stronger and our love deeper.

Peter gave me a quick hug and a "Hi Kate," and then turned to the boat captain to wave a thank-you as the crew unloaded our many boxes of various sizes. He took one look at the load and laughed.

"How'd you decide what to bring?" he chuckled casually, putting his arm around my shoulders.

I turned to look deep into his blue eyes. "I did the eenie-meenie thing," I replied as lightheartedly as I could. One day I would tell him how hard it had been, but not now.

Life On A Rock

On shore a few yards away stood six other Bahamians waiting patiently. I waved to the little crowd as I walked off the dock, trying to appear less apprehensive and self-conscious about my arrival. Peter pulled me closer and whispered, "The entire island has come to meet you—all seven of them."

After a brief introduction, Peter and Isaac loaded everything into Isaac's old pick-up and drove me 'home'—a small house atop a hill overlooking the southern exposure of the island and the sea. There wasn't much I could have said about this little house. It was dark inside with funky rattan paneling along all the walls and cupboards. The rug had seen better days, there was no dishwasher, no TV (something that would be rectified by Peter very quickly), and the dining table was an extended meal for the termites that called it their home. I was sure the legs would collapse at any minute. As I checked out each room, I thought the best place was the bedroom where in the months and years to come, we would find solace and badly needed sleep from the heavy workload. Little did I know that on my fourth night in the house, I was to get an unpleasant surprise.

I never even heard them enter the house. We'd only been there four days and our dogs hadn't acclimated themselves yet. As I turned from washing the dinner dishes in the sink, an unfamiliar figure leapt into the kitchen doorway, wearing a tam and gloves, with a sawed-off shotgun pointed directly at me.

"Where's da money?"

"Huh?" I just stared at him. Disoriented for an instant, I thought, 'Sorry Mister, but the gas dock is closed.' In a nanosecond, looking down the barrel of his gun, I figured it out. "What do you want?" I asked after what felt like an eternity.

"Git into da back room!" His words were sharp as he indicated with his gun where I should go. "Git in there, I said!" The masked intruder then moved his focus and the barrel of his gun to K.G., the largest of our two dogs.

"O.K., O.K., but please don't kill my dog!" I pleaded, resting a hand on K.G.'s head. I moved toward the office in the back of our house with the gun poking me in the back. The little office was an afterthought in the house plan and sat directly off the master bedroom.

Where the hell was Peter? Entering the little office, I found out. There he was, lying face down on the floor, with another intruder holding a silver handgun to his head. A third masked man in a green shirt stood by, caressing a bowie knife, the blade of which gleamed in the light. The first two intruders had somehow entered the house unnoticed, and caught Peter in the office.

"Geezus, what the hell do you people want?" I said, trying to keep calm. Only four days on the job and here we were, in a crisis.

"Give us da god-damned money, bitch!"

Thoughts ran through my mind. There were no police to help. Even the island's staff lived too far away to hear any screams.

"We don't have much. It's October—the slow season." I opened the file drawer and pulled out an old beat-up cash box. It didn't even lock. Opening the top, I handed the box to my captor. "Here, this is all we have."

"On da' floor, bitch," sneered the big guy, "and don't look up." As I lay face down on the floor, I could hear him pulling out drawers and opening cupboards. Papers were being scattered this way and that, and all the while his buddy continued to stick the barrel of the .38 into Peter's temple.

"OK bitch," he said, "where's da' fuckin' safe?"

With his face to the floor, Peter mumbled, "That's all we have, mister. We don't have a safe." His voice showed no emotion. Peter was always the level-headed one in our marriage—slow to anger, easy-going.

"Buddy, ya better come up with a safe real fast, or my friend here's gonna blow ya fuckin' head off!"

From face-down on the tile floor I screamed at them, "There's no more money! There's no more money! We don't have a safe! Geezus, we're telling you the truth! We don't keep a lot of money on the cay!"

Now, one of the burglars noticed my rings and gold chain necklace. "OK, bitch, take off da jewels," he demanded, as the barrel of his gun tap-tap-tapped on my earrings. With my face still facing the floor, I reached up and took off my earrings, a gold necklace and my heirloom engagement ring. I heard Peter unbuckle his watch. Was it going to stop there?

In those few seconds, I realized the deck was stacked against us with two guns and a knife. Now as I lay on the floor, I played the only card I had: my faith. I prayed out loud. "Lord, cover us with your precious blood and protect us now. Help us to forgive these..."

"Who you talkin' too!" my captor demanded and gave me a sharp kick in the face for good measure. I could feel the anger well up inside me; I'd have to keep my wits about me and stay calm or I'd never be able to survive.

"I'm talking to my God," I replied. Sweat trickled down my temples and my heart raced. This might be a life-or-death scenario, but I had to act strong—be strong.

The man with the bowie knife came over. "Yeah? Well then, why don't ya tell your god that me and my boys is gonna have us a little fun." He smirked as he reached down with his

14

knife and effortlessly cut the leg of my shorts up to the waist. "I'm gonna show ya how it's done," he sneered. My thoughts went rampant. They were going to gang-rape me right there on the cold tile floor of the office with Peter laying helpless, only a few feet away. I wanted to scream at feeling so violated, but I knew I needed to be tough. I needed to exude confidence.

"Geezus, why don't you be a REAL man!" I rolled my head around to try and face this dude. "*Real* men don't rape women." Where did I muster this courage? Maybe I inherited this from my dad, the dominant personality in my childhood. I never saw Dad back down from a situation.

Or, maybe it was my faith. I had a renewal of the spirit during my illness. This, coupled with a charismatic Episcopal upbringing, kept me close to God, so I continued to pray fervently and out loud. "Lord, thank you for the strength and courage you have bestowed upon Peter and me tonight. I ask for your shield of protection and to forgive…"

"Shut up, bitch!" said my captor. "Let's kill 'em or dey gonna talk," he added to no one in particular.

I heard one of the men take a deep breath. "I ain't never heard no white woman pray like dat before!"

"Yeah, let's just tie 'em up and get the hell outta here!"

It was a miracle! They were actually deciding to leave—and leave us alive. I marveled at the power of prayer. Maybe it reminded them of some childhood experience with the church. Maybe they thought about their own mother, reading her bible quietly.

"Go find somethin' to tie 'em up with!"

They rummaged around our bedroom. I heard drawers pull out and a lamp fall over. *Our* sacred bedroom. It was like a bad dream.

They tied and gagged us using belts, extension cords and anything else they could find. How could I keep one step ahead of them? When the big man hog-tied me (legs tied to hands behind my back), I was actually able to *fake* being tied tightly. In my innermost thoughts, I claimed the victory, hoping this fact would not be discovered.

However, I couldn't fake the gag: It was so tight and far into my throat I could hardly catch my breath. I would have to concentrate on my breathing, or I knew I'd retch. In—out. In—out. Concentrate. Relax.

From my position on the floor, I couldn't see Peter, but I knew they had tied and gagged him as well. Seconds later, they grabbed the keys to the truck and ran out through the bedroom. Were they gone? Would they be back? We didn't move. Breathe in—out, in—out. Don't panic with the gag. Relax. Breathe.

The next several minutes dragged by as Peter and I lay hog-tied on the floor. Then we heard footsteps. To my horror, the big man returned to check that we hadn't moved.

As he turned to leave, he laughed, deep and sinister. "Y'all better get some security 'round here!"

Then, they were gone. The extension cord that had tied my hands and feet was easily stretched. As the restraints fell away, I crawled over to Peter. They had tied his wrists so tightly it seemed an eternity before I could work the knots to make them give way. Finally freed, Peter and I sat on the floor, and looked at each other, bewildered by the circumstances and shaken by the experience. We held hands and dropped our heads to thank God our lives had been spared.

Still frightened that our intruders would return once again, we crept out of the bedroom and into the main part of the house, which now seemed far too quiet. With eyes darting back and forth, I walked into the kitchen and picked up the mike of the big VHF (very high frequency ship-to-shore radio) to call for help. The radio was our direct line of communication to boats in the area. "This is Highborne, This is Highborne. We have a may-day situation!" There was pleading in my voice. No response. "This is Highborne, please, anyone, come in!" Not a sound. Peter came up behind me to investigate. He grabbed the radio wires and held up the cut ends. Our eyes flew to the phone; We saw this line, too, has been cut. Our two hand-held VHF radios that we always wore clipped to our belts now sat in the dish water in the sink.

It was then Peter noticed my cut shorts. This was his reality check—that I had almost been raped. He wrapped his arms around me, and I lay my head on his broad shoulder as he gently stroked my hair. My body racked with sobs as we held each other tightly for what seemed like an eternity. "I love you, Kate," he said softly through his own tears.

Both of us, over the past hour, had managed to stay so strong and calm; Now we absolutely fell apart. In all our years together, we had never been so close to danger—or death—as we were this night. We knew the experience would change us forever. Whether it strengthened us or weakened us was an unanswered question.

When we finally gathered some composure, Peter coaxed me to walk with him to the staff quarters. He banged on a window at Isaac's house and yelled. "I need to use your phone, Isaac! We've been robbed and they've cut every form of communication we have."

Isaac, and his wife, Becky, both came to the door. "Wha' happened?" was all he could say as he saw my cut shorts and our look of dismay.

Life On A Rock

Using Isaac's phone, Peter called the Criminal Investigation Department in Nassau (the branch of the Royal Bahamas Police Force that dealt with felonies.) I heard him relate the happenings to the officer on duty. Once he hung up, he turned to me. "They've promised to send a helicopter, Kate. It'll take about three hours to get here."

Becky walked out of the bedroom holding another pair of shorts. "Here, Kate. Put these on for now. You can't go runnin' around with ya shorts half off."

I was exhausted and not looking forward to a three-hour wait for the police. When they finally arrived by chopper, it was after 3 am. We both gave our statements to two very sympathetic officers, but what good was that? It was three hours after the fact, and the burglars had gotten clean away. We knew one thing for sure that night: We had much to do in the coming days to secure the island, and more importantly, to secure our home.

By coincidence, early the next morning, the phone rang. The connection wasn't the best, but through the crackle, a voice said, "Is this Kate?" I didn't recognize the voice. "This is Mary. Welcome to Highborne." It was Mary Smith, the owner of the island and our new boss. "I hope you and your husband will enjoy working on the cay," she said. "I wanted to be the first to say how happy I am you accepted the job, and I look forward to having you both with us." I hadn't called her yet, so she had absolutely no idea of the past night's happenings.

"Thank you," I answered, not knowing quite what to say, but knowing I had to say something. I took a deep breath and pressed on. "Mary, we had some trouble last night. Three men walked into our house around suppertime and robbed the cay and us." I explained some of the details of the previous night. "The burglars took over three thousand dollars of the cay's money, plus all our jewelry and my Nikon camera." I didn't give her any more specifics. I knew if I had to tell her *all* the details, I probably would have broken down.

She was astonished. "Is everyone O.K.?" She seemed sympathetic and concerned at first. "Where did these people come from?" We talked together about the robbery. Somewhere in the course of the conversation, however, I detected a minute vein of doubt. Maybe she was wondering if we, as the newly hired employees, had set the whole thing up.

"I'll write up a report for you soon, but I'm still pretty shook up," I told her. She seemed to understand, but I could tell she had many unanswered questions. She suggested we buy a guard dog.

Later that morning, Peter and Isaac found the stolen truck. It had been driven down a precarious trail that ended at Horseshoe Beach. The burglars had come by boat and landed at the north end of the island. The terrain was a steep, rocky incline with lots of brush. Amazingly, the truck had survived with only a dented fender.

I had not fared as well. My mental state had deteriorated. The days following the robbery were very difficult. I found it hard to sleep. For many nights after the robbery, I climbed into bed almost fully dressed when retiring. I had dreams of being sexually molested. Noises in the night frightened me. Making love was out of the question. I prayed for bad weather, knowing that high winds and seas would prevent vessels from reaching us.

Dad, now a widower living in Nassau, called several days after the robbery. He had been concerned about our move to Highborne in the beginning. Now he saw the front page of the newspaper and phoned. "Kate, why don't you guys just come back home? Just leave that damn job and return to Nassau."

Life On A Rock

Dad was a man's man, a bit rough around the edges as military men usually are. I always admired and respected him. He was a good hunter, a good boatman, and a good father. He could build anything, fix anything. He always had solutions for problems. "I'll help you and Pete find work when you get back." Now he was trying to solve our dilemma with his powers of persuasion. "I don't want anything to happen to you, honey." The pleading was out of character for him.

"We're O.K., Dad. We're O.K." I paused, remembering something he had said to me as a kid: Never quit a situation that can be solved, or you'll be quitting the rest of your life.

"Dad, we *have* to stay. We have to work through this thing. If we come back to Nassau now, not only will we have failed in the job. We will have failed ourselves. We have to heal the fear and the doubt, and we have to do this here, where it all happened." For once, he knew I was right.

What concerned me most was the fact that the local newspaper had published the story. Now every criminal and punk in Nassau and the out islands would know that Highborne was ripe for robberies. It was practically an ad for the island's vulnerability.

Over the coming days, we tried our best to secure our little house. The communications equipment was repaired. New locks were installed, the old sliding glass doors were replaced, and halogen lights were purchased and attached to the exterior of the house. However, my nerves were shattered. I lost my appetite, and over the following three weeks, I dropped twelve pounds. I couldn't understand how I had stayed so calm during the incident, and then fallen apart in the days that followed.

Peter and I have always been familiar with guns. He loved to shoot clay birds, and, in Nassau, he belonged to a club at the local skeet range. I was raised in a family where my dad and both my brothers loved shooting, whether it was ducks or clay birds.

They all carried membership cards of the NRA. I'm an animal lover and an advocate against such boorish behavior, but under such pressure from my brothers and my father, I was forced to learn about pistols and rifles: how to place a stock tight into the shoulder to ease the "kick," how to "sight" a target. Much to my family's pleasure, I became a decent marksman, although I always hated the sound of the shot in my ears.

When Peter and I arrived at Highborne, we brought two shotguns with us, which we stored in the attic of our little cottage. We never thought we'd have to use them. We were wrong. The day after the robbery, the guns were retrieved and loaded with shells in the chambers. Each weapon was then placed strategically: one in the kitchen by the frig, and the other next to our bed. I knew then that I had my father to thank for the training I received earlier. Now, handling a gun no longer frightened me.

The guard dog that Mary suggested, arrived by plane several days later with her trainer. She was a beautiful and responsive German Shepherd, and she bonded immediately to me. However, she did not like anyone who wasn't Caucasian, and she indicated that she wanted to eat my cat for dinner. I could see it wasn't going to work, and I sent the dog back to Nassau in five days.

Julia, our miniature Schnauzer, and K.G., the big shepherd-mix, had been confused by the move to Highborne. They had always been great watchdogs before we came to the island, but the move disoriented them; They had trouble deciding who was friend and who was foe. The burglars had walked right in the front door, and neither dog had made a peep. In the weeks that followed, however, the dogs became familiar with the staff and our surroundings and began to acclimate themselves to their new home. Little did we know that in the near future, Julia and K.G. would prove to be our saving grace.

Life On A Rock

Meanwhile, Peter and I tried to keep occupied with the work at the marina. We scrutinized all the fishermen who came in for fuel, and we worried when four or five locals arrived for groceries at the store. It was frightening to realize we were overseeing five hundred acres of land in the middle of the ocean with five miles of unprotected shoreline and yet were thirty-five miles (and a proven three hours by chopper) from the nearest police station. I continued to feel uneasy, as the robber's last words haunted me. The comprehension of 'us' against 'them' began to dawn on me as I reminded myself: There are no police on Highborne Cay. We *are* the police.

Hard-core reality began to sink in. To survive the experience of living on Highborne Cay, we would have to muster the courage and fortitude necessary to do so. I had found courage before—been scared and then drew up the courage to go on. I had battled the 'Big C' eight years prior to our arrival at Highborne. I had found my courage with cancer. Now I needed it for Highborne. I vowed then and there I would never, ever, be put on the floor with a gun to my head again. I would fight till the end.

No sooner had I made that commitment to myself, then my life became mine again.

THE FIRST YEAR

"Highborne Cay, Highborne Cay, come in..." Our marine radio squawked before seven a.m. each day from boaters in the area with requests for weather, reservations, fishing reports and often for general advice about the Exuma Cays. The radio or VHF became an integral part of our life on the island. It connected boat-to-boat, boat-to-shore, and shore-to-shore, depending on who was transmitting. In a very short time, I learned to communicate by this big VHF radio that sat on a shelf in the kitchen, (and a smaller version that was always clipped to my belt).

Channel sixteen was the hail-and-distress channel, and once contacted, vessels were required to move to a working channel for further discussions. We realized shortly after the job commenced that this was the most important communication equipment on the island. Our business at Highborne Cay depended on VHF radio communications, and in some cases, lives depended on it. This point was driven home after the robbers had cut the radio wires.

Now, as I stood next to this big black box near the back door of the kitchen, I discovered I could hold the mike and still look out of the window to see the staff quarters below, the road to the store, and the remainder of the island to the south. Our

Life On A Rock

house's elevation provided a magnificent view, and the extra antenna height gave us a clear radio signal for miles around. Occasionally I could reach boats as far away as Nassau's harbor.

Looking south from the kitchen window

Soon after I learned to operate the mike (i.e. push the button to speak, release to listen), Peter warned me that whatever I said could be heard by anyone tuned in on the same channel. "Everyone who has a VHF radio within the sound of your voice— and that can be up to thirty-five miles—is standing by on Channel sixteen, the 'hail and distress' channel. Your conversations are never private."

I was so accustomed to the privacy of a telephone, this sounded crazy. Peter explained further. "You'll have to use your judgment, Kate. The VHF creates sound waves that are picked up by every other VHF radio in the area. This is known by the locals as 'copying the mail.' In the islands and on the high seas,

24

if someone eavesdrops on a vessel that is hailing another, the eavesdropper can 'follow' the transmitting parties to their working channel by a mere turn of a button; The whole conversation now becomes public."

I thought for a moment. "Maybe so," I retorted, "but in some cases, this might be good, especially in an emergency when someone needs help. Of course," I added with sarcasm, "that could only happen if the radio wires weren't cut."

Peter smiled. "Look, all I'm saying is, you need to use your judgment."

Big VHF radio (top) and single-sideband radio near the kitchen door.

Highborne's telephone service was less than satisfactory on this island in the middle of nowhere, even though the main Batelco (Bahamas Telecommunications Corp.) tower for telephone communications between the Exuma Cays and Nassau sat seven hundred feet from our house. The mass of guy wires, satellite dishes and iron rose over three hundred feet in the air, and its flashing red tower light could be seen for miles. Peter always grumbled that we were getting exposed to radiation with our close proximity to the tower. For me, however, I just liked the way the wind whistled through the guy-wires and produced an eerie sound, the pitch of which changed with the strength of the wind.

Thoughts of the robbery finally began to subside, and we settled into our new home on the cay. Our two dogs were now getting used to their new digs. The cat, Udder, had a tougher time adjusting. She was older, and did not acclimate quite as easily. Oscar, our parrot, fared well except for his inherent fear of seagulls. He would squawk and flitter around his cage if one got too close to the window. Later, I would bring Woody, my old Thoroughbred; For now, he remained in Nassau with trusted friends.

Peter had learned to deal with the fact that I was an animal lover, and much to his chagrin, we always owned various and sundry animals throughout our marriage. In high school, I had aspirations of becoming a veterinarian, but in those days, women in that field were rare. Veterinary colleges set the bar extremely high scholastically, and my grades were only mediocre. I remember when Dad had secured a summer job for me at a local vet's clinic. I had to clean kennels, bath dogs and put animals to sleep. I resented this intrusion on my dream of saving animals' lives.

But Dad had been right, again. I moved forward in the field of business and, over my career, worked at several lucrative jobs. I grew to love the business world, especially in finance and investments. But, I never lost my first love: The love for all animals, especially horses.

For the first few weeks, Peter and I worked hard to meld with the rest of the little settlement. Each resident was a grass-roots Bahamian, and most were born in the settlement of Black Point, Exuma, forty miles further south. Each small family had been on Highborne for the past twenty years or more with every individual having his or her own responsibilities and contributions to the running of the cay. To my dismay, I learned an important fact within a week of our arrival: none of the staff could read or write past the third grade level. This meant other than physical labor, no one could assist us properly with any of the paperwork at the dock, in the store or in the office. However, I found it interesting that when it came to money, *everyone* knew how to count out their pay packets.

Several weeks passed. We had arrived in the fall, a slow time for the cruising industry. We had time to acclimate ourselves to our jobs and our surroundings without the stress of a full marina. I focused on unpacking the many boxes that I had brought with me. I made some minor changes in the house, and Peter started fixing up a garden area at the dock. We were slowly beginning to heal from the ravages of the robbery.

I was walking to the store one morning when I passed Isaac at the staff's quarters. Isaac was fixing a flat tire on his truck which sat disabled in front of his house. As I approached, he looked up from his work. "Hey, Isaac," I said, thinking this might be a good time to ask him to fill in some of the details about the cay.

He laid down the tire iron and stood up. "Hi there," he replied. "How's it goin'?"

I stopped. "Well, o.k. I guess. I was on my way to the

store…" I paused. "Would you have a couple of minutes?"

Isaac pulled a handkerchief from his pocket to wipe his hands. "Sure," he said.

"Well," I said, trying to appear casual rather than nosey, "I'd love to get a better background of the cay and our boss, and I thought you might be just the person."

He leaned an elbow against the truck. "Mary inherited Highborne Cay from her late husband," he told me. "I knew Bill from when I was just a kid. He hired me to work on the cay. I guess I was around ten." I listened, amazed that Isaac, who appeared to be around thirty-five or so, had been on the island since he was a little boy.

"When Bill died," he continued, "Mary got the cay." He turned and picked up the tire iron. "Mary loves the island. She only comes about twice a year—usually flies in by sea plane and brings family members with her. And, when she's here," he looked up at me as if to emphasize the point, "she gets our full attention." With that, he went back to changing the tire. I got the picture, though. I thanked him and continued my walk to the store, only a couple of hundred yards further down the road.

This small but well-stocked commissary which sat about a half mile from the marina (and about three hundred yards from my house) was not only used by Highborne's staff and near-by islanders, but occasionally by a cruiser who had forgotten to put some salt or soup in his larder. The little island van would carry customers back and forth from the marina area to this broken-down building that was known throughout the area as merely "the store."

The store was an interesting entity. It was a pre-fab metal building whose roof leaked during the lightest rain, and its entrance door was about to fall off its hinges. The store carried about four hundred inventory items, but it wasn't your favorite supermarket by any means. There was no organization to the shelves and the stock room was a mess. I envisioned that this would be under my umbrella of responsibility.

Because I have always been obsessed with organizational skills, I knew this store was going to be a major project. Peter had learned to live with this fetish of mine over the years, and now I believe he was thankful for such a quirk. I'd have to expand the inventory to include such luxuries as two percent milk and Romaine lettuce. Other fresh produce would also be a nice start. The shelves needed painting. The store room needed palletizing. There was no inventory control. The cooler and freezer needed defrosting and re-organizing as well. It looked like a huge job. In addition, there was no cash register—just a cigar box to hold any funds. The can of 'Off' that rested on the counter was attributed to the fact that the back door at the store's stock room had no screen. I found as time went on that mosquitoes were often my best company when I worked there.

Every day I gave the majority of my time to the store, following a set pattern in how it should be upgraded. We only had a couple of months before the season would be in full swing, so I enlisted Ritchie's help. Ritchie was the oldest employee of Highborne Cay—oldest meaning not just in age, but in the length of time he had been working there. He was a little wizened man who talked so fast very few people could understand him. He was also the most outspoken person I ever met, although he never looked me in the eye when we talked. He and his wife, Chandra, had lived and worked at the cay for more than thirty-five years.

To most people, Ritchie was grouchy and grumbled a great deal. In *my* opinion, he was our best and most reliable employee, and he and I got along famously. His talents at painting, weaving thatch for roofs, and building stone walls couldn't be matched, and I was thankful for his help. Soon, at the end of each day, I began to see progress, no matter how small. While Ritchie was busy painting the store room and making new shelves. I worked over the inventory to decide where to expand the grocery lines in order to produce a better profit margin. Peter had been in the wholesale grocery business for many years, and his suggestions on improving the inventory were invaluable. To spruce up the exterior of the store's rusty building, I planted Bougainvillea, with its vibrant purples and pinks, along the front wall. It wouldn't be long before I would be able to call it 'the store' and be proud.

It was well into December when I took my first break. I wasn't familiar with a 24/7 work schedule, and I needed a day off. I was getting cranky, and Peter saw this long before I did. "Why don't you go into Nassau and have lunch with the girls?" he suggested. I admitted to myself he was always full of good ideas. Besides, it was my birthday.

I arranged to fly to Nassau with "neighbors" from Staniel Cay, another island about thirty miles south of Highborne. Rosie had a sea plane, and she was very adept at flying. Rosie was a real island gal. She always stepped out of her seaplane in bare feet with her brown, curly hair askew. Her skimpy shorts barely covered her butt, and she was usually disheveled—not your usual pilot, by any means. But, she was constantly making jokes, and she loved to fly.

In my years at Highborne, even though we only saw each other occasionally, I still counted on Rosie as a friend. She flew to Nassau on a regular basis, so that day I begged a ride. Sea plane transportation was the best way of getting to civilization in Nassau in a timely manner. I had only one day off, and I didn't want to waste four precious hours each way on a mailboat.

Seaplane taxiing in to the Dock Beach

Rosie deftly landed her sea plane into the southern harbor and glided it up to the beach near the dock. It was the most convenient place to pick up passengers and always provided entertainment for those people watching from the marina. Her little seaplane with a black witch painted on the tail was a familiar sight.

As we flew low over the sea on our way to Nassau, the brilliance of the blues and greens always fascinated me. The waters of the Bahamas are some of the clearest and most spectacular in the world. From the air, a person can look down into thirty feet of water and see sharks, coral heads and even starfish on the bottom. The clarity of the water is only exceeded by the colors. The varying shades of aqua, blue and lavender are like the palette of an artist as he mixes his colors for his next stroke. Flying was always fun for me, especially when I could view such beauty. I really wanted to learn how to fly, and I vowed that someday, somehow, somewhere, I would do it.

"Take the stick!" she yelled above the prop noise. I turned and tilted my head with the question. She smiled. "I thought you said you wanted to learn to fly."

"Rosie, …er…., me?" I couldn't believe she'd let me take the controls.

"Go ahead, take the stick. Have a go, kiddo! Just move it around gently until you figure out which way is which!" She laughed. She was always laughing.

Tentatively, I held the little half-wheel in both hands. A slight push and we went down; a pull and we came up. Turn left, we went left. Turn right, by damn, we went right!

"Get a feel for the pedals, too," she yelled. Then she pointed to the little knob above us near the windscreen. "This is the trim gear. If you turn it, you can raise and lower the nose of the plane a little so you don't fight the stick so much!"

I tried everything she suggested and caught on fairly quickly. This was more than fun; This was exhilarating! By the time Nassau came into sight, all my cares had been left behind at the cay. I was a new person, flying high. As we neared the harbor, I turned the controls over to Rosie, but I was just busting to tell Peter that he would have to start saving his money, because my next learning experience was to become a pilot!

As Rosie glided her 'witch' down into Nassau's harbor and under Paradise Island Bridge, she was careful to miss the anchored sailboats whose masts stuck up in the air like matchsticks and dotted the water on her approach—a true obstacle course. The harbor was busy with yachting traffic, but she managed to guide the 'witch' to the sea plane ramp and promised to see me again, promptly at four o'clock for the ride home.

My old friends in Nassau hadn't forgotten my birthday or me. We all met for lunch together. It was wonderful to be with them, again. Up until then, I hadn't realized how important my friends were in my life. We ate good food, drank fine wine and laughed together for most of the afternoon. The hours flew by, and soon it was time for me to catch Rosie's ride back to the Cay.

All of a sudden it hit me: As I stepped onto the pontoon, for the first time since moving to Highborne, I became acutely aware of how much I missed my old life. I missed my dad, our daughters, Peter's family. I missed my friends. I missed my church. I missed not being able to run to the supermarket for a carton of cottage cheese. It was then I also realized I would miss an opportunity to learn to fly, since instruction took place in Nassau. After such a wonderful day, I was definitely feeling blue at the thought of having to return to the rock. I knew the wine had exacerbated these feelings that were hard to shake.

After takeoff, Rosie again offered me another chance to fly her plane. She was surprised when I shook my head. "Too much wine," I said. No amount of flying would fix my somber state. The flight home was very quiet.

It took several months to really settle in to the job at hand. Living in such a remote area presented its own set of challenges. As the managers, it was our job to insure that the island's business activities were run efficiently. Yet, it was like running a small town. We had our own electricity, supplied by the two big generators that were located near the store in a well-stocked machine shop that was under the command of Isaac. The island had its own rainwater supplies (before the days of the reverse-osmosis machinery), and each house on the island had its own little cistern to collect the water when it rained. The rainwater would fall from the rooftop into the gutters around the house, and finally drain into the cistern. A bigger cistern was located near the store, and we depended on this for our major supply to make ice. Garbage, like anywhere, was an issue, but we dug and burned our own landfill, turning it over several times a year with the tractor. These were no small issues; The island was an independent entity. Therefore, its managers were like a town's mayor: responsible for governing its people and their well-being.

Then there was Cheap Charlie's, a conversation piece in itself. Whatever purpose the building had in its past seems to be a mystery. Even Isaac didn't know. However, in more recent times, this little building which sat at the base of the main dock, served as the marina office. The walls had been built of cream-colored limestone rock, and my guess was that these were probably quarried from the island many years ago. The roof was genuine thatch, cut from the brush on the north end of the island. The thatch had been professionally overlapped and woven by Ritchie, so it was secure and water-tight. The little building's interior provided a rudimentary office for the marina.

Peter opening Cheap Charlie's for business.

Cheap Charlie's was always the center for international entertainment. Since the only public phone on the island hung on the wall there, and since there were four white plastic chairs that sat near this phone, it was easy for clients to relax with a drink and eavesdrop on very important phone conversations of others.

There was no doubt about it. Cheap Charlie's was the island's hub. Clients could settle their bills, hear local gossip and possibly get a hair cut, or just gather there to shoot the bull. Inside the little building was a desk that served as Peter's check-out counter, a VHF radio for communication, a refrigerator full of cold beer and soda pop, and a locked cupboard with a stash of cigarettes which, at the time, was a popular item. There was a small bookcase against the front wall that served as a book exchange: Bring a book, take a book. Though most of those on the shelf were tatty and worn, boaters often stopped in to get a 'new' book and leave an 'old' one. Cheap Charlie's was so renowned in the area that the VHF call sign for the marina office was just exactly that: Cheap Charlie's

Cheap Charlie's interior provided a rudimentary office.

Life On A Rock

As Peter and I continued to adjust to our island situation, there was always the fact that, indeed, we had no one to assist in any sort of emergency situation. This fact was never more prevalent than when we were robbed at gunpoint, or when Günter, a guest at the marina, had a serious mishap at the fish-cleaning station.

It was a quiet November day when things were slow and yachts were few at the marina. The weather was beautiful. Günter Solomon, a regular visitor from Washington D.C., said this marina was just what he was looking for—a quiet place to tie his boat for a few days before heading south to the fishing grounds for some Blue Marlin. That day the ocean was calm, so he decided to do a day's fishing for dolphin (mahi-mahi) in Exuma Sound. Over the radio, we could hear he was having a good day. By the time he returned, he'd dropped five large dolphin and one Yellowfin tuna at the fish-cleaning hut. We thought no more of it and continued to go about our usual business at the marina until we heard a blood-curdling scream at the end of the pier. Stumbling over the rough path, I ran out to the fish-cleaning hut to see about the commotion.

Blood was everywhere, and it wasn't fish blood. It had spattered onto the table and the concrete base beneath. Günter was bent over, holding his hand. His shorts were stained, and some blood had dripped onto his sneakers. "What the heck happened?" I asked. He just groaned.

"Let's have a look," I said, trying to be casual, yet steeling myself for what was to come.

"I was just trying to clean the fish," he replied. "The knife slipped as I was doing the final fillet."

When I convinced Günter to let me see the damage, I immediately regretted it. As he slowly took his other hand and carefully opened his fingers enough for me to see, I felt like retching. The four fingers of his right hand were severely sliced, and I knew he needed immediate attention. As I regained my composure, I thought about the veterinary practice I never had; Even if I had made the grade, I'd probably never have been able to stomach the inevitable blood.

"Listen, we need to get you into Nassau for this," I said, swallowing hard. "C'mon back to Cheap Charlie's with me, and we'll get Peter to call for a plane." I tried to sound casual, but I could hear my voice on the edge of panic.

It was still going to be several hours before we could get Günter to the hospital. It would take an hour before Rosie arrived at the Dock Beach, another forty minutes to fly Gunter back to Nassau and then yet another half hour or so for the ambulance to get him to the emergency room. While we had a full medical kit at the house, this injury was way beyond our skills. Peter, always the level-headed one, had the forethought to fill a small cooler with ice that we kept in supply at the store. "Günter, stick you hand in here," he said, pointing to the little cooler. "See if we can stop the bleeding." Men are so nonchalant, aren't they? As for me, I didn't want to take another look at that hand which was looking more and more like a piece of meat, the soft red flesh and white grizzle.

While Günter waited for the plane, I hopped in the golf cart and sped back to the house for some pain meds. I grabbed the Percocet and called ahead for a surgeon at the local hospital in Nassau. I wanted them to be ready for this emergency, as well as send an ambulance to meet the seaplane.

As the seaplane charter glided into the harbor, Peter and I glanced at each other with unspoken words. I prayed everything would go according to plan. "Call us, Günter!" I cried out as he waded in the water towards the sea plane pontoons, still holding his bandaged hand high above his head. He looked back briefly and waved with his good hand.

Shortly after the excitement died down, Günter's boat captain came into Cheap Charlie's, and we learned that Günter was a well-known graphics artist. How was he going to fare with so much damage to his right hand? We'd never know until the following spring when we got our answer.

That's when a large package arrived by mailboat. Peter tentatively un-wrapped the box to discover, among layers of tissue paper, a fine penciled drawing of Cheap Charlie's, complete with frame. A note from Günter told us that the surgeon in Nassau had done an excellent repair job on his hand, and the doctors in D.C. were very pleased with the results. The drawing was living proof that he was really ok, and the package was a thank you for saving his hand.

We were astounded. I carefully hung the drawing in our living room. It certainly deserved a place there. But, both Peter and I were somewhat embarrassed. We had merely done our job—to look out for the safety and well-being of our clients.

I had no idea that similar scenarios would happen again and again during the next five years. No police. No emergency technicians. No help. It was a hard fact to accept.

In the late fall, I finally got the call. Woody was coming! A local shipping company called to say they had room on one of their freighters for my old Thoroughbred horse who was still in Nassau, patiently waiting for a ride to Highborne. He had been under the watchful care of my good friend, Sarah, over the past several months, and it now looked like *The Cavalier*, a local freighter, would be the only opportunity I would have to bring him to the cay.

This required me to make a trip to Nassau to organize such an affair. The job at hand was to load Woody into a horse trailer, get the trailer onto the deck of the ship, accompany the horse on the trip, and unload him at Highborne. More of a challenge than I had anticipated.

Woody really didn't want to step into a dark trailer at five a.m., and finally, after loading him with the help of half of Nassau, the truck to pull the trailer wouldn't crank over. Thankfully, one of our helpers was a mechanic. He went under the hood for quite a few moments before he got the truck to start. We finally arrived at the wharf in downtown Nassau to learn to our dismay that due to our late arrival at the port, the ship might not be able to get into the marina at Highborne Cay. The Captain has calculated that our arrival time there would now be at dead low tide, and there might not be enough water under the boat when they arrived in Highborne's harbor. But, Woody, Sarah and I had come too far now to turn back. I took the gamble, and we left Nassau with a cool breeze at our stern. Thankfully we were blessed with good weather and a calm sea that day.

The six-hour trip was happily uneventful. Sarah had volunteered to make the trip with me, and I was glad she came. She was excellent company on the journey, knew a great deal about horses, and was a big help. It was hot inside the horse trailer, and I had brought several large containers of drinking water for Woody and us, but Sarah had brought the most important thing: a spray bottle filled with water and alcohol in a 50/50 mix. By frequently misting all of us with this mixture, the evaporation of the alcohol kept us cool and comfortable during the trip. In addition, I kept Woody's hay net constantly filled so he would stay calm and distracted.

Upon arrival at Highborne, the captain was able to lower the front ramp of his craft onto a corner of the quay—an amazing feat considering the precise maneuver of a two hundred-foot vessel in very shallow water. It was now time. Woody stepped out of the horse trailer onto the main deck of the ship. With ears pricked forward and wide-eyed, he glanced at the shore and there was no stopping him.

Woody was ready for dry land.

I held my breath as the big chestnut horse headed down the ramp with Sarah and me in tow. His shoes resounded on the metal base of the ramp. Bam! Bam! Bam! My fingers, firmly curled around the halter strap, held tight, but my feet barely touched the ramp: The noise had spooked Woody, and his head flew up in the air as he came prancing down the incline. With the ramp resting on only two or three feet of the pier, I prayed we wouldn't miss our narrow pathway to dry land. Finally, in what seemed like an eternity, Woody's front hoofs touched the concrete of the pier. He gave a little buck, shook his head and seemed to indicate that he was grateful we had arrived at Highborne. I took a deep breath; I knew I certainly was.

Luckily I'd made some plans for the horse the month before. Ritchie was the person who helped make a little paddock for Woody up near the old barn across from the store. As we worked together those several weeks prior to Woody's arrival, Ritchie gave me a further history of Highborne and some of the interesting trivia associated with the cay, including the fact that the island had been a pineapple plantation back in the 1800's. As we worked together to prepare for Woody's arrival, I was grateful for his help.

I smiled to myself as Sarah and I led my horse up from the marina to Woody's new home. It most certainly wasn't his fancy stable in Nassau. No, this was a rudimentary paddock with a little lean-to to help shade him from the sun and protect him from the rain. It would have to do. We were making sacrifices; Woody would have to do the same.

He was a wonderful horse. I had bought him from a hack stable in central Florida the year I got cancer. When I bought him he was thin and lame, and I took a big chance when I laid my money on the table to pay for such a bedraggled looking animal. But, I could see he had a kind eye and, with good care, he could become a beautiful animal once again. Right then, I made a secret deal: I promised God that if He would rid me of the cancer, I would bring Woody into a loving family and give him the very best care and affection for as long as he lived. Woody would be "God's horse," not mine. (He was, from that moment on, God's horse until he passed away at the ripe old age of 36, many years after Highborne Cay.)

As I turned him loose in his new digs, in private thoughts, I secretly hoped Woody would help keep me happy here on the rock.

Life On A Rock

With Sarah on the island, I was overjoyed. Sarah, now entrenched in the legal profession with her husband, was one of my best friends in Nassau, and I was glad she had an opportunity to accompany Woody and me to the cay, even though she could only stay over for a few hours. Soon Rosie would be flying in to pick her up.

Sarah had never been to Highborne—nor any of the Exumas—and she was glad to be able to see where her friend had moved. With the help of our walking shoes and the golf cart that I commandeered from Peter, I took her on a tour to survey this five hundred-acre island of coral rock which we now called 'home.' The rough road from the marina went north/south only. To go east or west, we had to walk.

The cay had a diverse geography. I started at the north end. The road took us to the highest elevation at the top of the island. The view was over a hundred feet above sea level with a truly breathtaking three hundred sixty-degree panorama of the surrounding cays and ocean. Sarah was in awe of the beauty that surrounded us…the breakers on the East Beach, the serene waters of Horseshoe Bay on the west, Allen's Cay to the north where we could see ten or fifteen boats at anchor. Sarah wanted to stay there and soak it all in; But it was time to move on. I wanted to show her the whole island before she left.

I soon found the trail that led off the main road to the east. The trail, which was merely an opening through the bushes with a rocky, uneven path, ended with another spectacular view. "This is unbelievable!" she exclaimed as we came out of the trail onto a magnificent sand beach that extended for almost two miles down the length of the island. As we walked along the powdery white sand, a variety of shells were visible, having been washed up onto the beach by the waves. The ocean rollers came onto the beach with the grace of a gymnast, and a solitary sand piper strutted along the high water mark, looking for crabs or other crustaceans for his dinner. A flock of shearwaters flew low, a hundred yards away as the sea grass on the dune swayed with a light breeze. This was Nature at her best.

We retraced our steps and returned to the golf cart. "C'mon, Sarah," I called as Sarah lagged behind, not wanting to leave the beauty of the beach. "There's more! We'll need to hurry if we're to see everything before your ride gets here."

The south side of Highborne was equally striking. With jagged honeycomb rocks running along the ocean's edge, the rocks dared anyone to land there and risk being torn to shreds, because the sharp coral shoreline on this end of the island was continually being thrashed by the waves. "I want you to see the blow hole," I said as we travelled south.

When we approached, I could see a high energetic geyser of sea water knife through the air, spewing foam and spray far above all the vegetation that grew around the narrow hole in the coral rock. As the power of the ocean's waves hit the rocks, the water was forced underneath the coral ledge with a blunt 'thump' and up through the blow hole with a distinct 'whoosh.' Thump. Whoosh. Thump. Whoosh. We could have stayed there for hours watching this magnificent scene. But, we had other places to go, and the afternoon shadows were getting longer.

To explore the west side of the island, Sarah and I trudged through scrub and prickle bushes. We laughed together as we tripped over thick vines and scrub. "Where the heck are you taking me?" Sarah joked, as we beat our way through the bush and rough land to finally arrive at some caves near the western shoreline.

This was a fascinating area. Near one of the caves' mouths was a deep pool of water surrounded by coral rock. The water was clear as gin, and I could see several varieties of beautiful fish

43

swimming there. "This," I said, "is a blue hole—an underground cavern that flows out to the sea somewhere in the region." Sarah perched her long, lanky body precariously over one of the rocks so she could see better into the pool. "It's like a tunnel, Sarah. Fish can swim from the sea into the tunnel and end up here, in this blue hole, an opening in the land that surrounds it."

Sarah was mesmerized. "This is incredible, Kate," she said, in almost a whisper. Our day together was coming to a close. It had been wonderful to be with my good friend again. Now, as I drove her back to the marina to await Rosie's arrival, I felt the pangs of homesickness once again. As the seaplane coasted into the beach at the marina, I knew this had been a special treat, and I wished I could extend Sarah's visit a little longer. But she had a desk full of legal documents to which she had to return. With a hug and a wave, she waded out to climb aboard 'the witch' for her ride home.

❦

I recalled during my childhood, probably in grade school or in Mr. Kaiser's history class, reading about the North American settlers who pushed westward in the 1800's. What stuck in my mind was the fact that those homesteaders who, along the way, settled on the plains of Nebraska or Kansas—places of nowhere—spent their lives trying to resist feelings of loneliness and fear, and who, forever, had to listen to howling winds through most of the year—blizzards of winter or sandstorms of summer.

That's how I found my mental state as winter approached: the loneliness of the cay, the fear of the isolation and recalling and reliving the robbery experience continued to plague my mind. And then there was the wind. It blew for days at a time, howling incessantly from the northeast. It whistled around our little house and through every window that wouldn't close properly. The howling was eerie and evil-sounding. It made me feel uneasy, and served to reinforce the fact that I didn't feel good about my job or about the cay. I wondered if the solitude was causing such feelings, and I hoped that Peter and I hadn't made a big mistake in accepting this job. I pressed forward, trying to shove such feelings into the deep recesses of my mind, but the old saying kept popping up: You make your bed; you have to lie in it. We had left the comforts and security of our former life; now, we had to figure out how to stay on top of these feelings and just get on with the job at hand. I was *not* going to be a quitter, and it was too late to look back.

Living in the islands, the weather became an important and integral part of our lives. With thousands of square miles of ocean surrounding our little cay, rough seas meant everything changed for the day—boats that were planning to leave the marina decided to sit tight; Boats that were planning to arrive that day usually decided to stay wherever they were. The VHF radio was always yakking with yachts contacting each other, trying to decide if the weather was going to break or be an issue for them that day. Our VHF radio was such an important means of communication that it was imperative it be left on twenty-four hours a day, both at Cheap Charlie's and at our house.

Peter and I awoke every morning by six-fifteen a.m. We always grabbed a cup of coffee and sat quietly on the porch together for a few minutes to meditate on the beauty of the island that lay within our view. It was our quiet time together at sunrise before the day started to get crazy. Then, Peter left for his daily staff meeting at six forty-five a.m. and I started my job with the weather. I had to be at the VHF promptly at six-fifty a.m. for this daily morning task. Since there were no computers and no internet on the island, I had to laboriously make notes in longhand from the information provided by the Nassau Meteorological Office's report that was faxed to us around that time. Shortly thereafter, I received the Nassau Boaters' Report given by Bahamas Air Sea Rescue Association (BASRA) at seven a.m. sharp over the VHF. From those two reports, I gleaned a weather report for Highborne Cay and the northern Exumas. I then transmitted this twenty-four hour weather information over the VHF promptly at seven-fifteen a.m. I never knew until many months later how valuable this information was to boaters within a twenty-five-mile radius of our island. Most were out of range to hear the Nassau reports, and many just liked to check in with us as they cruised the waters in our area.

For me, it was a great way to start my day. I'd give a detailed weather report, followed by a brief hail from each boat that had picked up the VHF signal. Thank you, Highborne. You're welcome, *Sea Dragon*. Thank you, Highborne. You're welcome, *Charade*. Some days, up to twenty-five boats would check in. It was a good way to keep current with who was in the neighborhood, and it was fun to welcome them back when they had come through the area previously.

As much as I hated leaving my bed early in the morning to do the preparation, the weather report, itself, was a task that I really loved to do; People seemed to appreciate the effort. Guests who pulled into the marina for supplies or to tie up at the dock for the evening would say to me, "Hey, you're the Weather Lady. I recognize your voice." Or, "Thanks for your efforts with your reports each day." Boaters always made me feel important when I did this job as if it held great significance to all within the sound of my voice. They were the ones who gave me the encouragement to continue the task every morning, day after day, year after year.

As the days melded into weeks, and the weeks into months, we found time to ourselves on the island was rare. During that first year, Peter and I made the mistake of working 24-7. Our days were long, and often I could be found in the little office late into the night working on the books. Most of our staff only worked Monday through Friday. However, Isaac, the mechanic was the exception. One Sunday afternoon a month, he covered for Peter at the marina for a couple of hours, so Peter could watch a Sunday football game. A welcome break. Isaac was a big man, tall and muscular with an infectious smile that revealed a perfect set of gleaming white teeth. His strength was impressive as I saw him lift the heaviest cases from the mailboat or move machine parts in the generator room. He had been the first person I met when I arrived, and he had impressed me as a born leader. He was extremely intelligent. It amazed me how he could be such an expert on engines and generators, just by interpreting the diagrams of his equipment manuals.

Isaac's realm of responsibility was great; He cared for the island's power plant with its two big generators, all the vehicles and anything electrical that could be rewired, rewound or restored. He was a personable fellow and an excellent ambassador for the cay, so he was the perfect person to relieve Peter for those precious couple of hours occasionally, even though our VHF was never off and we were always 'on call.'

During one of these infrequent breaks, we were trying to catch the last quarter of the Dolphins/Patriots game on a Sunday afternoon when the radio began its summons. "Highborne Cay,

Highborne Cay. This is the yacht *My Venice*." There was a pause, and then, "Highborne Cay," the voice pleaded, "please come in!" The calling vessel had arrived several days ago and was securely tied to the pier at the marina. What could be the distress? The caller was persistent with panic in her voice.

Begrudgingly, Peter hoisted himself from his favorite chair and grabbed the mike, holding his eyes on the screen as the Dolphins scored a touchdown. "This is Highborne. Go ahead." The radio snarled with static as he released the transmitter.

"Please help me," the voice wailed. "We're tied to your dock at the marina, and my husband is very ill! Please...can you come?"

"OK." It was more like a sigh. "We're on the way," he replied as we grabbed our foul-weather jackets and headed out the door. It was only a 4-minute drive to the marina by truck, but to me it seemed like an hour. She was standing on the dock waiting for us. Isaac stood next to her, looking helpless.

"What happened?" I yelled above the squally weather.

"My husband! Can you help? Please!" she sobbed. "He's stopped breathing!"

Peter and I jumped aboard the vessel, and as I entered the main salon, there, on the floor, lay her husband. With only a few seconds to assess the situation, I felt for a pulse, found none, and saw that he was, indeed, not breathing. I immediately knelt and started mouth-to-mouth resuscitation. As I applied CPR, one thing was sure—the boat was an absolute stinking mess. I could smell the rotting food and the stale air in the cabin. As my mouth touched the dead man's every few seconds, thoughts began to creep into my mind: what if this man was really sick when he died? Maybe contagious? A frightening thought. The minutes seemed like hours. Finally, after what Peter called a gallant attempt, he pulled me off the rescue effort. I guess he was thinking the same thing, but he was kind enough to keep the thoughts to himself.

We finally had to come to grips with the fact that we had a dead man in a boat at our marina, a new widow who didn't know anything about boating, and a filthy boat that had no captain. This difficult situation presented us with a whole new problem. We now faced the unfamiliar task of dealing with a corpse.

I telephoned a doctor friend in Nassau, only to learn that any foreigner who dies on Bahamian soil requires a police investigation and a mandatory autopsy. This presented a two-fold problem: (1) we had to get the police here, and (2) we had to get the body to Nassau for the autopsy. Peter knew there were several police officers on an island a few miles south of us where they were stationed to protect a local airstrip from drug traffickers. So, he ran his own boat, *Bookalukus*, a high-powered thirty-one-foot Morgan, to Norman's Cay to try to convince the officers to leave their post and come to Highborne with him.

With about an hour to kill before Peter's return with the officers, I went to work on the problem at hand. I learned the widow's name was Lillie von Straggart. She and her husband, along with her little dog and two caged canaries, had come from Florida to cruise the Bahamas. I also knew her husband had been a drinker because, each day that they had been guests at the marina, he had come to the store for a bottle of brandy. Five days. Five bottles of brandy. It had been like clockwork.

Naturally, Lillie was distraught about her husband's untimely death, and I was grateful when one of our guests kindly took her aboard their yacht for a while. That gave me an opportunity to work through the issue at hand, namely getting the body to Nassau for an autopsy. I called several charter seaplane companies but the weather was too squally for them to fly out. The earliest they could come was the next day. Twenty-four long hours. The big question, of course, was: what do we do with the body until then? It was at that very moment that I had a horrible thought and grabbed the VHF that hung on my belt. "*Bookalu-kus, Bookalukus*, this is Highborne. Come in."

Now eight miles away, Peter picked up the call and answered. "This is *Bookalukus*, go ahead."

"*Bookalukus*, please switch and answer One-Four," I said. (That also meant that everyone who was copying the mail that day was now switching to channel fourteen.)

"*Bookalukus*," I said slowly, "Lis-ten ver-y care-ful-ly." There was a long pause. "If the police ask about our storage facilities, remember…the freezer…. in the store…. . is full." I hoped that was all I needed to say.

Within a few minutes, the captain of a ketch that was anchored in the harbor came by in his dinghy to offer us an extra sail he had on board. Almost apologetically, he reached over the gunwale of his dinghy to hand me the folded sailcloth. "I know you're in a tough situation. I followed your conversation with *Bookalukus*. You could use this as a shroud." Now I remembered Peter's conversation about eavesdropping on the VHF. This was one time I was happy about it.

Isaac and I then drove to the store to load a dozen twenty-pound blocks of ice in the back of the pick-up. We lugged them, one by one, down the pier to *My Venice*. My plan was to rest the Late Mr. von Straggart flat on the shroud, pack the ice tightly around his body, and roll up the sailcloth to secure its contents.

Isaac looked at me, long and hard and then at the body. "This is not my idea of fun," he said through clenched teeth. Touching dead people was something he'd never done, and he didn't like it. I couldn't blame him.

"I'll get you some rubber gloves, Isaac. Would that make it any easier?"

"Yes, m'am, it sure would."

I drove back to the house and grabbed my kitchen gloves, praying they would fit Isaac's big hands. I needed Isaac's help. The gloves better damned-well fit!

Returning to the marina, we followed the plan. First we chipped up the ice blocks into small pieces. Next, we packed the chips firmly around the corpse as we simultaneously wrapped the shroud around it. It was a bigger job than I thought. With the heat of the day, we had to work fast with the ice. Afterwards, Isaac and I were both drenched in sweat, despite the fact that our hands were cold from handling the chipped ice. Lastly, I found some baling twine in Cheap Charlie's cupboard to secure the shroud at each end. Only then did I stand back to assess our handiwork. What type of barbaric place was this?

Peter finally arrived with the two police officers. As they stepped off the gunwale of *Bookalukus*, one of the officers pulled me aside. "M'am, we'll need to stay here until you've flown the body to Nassau for the autopsy."

"Here?" I asked. "On Highborne?" This was getting complicated. "How come?" I was looking for a reason why, at that moment, I not only had a dead body to worry about—I had two policemen, as well.

"Yes M'am. It's the law, and we'll have to take statements from everyone connected with this man's death." The officers moved off to do whatever official things were necessary, and I was left standing there on the dock, near the body of the Late Mr. von Straggart, wondering what the next step would be.

It was Peter who finally got everyone settled into Harborside—the cops, the widow, her dog *and* the canaries—to spend a long night in anticipation of the next day. Unfortunately, I spent *my* night worrying about what I might have contracted by way of disease.

The next day when the weather had cleared, a plane was dispatched to Norman's Cay. *Bookalukus* left the harbor for Norman's Cay airstrip eight miles south of us with the Late Mr. von Straggart, still in the shroud, strapped in the fishing chair. As *Bookalukus* pulled away from the dock, it was a strange sight to see. I wish I had been privy to watch Peter, Isaac and the two policemen get Mr. von Straggart's remains plus his widow and her dog into a five-seat charter aircraft at the Norman's Cay airstrip.

After they returned, Isaac and Peter turned their hands at cleaning up *My Venice* so the boat would at least be somewhat presentable for a hired captain to take back to the States. As Isaac and Peter grumbled about this job, they piled the old food, soiled carpeting and smelly linens onto the dock beside *My Venice.* (As the pile rose higher and higher, I wondered how anybody could have lived in such filth.) While they were working at that task, I made some calls to several marinas in Nassau. I finally found a young Bahamian captain who was free and willing to take the job of running this vessel back to Fort Lauderdale, its home port. I hired him, knowing it would only be another few days before the boat was finally gone.

When we looked back on the experience, Peter and I decided that we had lived through the ordeal relatively unscathed. Both Peter and Isaac admitted to the fact that this was the closest either of them had been to death in the flesh, and neither of them were happy about handling a corpse. Nor was I happy about having to wait six days for the autopsy report, which finally arrived by fax, showing cirrhosis of the liver, and giving me great relief that I had not been exposed to any contagious disease.

It had been a tough few days. In the end, we inherited Mr. von Straggart's two canaries and learned a great deal about handling such a situation. The island continued to teach us that we really could cope under the most extraordinary conditions.

That first winter at Highborne provided new experiences at every turn. Woody, had managed the trip to Highborne and had fared very well here. He actually surprised me. As old a horse as he was, he was still full of life, and took every opportunity to lift the latch on his gate and saunter down to the beach, about a quarter mile from his stable. When I had purchased him ten years prior to our move, he stuck me as an extremely intelligent animal with a kind disposition. As the years passed, we bonded well, and he became a faithful friend to me. But his intelligence often got him into trouble. Unlatching the gate was no feat for him whenever it became hot and muggy. He knew where the beach was, and he loved to swim, but his shoes were always an issue. The sand would suck those shoes right off his hooves! And, since I was also the local 'blacksmith' on Highborne, his jaunts to the beach often exasperated me.

One day I was sitting in the office doing the books when I looked out the window to see Woody's rear end heading down the road toward the beach. My common sense said to rush out and catch him; Instead, I slipped into a pair of beach sandals and crept down to the beach behind him to spy on exactly what he was going to do once he got to his destination. He plodded down the path to the beach, looked up and down the stretch of white sand, and without another moment's hesitation, kicked up his heels with amazing dexterity and flew down the beach at a flat-out gallop. I stood, hidden by the bushes, and watched in amazement. With the beach almost two miles long, he galloped until he was almost to the end. He was traveling fast. Then, all at once, he slowed down and made a sharp right turn, directly into the ocean. As I watched him splash into the sea, it was troubling to see he had no regard for the distance he was putting between the land and himself. Against all instincts to run down the beach after him, I held my position at the top of the path, hoping against hope that no cruising shark would be interested in his toothpick legs that were thrashing under the water's surface. Just when I could stand the anticipation no more, Woody realized that Africa was going to be a longer swim than back to shore, and he made his turn. He was coming home. Like a mother with a small child, I never let him know I was watching him. I stayed hidden until he reached the beach path once again and headed for the stable. A turning point for both of us had occurred. From that moment onward, Woody's gate was always open during the daytime, and I never worried about him again. Often I would come back from the marina and find him sound asleep on our front porch, the cool breeze ruffling his mane.

Woody catching the cool breeze on our porch

His shoes, on the other hand, were always an issue. Because he was a finely bred horse, he could not go barefoot on the coral rock footings of the island; He would go lame in no time. His feet needed the protection of the standard iron shoes used on most horses these days. This presented a major issue for me. In Nassau, I could call the local blacksmith once every six weeks to have this painless job done. However, such a skilled craftsman was not available to me any more. The solution came down to one choice only: I had to learn to do the job myself.

Luckily, Monty, Woody's blacksmith in Nassau, was also a good friend. He had actually started the instructions several months before we moved to Highborne Cay in anticipation of the issue, and the background and practice he gave me during that time was invaluable. When Woody was ready to leave Nassau, Monty felt confident I could do the job. He agreed to come to Highborne if I got into trouble, but he assured me that I now had enough knowledge to perform this very specialized work.

The process of shoeing a horse is difficult for any layman. The main objective is to trim the hoof, itself, and then shape a piece of iron (the shoe) to replicate the bottom of the hoof. Each horse is different, and the shoes need to fit properly to be comfortable (like our own shoes). I worked around this challenge by taking a paper tracing of each foot, and then faxing the sheets to Monty in Nassau. From these tracings he would make the new shoes to send back on the mailboat. The whole procedure was still an ordeal. And, I always tried to keep at least two pair of spare shoes at any given time. The most discouraging thing, though, was to see Woody coming back from the beach with a bobbing head, which indicated that he had thrown a shoe somewhere in the sand.

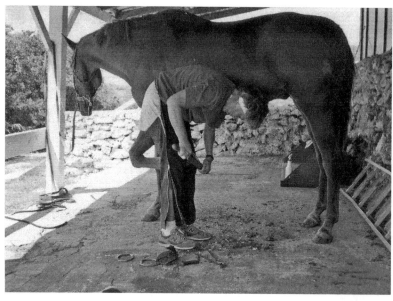

Shoeing Woody was back-breaking work.

Shoeing was back-breaking work. It didn't take me long to realize that whatever a blacksmith charged to do the job, he earned it. To remove two shoes, shape the bottom of each hoof, file off any rough, uneven spots and then tack the shoe back on properly would take a skilled blacksmith about twenty or thirty minutes; it took me almost two hours. As the months wore on, I found if I took three Advil before starting the job, I could still stand up straight at the end of it. I was proud to say that in five years of shoeing my horse, I never once put a nail in the wrong place. But, it was a task I never relished and sometimes, as I bent underneath the horse with my back in spasms, I wished I was back in Nassau where a professional farrier was only a phone call away.

✲

When we started work at Highborne, Peter and I never knew what real physical labor was in a job. We had both come from office employment where there was a comfortable room, a nice desk and air conditioning. The job at Highborne, however, proved to be a shock to our bodies, soft from a poor exercise program, pale from lack of sunshine. We were immediately thrown into heavy physical labor: lifting cases of canned goods in the store, yanking on yacht ropes at the marina and walking back and forth in the hot sun in what seemed like endless miles: from the dock to Cheap Charlie's, then back to the dock, from the dock to the gas depot, from the gas depot to Cheap Charlie's. It wouldn't surprise me if the miles we walked each day were double digits. And the sun, endlessly beating down to sap every bit of strength and energy from a person's body, left both of us totally drained as each day came to a close.

We were now three months into the job, and with the help of Ben Gay, Advil and a sunburn lotion, our bodies were starting to meet the challenge. Pete's arms became bronzed and his shoulders started to muscle up. My clothes began to fit more loosely as fat turned to muscle, and my skin took on the natural glow of a permanent suntan. We were becoming acclimated to the long hours and the physical work, and it seemed to be agreeing with us. However, the mailboat job was one I wished was not mine.

The mailboat, *Emmett & Cephas*, arrived once a month, not only with mail but with everything including groceries for the store, lumber and building supplies, propane tanks, generator parts, horse food, cases of water, soda pop, liquor and anything that the cay required that month.

She was an old wooden vessel, less than 80 feet long, that traveled weekly between Nassau, the Exuma Cays and Aklins

Life On A Rock

Island. Highborne Cay was always an "unscheduled" stop since it wasn't on the regular route. On that accord, her captain always charged us double freight. She had a large cargo hold beneath her deck and a walk-in freezer and cooler above deck to hold the perishable items. The freezer was a joke, barely holding at 32 degrees. Perishable items such as ice cream usually arrived in a disastrous state with the now-thawed product dripping out of the corners of the case.

Dry cargo had to be manually lifted from the freight compartment below deck, item by item, and set on shore where the goods were transferred to a rudimentary flatbed trailer that was hitched to Highborne's old Farmall Tractor. The tractor, itself, had seen the turn of several decades and looked like it might give up the ghost at any time.

Unloading the mailboat

To make the mailboat situation worse, her captain was cantankerous, so it was difficult to discuss with him the various delivery errors, issues with thawed cargo that should have arrived frozen, and to set a scheduled delivery that would be some time other than midnight.

The job required all-island participation in the unloading process, which often happened after dark, since the mailboat's stop at Highborne was seldom on schedule, and the tide played a large role in whether the vessel had enough water beneath her hull to get into Highborne's harbor. When the mailboat arrived, the mosquitoes gathered in clouds to feast on human blood. We suffered through our work, covered in Off or Skintastic, and wondered why we had to be so tortured in our labors.

Once unloaded, the mailboat departed in the darkness with only her cabin lights aglow, and the old tractor chugged and coughed up the hill, pulling its load to the store or the machine shop a mile away. Here a second unloading took place, this time off the flatbed and into the store. As the young men tossed the cases off the trailer, we were at the warehouse door, catching and sorting, with this case to go on this shelf, that case to go on that pallet.

Sometimes, after a long day, I could hardly face this job. It always took the entire island staff, working together late into the night, to complete the task. When we put the last case of goods away, everyone said good-night and headed home—everybody, that is, except Peter and me. Each invoice from every supplier had to be checked against the goods received, and a selling price for each item was calculated and recorded on the store's master price list. It was a known fact: When the mailboat came to Highborne, it meant a very late night for both of us.

The mailboat, itself, was only part of the issue. Month after month the cycle continued: Before faxing the orders through to the suppliers in Nassau, we had to take a physical inventory of the store items and building materials or machine parts that might be needed. The orders were then placed with about fifteen or twenty different suppliers. If I missed an important item on an order such as a new carburetor for the truck, or screen for a porch, that item would have to wait until the mailboat arrived again, a long month later.

I was convinced: The mailboat with its related jobs was one of the most tedious and thankless jobs on the Cay, and I hated it. Yet, it was our thin thread to survival. The mailboat held a lifeline between Highborne Cay and Nassau. Without her, we had no other way of getting the necessary food, supplies and mail. Yes, the mailboat was irreplaceable. No creative problem-solving could eliminate this necessary evil, no matter how long and hard we thought about it…but we kept thinking.

As winter approached, so did the "snowbirds" from the north. Sailboats, motor yachts and large cruising vessels began to arrive, bringing with them business for the store, the marina, the guest houses and stress. We worked twelve-hour days regularly with additional hours being put in at the house, where we often found ourselves working over the accounts well after midnight. Early in December, after a long day at the dock, we were looking forward to sitting down to some fresh steamed snapper and a nice glass of white wine for supper. While Peter set the table for dinner and I was hard at work over the stove preparing the meal, suddenly and without provocation, KG and Julia started barking as if they'd both gone crazy. As they ran back and forth in the living room with their hackles up and scratched at the door to go out, they put up an alarm that was frightening and couldn't be ignored. After what we'd been through several months before, Peter had made sure we were as prepared as we could be; Our loaded shotguns were within easy reach. With alarm in his voice, he gave me a quick glance. "Get the guns, Kate!"

With both of us now gripping our firearms, Peter disappeared out the back door, his voice trailing, "You go out the front... and...take the safety off!" I grabbed a flashlight as I flung open the front door, giving my eyes a chance to adjust to the darkness. I quickly repositioned the light in my hand with the barrel of the Winchester resting on top of the flashlight. In this way, wherever the beam was aimed, the barrel of the gun followed. My heart was pounding and adrenaline was up. As I stepped into the darkness, I vowed to myself that I would never go through another terrifying experience like last fall; I would rather die first. So, I worked the light beam, first through the shrubbery at the edge of the property, then under the Hibiscus bushes at the base of the house, and finally along the top of the low stone wall that bordered the road. To my surprise, the light allowed me to catch a glimpse of a little black dome tucked behind the wall. It took only a second to realize that was the top of someone's head.

"Get up, you Mother Fucker! Get up there from behind that damned wall!" I screamed. The words and tone disguised my true feelings of panic. Throwing the barrel of the Winchester up towards the sky I pulled the trigger. I'd forgotten how loud a twenty-gauge shotgun could be. Hearing the gun, Peter rushed back in a panic, not sure of what he might find and hoping I wouldn't shoot him as he banked around the corner of the house.

Up jumped a small man, hands raised, yelling, "Don't shoot, don't shoot! I'm a poor fisherman," he pleaded, "and my boat did sink." There was a pause. "I swam to dis here cay."

Of course this fact could easily be true. Out here in the middle of the Exuma Cays, people got stranded; Rescues happened. We quickly analyzed the situation. "Yeah?" Peter quipped. "How come your clothes aren't wet?" As Peter and I struggled with these questions, we stood there with both barrels of our guns aimed at the man who had disturbed our evening tranquility. Each moment that passed made us more paranoid, yet we had to admit that we could be over-exaggerating…over-reacting. It was hard to make the call, until the VHF radio inside the house started blaring "Highborne Cay, Highborne Cay, this is the yacht *Damselfish* with urgent traffic." The sound echoed through the open door of the house and reached our ears as we stood in the yard. I couldn't take my eyes off our prisoner; I wasn't moving. Again and again the radio called to us. Peter broke the ice. "Answer it," he said.

The voice on the VHF was that of Tom Jantz, captain and owner of the motor yacht *Damselfish*, tied at the marina. Tom was a good client of the Cay, and was very aware, hearing the shots, that there was a crisis at the house. I filled him in on the details.

"There's something going on down here, too," he replied. "A small boat just entered the harbor, and it's circling around the dock area." It was now pitch dark and very unusual for a small boat to approach at night. When Tom heard the shots at the house, he knew this was too coincidental. "Don't worry," he assured me, "I'll take care of the situation down here."

He quickly turned the mike over to his wife, Lynn and retrieved his . 357 Magnum from the closet aboard *Damselfish*. In a bold move, Tom stepped off his boat with his gun in his right hand and a flashlight in his left, the beam of which he pointed directly at the weapon. With his handgun now in the spotlight, he yelled, "I'm from Detroit! This is my gun and I know how to use it!" The driver of the boat hesitated. "Dock your vessel or be shot!" Without further incident, the little boat came alongside, and Tom single-handedly placed the driver under citizen's arrest; But Tom, too, wondered what the next move would be.

Back at the house, things were beginning to unfold. Peter searched the area where our perpetrator had been hiding, and to our amazement and shock, on the ground lay a .9 mm handgun, a roll of duck tape, a croaker sac, and a black tam and gloves. It was at that very moment I looked directly at Peter. "My God, they were coming to do the whole thing again!"

With two persons now in custody, it was time to call Nassau. A fellow Rotarian, Supt. Basil Dean, headed up the Criminal Investigation Department there; Basil gave us needed encouragement. "We'll get a helicopter dispatched as soon as possible," he said. We should have remembered from the first robbery that it would be a very long three hours before they arrived.

Time dragged by. I thought my arms would give out. Peter and I took shifts, but holding the heavy Winchester to my shoulder with the barrel aimed at our captor was proving to be a bigger physical effort that I thought. The ache went across the back of my shoulders and down my left arm. It was imperative to keep vigilant, but it was a real task to make my body do the work without cramping. The only encouragement was the thought that *this* time the tables were turned; *this* time we were the captors instead of the captives.

By the time we heard the thump, thump, thump of the police chopper, Tom was still holding the boat captain at gunpoint at the marina. Finally, Lynn called from *Damselfish*. "The police have arrived, Pete. They are taking our man into custody." I overheard the conversation from my position on the porch and breathed a sigh of relief. She continued,

"Isaac is driving the officers and the suspect up to your house right now. We'll stay down here and be vigilant for anything else."

Not long after Peter and Lynn signed off the radio, the inspectors arrived and took over. Now I knew we had plenty of backup firepower. I could finally put my gun down. I was beat. The stress of the night, coupled with the fact that it was a second robbery attempt, crushed my spirits. I sat down on the porch step and, with my head in my hands, quietly wept.

Peter, too, was visibly shaken, and his face was drawn as he sat down beside me. "I dunno," he whispered, "we seem to be getting a lot of practice at this." He reached for my hand and his grip was firm. As we both rested there on the front step, we realized we had risked our lives to capture these people. We could have been shot. Worse, we could have been killed. But, this time we did what we had to do in order to protect ourselves. The island was teaching us well.

The inspectors arrived in the back of Isaac's truck with the suspect that Tom had apprehended. They took our suspect into custody as well, and after intense interrogation, learned there was a third suspect involved. With this information, they handcuffed the two men and took them towards the East Beach where the police chopper waited. The inspectors then returned to our house to take statements from Tom, Lynn, Peter and me. It was a long night. Peter and I could hardly wait to crawl into bed at four a.m. for the precious few hours of sleep before the next sunrise. And, we knew we would never be able to repay the kindness and courage of Tom and Lynn for their help in securing the island. They would remain our special friends forever.

Early the next day the officers who had remained on the cay were knocking at the kitchen door. "We need your assistance," they said through the open jalousie windows. "The third person involved in last night's attempted burglary is still loose on the island, and we need to track him down."

I knew this would be an arduous task on this 500-acre island since much of the area was in heavy undergrowth and bush.

"I know all the island's trails and paths," I told them, "but, these are only accessible by foot or horseback." They'd never be able to cover the ground without one of us as a guide. "I could walk you through the area, if you like."

"That would be good," said one of the inspectors.

Peter scowled. "It's too dangerous. Something might happen."

"She'll be safe with us, Mr. Albury. We just need to be shown the trails near the front of the island." After some discussion, Peter finally agreed. He would open the marina office as usual to quash any rumors or gossip. I, on the other hand, would walk the officers along the trails.

"Can I bring my gun with me?" I asked. After the happenings of the night before, the Winchester was my comforter. The inspector nodded.

It was an adrenaline rush for me—a feeling that it was payback time for all the fear, the uncertainty—the feelings of violation the robbers had caused months ago. Carrying the Winchester with the trigger guard resting in my right hand and the barrel in my left, I led the inspectors into the remote parts of the cay. Finally, as we came to the landfill on the northwestern side of the island, a red cap popped up from the bushes about two hundred yards away. Once Redcap caught a glimpse of us, he disappeared into the thick undergrowth again. The inspectors signaled me to move out, and as I jogged towards home along the dirt road, I could hear guns firing.

Peter met me on the road about half way home. "Are you okay?" He had heard the shots and was clearly shaken. I nodded as I handed him the Winchester. "C'mon," he said, "let's see who they caught."

We walked back to meet them. The suspect, now flanked by the two officers, was being escorted in handcuffs, back to the house. I couldn't restrain myself. As I walked towards him, I held his stare. "You bastard," I snarled, and hauled back, slapping him with the full force of my hand and simultaneously giving him a knee to his groin. The inspectors casually looked the other way.

Peter was close behind me, and I could hear the shells being ejected from my gun. He jammed the barrel of the Winchester at the base of the suspect's nose. One of the inspectors gently pushed the barrel away, but not before Peter growled at their captive. "If you ever set foot on this cay again, I'll kill you."

Later that day the chopper returned to collect the CID officers, along with the last suspect. We were done with another chapter in our lives, but this time the experience turned our fear into courage, and it helped to heal the scars left by the first robbery. The island had given us another life-changing occurrence that taught Peter and me about our capabilities and helped us understand ourselves. Never would I have dreamed we could both muster the courage necessary to put our lives on the line and rise above such a grave situation. Tonight would not be forgotten.

Over the years, Christmas has always been a big deal for our family. Both Peter's family and mine were close and took turns alternating Christmas dinner, year after year. My mother and Peter's mother had been good friends since their childhood, so it was natural for this to happen. It was truly wonderful to have such a loving extended family, and Peter and I both missed everyone, especially as the holidays approached.

This year, Christmas would be totally different. There would be no family; Peter and I were alone for the first Christmas ever. Since we had to work through the holidays, I decided I wouldn't even bother with the usual holiday stuff. But, as December 25th drew closer, I felt the need for a little holiday spirit. I got motivated to make some decorations for a little three-foot artificial tree I had found in the attic of one of the guest houses a few months before. The little tree was tattered and dusty and wouldn't have made the grade as a Christmas tree anywhere else. However, I had a few strands of tiny lights, made some bows out of left-over birthday ribbon, and tied up some sand dollars and white shells to hang as decoration. Peter popped some popcorn to string up as garland. Voila! It became the prettiest Christmas tree on the island, and each night that we lit it up, our spirits rose to the occasion.

Christmas Day we decided to close the marina and store at noon. It was the first time in almost four months we indulged ourselves in a half-day off. At first I felt guilty. Maybe this was because I was such a workaholic, or maybe because I just wasn't used to the time off. Peter appeared about thirty minutes later in his genuine Santa suit.

I chuckled as I recalled when Peter had packed his old Santa suit in the box marked "to take to Highborne." At the time, I was dumbfounded.

"What in hell's creation do you need to take that for?" I asked, worried about the space the suit was going to require in packing, and the fact that he'd probably *never* use it.

"Don't you worry yourself about that, Kate," was all he said.

Now I understood. He knew sometime, somewhere, he would be able to put that suit to good use. He donned the suit, boots, and beard in eighty-degree weather and we headed south by boat to Norman's Cay. Word spread fast by VHF that Santa was on the way. Boats at anchor near Highborne's harbor honked their horns, and people waved as the big man in the red suit drove by in *Bookalukus*.

Santa landed at Norman's Cay beach, carrying a case of beer on his shoulder for the residents there. It was a good laugh for everyone and certainly broke the monotony for us, as we all sat on the sand and drank Kalik. When Santa and Mrs. Claus were invited to join in Christmas lunch at one of the homes on Norman's Cay, we couldn't resist. It was nice to be off Highborne for a few hours.

For me, aside from being affectionately called the Weather Lady, I was also known as the Store Lady, driving people back and forth from the marina to the store, keeping the shelves stocked, and manually tracking inventory for the next mailboat. It was my job, also, to keep good public relations with the clients.

One day in February, I happened to drive two guests to the store for some supplies. We drove and talked about the island and the weather, where small talk would suffice. Once at the store, they purchased several bags of groceries and were about to pay for these when the gentleman asked me to take a U. S. one-dollar bill out of the register. Perplexed, I asked him why.

"I'd like to autograph it," he answered. I was bewildered. I thought this person might be a rock star or a Hollywood celebrity, and I was embarrassed I hadn't recognized him. I pulled a U. S.

one-dollar bill from the register. He proceeded to sign his name on the bill and gave it back to me with a big smile.

"Oh, thanks!" I said, first looking at the bill and then to him. I guess my confusion was obvious.

"See?" he repeated, pointing to the dollar bill that now lay on the counter.

"See what?" I answered, peering at the face of George Washington.

"That's my signature.... the same as the one on the bill. I'm Nicholas Brady."

Slightly exasperated, I slid the note back into the cash drawer. I didn't quite know what to say, but I knew I'd better say something. "Oh, you're THE Mr. Nicolas Brady!" That was good enough for Mr. Brady, and it covered my tracks of looking totally stupid. As I drove him back to the marina, we laughed about the fact that I was a Bahamian and knew very little about the U. S. Secretary of the Treasury.

All in all, I liked the store job. Even though the building, itself, left much to be desired, the interior was my responsibility. Sets of whitewashed wooden shelving bordered the inside walls where there sat rows of dry goods, canned goods, cleaning supplies, snack items and soda pop. An old chest freezer near the entrance door held a few self-serve items such as steaks, cuts of chicken, pork chops, hot dogs, spare ribs and various packages of frozen vegetables. We had a small room off the main floor where a customer could find liquor of all descriptions, and cases of assorted beer were meticulously stacked beneath the lower shelves. A small storage area off the back of the store was jokingly called the 'warehouse,' and this little area somehow held all of the remaining stock not displayed out front.

Near the check-out shelf stood the big walk-in coolers with a heavy latch that needed brute strength to operate.

Inside were cases of fresh fruits and vegetables, and candy of all varieties. In the freezer section sat cases of frozen orange juice, frozen vegetables and the bulk of the meat and poultry supplies; anything that needed a hard freeze was stored inside, including milk that had been delivered by the mailboat. (Freezing the half-gallons of milk was the only way the cay could have a steady supply between mailboat deliveries.)

Then there were the bags and bags of ice that lined the freezer shelves. Ice on the cay was a precious commodity. In the beginning, there was no ice maker. Ice had to be made by manually filling large plastic bags from the spigot at the cistern, and then gently loading the bags into the back of Peter's truck. The truck would then back up a hundred yards to the store and one by one, the bags would be hand-carried into the freezer and carefully laid out on the shelves. Ice sold for five dollars a bag; it was a cheap price to pay for the intensive labor that was involved.

The new cash register machine sat proudly behind a little counter near the door where, until recently, the space had been occupied by an old cigar box and an adding machine. The counter offered plenty of space to pack groceries for the customers.

I had never done retailing in my former career, so this was all new to me. Things like rotating the stock, keeping the shelves neat, tracking the inventory, planning orders and, of course, balancing the cash were my duties. However, there was the green-grocer business, too, and a messy business it was. To laboriously unwrap and pull the black and soggy leafs from the lettuce, or sort through some spoiled tomatoes or rotten potatoes was not my favorite job. A case of potatoes that needed work would require me to lug the case to the cistern spigot a hundred yards away, dump the potatoes on the grass nearby, sort through the rotten pieces, and then wash and dry each good piece before replacing these in a fresh box.

It was obvious, however, that green-grocer work was important. Since the mailboat only stopped once a month, I had to make the produce last as long as possible, and I could only do this if there were no rotten apples in the barrel, so to speak. Every staff member living on Highborne relied on the store for their groceries, so keeping the produce in good condition not only benefited the clients; it helped those of us who lived there.

All in all, the store was a challenge I liked. I found it rewarding to balance at the end of a good day. I loved counting the money. I convinced Peter that we should begin to expand the inventory items as business increased, and we branched out into a small clothing line. After I planted Bougainvillea along the front entrance wall, its beautiful sprays of fuchsia flowers gave the old metal building a facelift. Ritchie painted the floor to disguise the raw concrete, and I tried to palletize the store room for better organization. With the VHF radio close at hand, I was never out of contact with the marina office or the boats in the area. The store proved to be one of the good parts of my job, but I continually wished the store's building were in better condition. I hoped I could convince Mary Smith to spring for a capital improvement, although I seriously doubted if this would ever happen.

Meeting new people was always interesting and there was no better place to do this than at the marina. When *The Other Ten* first pulled in and asked for a slip for a few days, we were happy to accommodate. Little did we know that its owner would become one of our life-long friends in a place where long-time friends were few.

To meet Sandy Miles was an experience in itself. He drawled out a Southern greeting, had a new joke on the tip of his tongue and a laugh that was so contagious it made everyone around him join in. His smile spread over his whole face, and he adored life, even though he had serious heart disease, and smoked like a fiend.

Although he hailed from North Carolina, he loved The Bahamas and its people. I remember his story of an old cab driver he had met in Nassau many years ago when he first started coming to The Bahamas. Sandy had hired Smitty to take him around Nassau to shop for ships' stores before leaving for the Exumas. Smitty stayed with Sandy the whole day, suggesting places to shop and helping load *The Other Ten* for her next cruise.

When evening came, Sandy wanted to do a little gambling on Paradise Island. He asked Smitty to stay with him that evening and 'take care of him.' Throughout the evening, Smitty never left his side. As Sandy began to win big at the craps table (as well as get totally inebriated), he passed all of his chips to Smitty for safekeeping until the evening was over. It was ol' Smitty who counted the chips and cashed them in, and then took Sandy back to *The Other Ten* where he laid him out on the couch in the main salon to sleep it off. The next morning, Sandy awoke with a screaming hangover to find his winnings were laid on the table next to the couch.

From that time forward, it was Smitty who always helped Sandy when he was in Nassau, and many years later, it was Smitty, the cab driver, who traveled to North Carolina to attend Sandy's funeral.

Sandy's personality always put him in the best slip available because he was genuinely kind to us, and that's one of the perks of the job—giving and receiving. He was a true southern gentleman and with his compliments and winks, he always made me feel special. Over the following months, he became one of Peter's best friends, and we always looked forward to his visits to Highborne.

Like most of Highborne's clients, Sandy never tipped. We always gave him top service, never expecting anything in return. However, one Christmas he arrived with a package. Thinking it might be chocolates or a joke present, we all laughed together, and I took the unopened gift home. That evening, just before dinner, Peter gently untied the red ribbon that secured the box. As the wrapping fell away, our mouths dropped when we saw two shiny deep-sea fishing reels, each with our names engraved. This was Sandy: thoughtful, appreciative and caring.

Another of Sandy's trips followed closely on the heels of the death of Mr. von Straggart. Sandy had obviously heard about this encounter through the jungle drums, and the crisis impressed on him the fact that *everyone* should know and be able to apply CPR. Keeping this in mind, he met a nurse who was vacationing on a boat anchored in the harbor. After putting on his usual charm, he convinced her to hold a voluntary refresher course in CPR. Many of the clients and guests at the marina participated, and the forum was held on *The Other Ten* where it was all business for an hour or so. This was time well spent from the normal work day, and we had a chance to practice feeling for pulses and pushing on people's chests—something Sandy probably enjoyed the most! On another visit later that year, he brought a CPR mask to keep at Cheap Charlie's, just in case I was ever in such a situation again. "You'll never have to touch anyone else's lips like that again," he said with a wink, as a wide smile spread across his face.

We had come to Highborne for a sabbatical from everyday life. We weren't running away from anything, unless running from the mundane counted in the equation. Remembering the good times of our weekend jaunts in the past might have been influential in our decision to move here. However, actually *living* on the cay was a different kettle of fish from a weekend at anchor. I admit, we probably didn't do enough research before we accepted the positions, but we never thought we'd be blindsided by the amount of work that was required.

During the high season, sometimes I thought I would go crazy with days that went on and on without a break. Such was a day in early March, when so many things happened that were out of the ordinary; I began to wonder if that day would ever end. By five p.m. we had been on duty a full ten hours between the store, the marina and the houses, having wolfed down a sandwich for lunch on the run. We weren't prepared for the remainder of the day.

Just after closing, the Bahamas Defense Force's sixty-five-foot patrol boat #34, on a routine assignment in the area, tried to dock alongside the concrete pier near the fish-cleaning station. The south wind was stiff at about twenty-five knots that day, and after several unsuccessful attempts at a normal docking, the crew became desperate. With Cheap Charlie's closed and Peter gone, there was no one to assist, so the crew tried to help their commander by successfully pitching several bow ropes over two of the fifteen-inch diameter concrete pilings on the pier. With the bow of his vessel now secured to the posts, the commander thought he could reverse his vessel into the wind to bring the stern alongside. This maneuver managed to snap both pilings off at their bases, at which time the vessel made a u-turn and headed out of the harbor without saying anything to anybody! The only way we learned about this hit-and-run was because friends on the *Empress*, a yacht tied close by, saw the whole episode. It was Mr. Bladle, the captain, who called Peter to report the incident.

"Highborne Cay, Highborne Cay, this is *Empress*. Come in."

Peter, now back at the house and unaware of the commotion at the dock, took the call.

"Empress, this is Highborne. Let's switch to our working channel." This was standard procedure, and Peter clicked the knob to channel fourteen.

Peter," said Capt. Bladle in his thick British accent, "I have to report, old boy, that a Bahamas Defense Force vessel has just tried to dock at your pier and has taken part of the dock with them when they left. Bloody cheeky of them, I'd say."

Peter groaned. Most people failed to realize the time factor involved in repairing this type of major damage out here on an island. It would be a month before the mailboat stopped at Highborne, again, not to mention the expense for materials and labor. "Jerry, what's it looking like?"

Capt. Bladle continued. "I say, two pilings and part of the concrete dock have been demolished."

Peter swore under his breath. "Did you get the numbers, Jerry?"

"Number 34 and she's headed north from the harbor."

Peter thanked Capt. Bladle and immediately switched back to channel sixteen.

"BDF34, BDF34, this is Highborne Cay. Come in." Peter's voice could not conceal his annoyance. "BDF34, BDF34, this is Highborne," he repeated.

After several more tries, the vessel answered. It was the Commander who picked up the mike and asked Peter to move to channel seven-zero. No sooner had Peter flicked the dial when he heard, "Yes sir, Highborne, this is Commander Watson. I apologize for the damage we caused to your dock. Please send me a bill and I will pay for the damages personally." They were coming clean before Peter even got started.

"OK, Commander, but I would appreciate radio contact the next time you need help." They exchanged mailing addresses and signed off. Peter was still grumbling about the incident, and I thought that would finish the day. I was wrong.

Thirty minutes after the Defense Force incident, we received a distress call.

"Highborne Cay, Highborne Cay, this is a distress call from the motor vessel *Moortown*. Please respond and answer channel one-four."

I was close to the big radio in the kitchen and picked up the mike. "This is Highborne moving to channel one-four."

"This is *Moortown* on one-four. We've just picked up six men floating in a small dingy. The men are telling us their fishing vessel, *Black Point Lady*, has sunk about seven miles due west of Highborne. Over."

"OK," I answered. "Got it. Go ahead."

The transmission from the *Moortown* continued. "We have the dingy in tow with six men aboard. The men have been in this little dingy for about thirty-six hours, ma'm. We're headed for your marina."

"Is everyone OK?" I asked, wondering if I should call for a chopper.

"Yes, they're OK. Apparently their dinghy's outboard engine gave out at some point during the night, so they took the engine off the hull, tied it to a rope and dropped it overboard to use as a sea anchor until someone found them." As I looked out of the kitchen window, I could now see *Moortown* on the horizon.

"Thank you, *Moortown*. I have you in sight. We'll meet you at the dock when you come in." The vessel arrived about thirty minutes later, bringing in six bedraggled men who desperately needed food and water, not to mention a dry shirt or two.

Just as we were tying the *Moortown* to the dock and were attending to their needs, a fifty-five-foot sailing vessel which had come in earlier for fuel, headed out Highborne Cay Cut and, in the twilight, promptly ran aground on a nearby coral head. Peter took *Bookalukus* out to see if he could assist the vessel, now hard aground. And, right in the middle of all this confusion, the *Emmett & Cephas* appeared on the horizon with our supplies for the next four weeks. Her shipment was a big one: Thirty sheets of plywood and other building materials, ice cream and frozen foods, produce, canned goods, a mattress, cases of beer, liquor and sodas, horse feed, parts for Peter's truck, and two air conditioners.

By the time we unloaded the *Emmett & Cephas*, and then sent the survivors back to Black Point, Exuma on that same mailboat, (whose route happened to go that way,) it was after midnight, and my bed was looking better and better. As I crawled under the crisp, cool sheets, I knew the best part of the day had been when I realized the six survivors of the *Black Point Lady* accounted for everyone on that boat; No one was lost at sea.

I reached over for Peter's hand. "It's been a long day, huh?" I whispered.

"It sure has. I'm not sure if we should remember it, or forget it." In a nanosecond, he was snoring.

As April approached, so did the dolphin (the fish—not porpoise). By our standards these were definitely the sweetest-eating fish in the sea, and that was second only to their beauty. Their colors were deep sapphire blue along the dorsal fin, changing to beautiful chartreuse near the belly. The size of the fish usually ranged from ten to fifteen pounds, but Dolphin as big as fifty pounds were not unheard of. By late spring, we could count on their appearance in large numbers in the Exuma Sound as they began their migration north in search of the Gulf Stream. Occasionally working through these schools of dolphin were sailfish and marlin, billfish with huge leaps and matching energy to make a fisherman's dream come true.

Peter and I had been avid fishermen for years before coming to Highborne, and it was our love of fishing that occasionally woke us up at five-thirty a.m. to squeeze in an hour's trolling before opening the office and store. Having fresh fish on the dinner table was the norm, not the treat.

Once in a blue moon we'd actually get an afternoon off. It was usually 'football Sunday' as I used to call Peter's time off once a month. However, when the season ended, we decided to continue this once-a-month ritual, if possible, as we needed a little time to ourselves.

One Sunday, we decided to put some beers in a cooler and head out to the Exuma Sound for a couple of hours fishing—a nice break for us. Peter steered *Bookalukus* out through the southern cut into deep water.

I was always the 'stern man.' I loved tying the leaders to the big hooks, and people said my knots and baits looked as good as any professional's when they went into the water. Peter, on the other hand, was always the 'captain.' He would watch to be sure the lines never tangled as we trolled the baits about a hundred and fifty feet behind the stern. He was accurate with the gaff, a long-handled hook that was used to bring the larger fish into the boat. We fished well together.

"Lines in!" I yelled to Peter, as I tossed the baited hooks into the water behind the boat. I didn't care if we caught any fish or not. It was time off the job, and I was determined to enjoy every minute of it.

It was a beautiful day, but the seas were quite rough. When the marlin hit the line, nobody was ready. The reel screamed as the rod took the strain and the big fish headed down into the deep. Peter knew it was a Blue. He had seen the fin cross the water, making a wake of its own as it plowed across the stern of *Bookalukus* and crashed the bait.

Bookalukus was a great little fishing vessel. Sturdy, seaworthy, reliable. With two big outboards and a wide and roomy cockpit, the thirty-one foot boat was great in heavy seas, and today was no exception.

"Tighten the drag!" Peter yelled above the noise of the engines. "Get that damned rod out of the holder and wind it up!" The line continued to sing as it went off the reel in yards. I had also seen the big fish hit but was concentrating on reeling in the other lines that now lay loose in the water. "Forget them!" he hollered. "Just get the damned fish in!" Pete threw the boat in neutral and left the helm to come to the stern.

I had begun to work the fish, keeping the line taught, trying to be skillful as I held the rod. Go down—reel. Come up—easy. Feel the fish. Don't pause—just steady pressure on the rod. "Geezus, this is a tough one," I grunted to myself, and I worked to pull the big fish up to the surface.

Peter, meanwhile, quickly retrieved the other baits from the two outriggers. He knew if the fish decided to run, he'd have to back down, and having lines in the way would hamper the process. The seas were rough, and now, with no one at the helm, *Bookalukus* broached and wallowed, making it a hard job to stand and fight the fish. I persisted, working the rod to my best advantage. Peter and I always liked to fish with light tackle for big fish. A nice fish on twenty-pound test line was always a challenge.

Now it was the marlin's turn. I could feel him coming up. The line came in faster and faster, as the big fish headed for the surface. "He's gonna jump, he's comin' up!" I shrieked. While the reel's drag ratchet clattered, I tried to wind as fast as possible. But, the fish was coming up so quickly that, when he broke the surface, his beautiful shiny blue body caught the slack in the line. In a nanosecond, the fish was gone, leaving empty yards of line to wind onto the reel.

"Damn, that was a nice fish!" Peter exclaimed.

It had been a good day, however. Together we had boated three large dolphins, a thirty-pound Wahoo and a small mackerel. We seldom got time from our busy jobs on the island to have a few hours' fishing, so catching a few nice fish was icing on the cake. "We'd better head back," he said as he grabbed a Miller Lite and returned to the helmsman's station. Turning *Bookalukus*' bow southwest, we headed back through the heavy seas to the island.

The fishing was, as usual, hot in April and May. Peter thought now would be a good time to host a fishing tournament out of Highborne's marina. He invited all the members of the Bahamas Angling Club to come to Highborne on a Friday night in early April, to receive special dockage prices, and participate in the 2-day tournament that would culminate with a trophy presentation on Sunday afternoon. We had no idea that the participation would be so overwhelming, and the fish so plentiful.

Because this tournament fell smack in the middle of high season, we were run ragged, but the thought of a fishing tournament out of Highborne challenged us to put every ounce of effort into its success. And that it was. Twenty-five boats participated. The dock and pier were jammed with fishing vessels ranging from twenty to eighty feet.

For all the participants, we held a complimentary welcome cocktail party that included Peter's famous Jonestown Rum Punch, making it difficult not to have a good time. Rules were reviewed, and everyone was excited for the next day's start.

On Saturday morning at seven sharp, Peter blew the whistle, and it was quite a sight to see all of the sport fishing yachts steam out of the harbor with the outriggers waving and people frantically working in the stern of each boat in preparation for 'lines in!'

The fishing was extraordinary that day. Every boat caught a good quantity and variety of fish. With 'lines up' at four p.m., boats returned to the harbor and started to sling their catches up onto the dock. I was the weigh-master and record-keeper that day, using the big scales that hung at the end of the dock near the fish-cleaning hut. Captains were cleaning their fish, throwing the tidbits to the sharks and rays who patrolled the waters surrounding the area, feasting on fish heads and guts.

All went well until I left my weigh-station to get a Coke. As I stepped over dead fish lying on the dock to be weighed, with others still flopping around, one bull dolphin fish was particularly upset at being on dry land. With a belly flop, he shook his head and threw the big hook out of his mouth, where it flew through the air and, without further fanfare, effortlessly sank into my thigh. There I stood, looking incredulously at a #9 hook, the shank of which now dangled out of my leg. Luckily, the hook had not become imbedded in the muscle and had turned just as it entered under the skin. But it was a predicament, and certainly an embarrassment for me, that the activities now centered on who was going to cut the hook out of my leg, instead of who caught the biggest fish of the day.

All ended well. The usual drill for an embedded hook is to cut off the shank and push the exposed barb out through the skin. But, the thickness of the shank of a #9 hook was too much for anyone's wire cutters. In addition, the hook, itself, was over an inch wide across the curve. Finally, someone came up with the idea of using a single-edged razor blade which easily cut the skin that held the hook, and Peter jokingly stuffed a handkerchief in my mouth to prevent any foul words from escaping as the procedure was done. Everyone stood around to watch, and someone made a comment about urinating on the incision to keep it clean. It was obviously an unexpected piece of entertainment for those who came to fish! But it was also another lesson learned: take better care to avoid accidents. If that hook had become imbedded deep in the muscle tissue, the only solution would have been a trip to the hospital in Nassau. I was thankful it wasn't more serious.

After that short diversion, the tournament continued and the weekend proved to be far more successful that Peter had ever dreamed. People were pleased with the fishing, they loved staying at Highborne's Marina, and word was out that our prices were good. We decided we'd have to consider doing another tournament next year.

Easter weekend was upon us. It was a weekend as big as Christmas, with the slips at the marina chock-a-block full. The dock parties provided good food, and lots to drink. People kept themselves well entertained with backgammon tournaments or a game of beach ball. Anchored on one of the moorings was a sailboat, *Bosun Bird*, with a vivacious couple who had sailed down through the Exumas from Key West. Joe and M. J. were real party animals and always livened up any get-together. At one dock party on the Saturday before Easter, Joe brought his guitar over from their boat. As chance would have it, a visiting yacht had on board a professional musician from Canada who happened to have his guitar as well, so between the two of them, the show was on! For the rest of the day they jammed and people sang, drank, ate, and drank some more.

It was a great time had by all, and it was a needed break for Peter and me. During the past several months our work schedule had been fast and furious, and I had forgotten how to relax. This dock party was a quick refresher. I believe Peter may have poured me into the truck for the ride home late that afternoon.

Easter Sunday dawned with people arriving at the house at 7 am for an Easter Sunrise Service to be held in our garden with the beautiful view of the ocean. Gulping down a couple of aspirin, I moved right into this next phase of the weekend. This gathering proved to be more popular than my wildest expectations; sixty people turned up. A guest preacher on one of the yachts agreed to do the short service, and afterwards, Peter and I served raisin bran muffins, Johnny Cake (a Bahamian corn bread), and banana bread to go along with coffee, tea and orange juice. With Highborne's remote location, I was delighted in the turn-out, and I felt like I had repented for my frolicking the day before.

As boats left the harbor following Easter weekend, Peter and I breathed a sigh of relief, hoping that we might get a few minutes to ourselves before the next wave of visitors arrived. "Can we have an early dinner tonight, Kate," he asked as he closed the doors to Cheap Charlie's.

"You mean, like with candles and soft music?"

"Yeah, it seems like a month since we touched—since we made love." He reached over and pulled me to him for a kiss. His hands dropped to the small of my back and he pressed me close. He was right. Probably it had been a month.

"OK," I said. "It's a date." I turned to head for the golf cart. "Too bad it can't be spontaneous…. but lately we've had to book in by appointment," I added with a wink and trying to make my voice sexy. I found it hard to BE sexy when I was so damned tired all the time. Then I remembered my mom.

Mom was a lovely lady, born and raised under the wing of Nassau's finest society. When Dad finished his navy tour, they moved to upstate New York where Mom found the winters harsh and cold. She longed for her Bahamaland. She was a soft-spoken lady with much class. Her virtue was her patience. "Just remember one thing, Kate," she told me before I was married. "Do it, no matter what. Put a bag over your head if you have to, but do it!" I always thought that was funny…. Mom talking about sex that way. But, her marriage had lasted forty-seven years and never did either of my brothers or I hear a harsh word between Dad and her. When the voices got a little high or a little loud, one of them would say, "We're just having a discussion…"

In our marriage, Peter was the patient one. He was a B personality—easy going, with a long fuse. It took a lot to make him mad, and I thanked God for that virtue. Now I needed to be better aware of his needs and wants. Out here on the rock, it was too easy to ignore.

It wasn't long after Easter that Ray Darville phoned. Ray was the warden of a unique Bahamas underwater reserve called The Exuma Cays Land & Sea Park. Their headquarters were located about thirty miles down-island at Waderick Wells where the warden had a small office and accommodation.

This park was the first of its kind in the world and was established in 1958 by an Act of Parliament to put aside and protect an area of approximately 112,000 acres of land and sea for the replenishment of marine wildlife. Ray was always busy chasing poachers within the park, rescuing boaters in his area or hosting dignitaries of other conservation organizations, as well as managing eight moorings that were available to boaters within the park on a daily basis. He always came to Highborne for supplies, and he and Peter had become friends.

Ray always had his hands full with work at the park, but the day he called Peter, he was excited. Two windsurfers were trying to set a record by windsurfing from Trinidad to Miami. They had spent several nights with Ray at Park Headquarters and were on their way north, toward Highborne. Sure enough, that evening, the two young men sailed into Highborne's harbor, tired and sunburned, yet in high spirits.

From Trinidad, the small Caribbean island off Venezuela, all the way to Miami is a long way to sail. However, the idea of *wind-surfing* such an ocean trek was a challenge to the extreme. A wind-surfing board is only about eight feet long and two feet wide with a single mast and sail, plus a "wishbone," a piece of wood running horizontally along each side of the sail. The wishbone is held with both hands (on one side of the sail) to keep the board upright and hold the sail, itself, into the wind. Two small straps at the back of the board prevent the feet from slipping off. As easy as it looked, I tried it once or twice and found it required balance, sailing skill and dexterity, none of which I possessed. So, when I saw the two surf boards with their bright, colorful sails coming into the dock beach, I could appreciate the feat these two men were trying to achieve.

We greeted them, and they introduced themselves as Tim Smith and Michael Archer. They had left Trinidad at the beginning of January. Their top speed was twenty knots in big winds and rough seas, but they averaged about ten knots overall. Their biggest problem, they said, was good weather—calm seas and no wind. Michael told us they wore wetsuits when they traveled, and carried a small hand-held GPS for navigation. For added safety, each man had an electronic distress signal and a tiny VHF radio in a zip-lock baggie. Their provisions were stored in a small backpack with energy bars, dried fruit and water, but they also had to depend on strangers along the way to help them.

Upon their arrival, we had one rental house empty, which we gladly gave them. As one day moved into the next and the days wore on, however, the winds continued to remain calm. Tim and Michael now found they were, in fact, marooned on Highborne Cay. When the rental houses filled up with guests and Harborside was no longer available, Peter told the men they could sleep on *Bookalukus*. She had two comfortable bunks but no air conditioning, so the mosquitoes were always an issue.

The young men joined us several times at the house for dinner, where we learned that Michael was a veterinarian. It was a great opportunity, since the new island dog, "Jumpy," needed to be castrated. What better time to do the job than when a veterinarian was in residence!

With tranquillizer, Xylocaine and a scalpel in our Highborne Cay medical kit, we turned our dining room table into the veterinary surgery. It wasn't the most ideal of circumstances, but Jumpy needed to be fixed, and we had the person to do the job. Here I was, actually assisting in the surgery—not cleaning kennels as I had thirty years ago. I stood at the dining room table with confidence and composure. That evening, blood did not upset me, and the burden of doubt was suddenly lifted. As Michael tied the final suture, I realized maybe I could have made it after all, despite the setbacks. I was, for that short period of time, living my dream of being a veterinarian.

I went to bed that night once again feeling good about myself, and again amazed at how we made do with living on an island in the middle of nowhere.

Several days later, the winds came up and our windsurfers had enough breeze to sail off. When completed, their course would take them to twenty different countries and fifty islands throughout the Caribbean. The day they left us, they were planning to sail to Nassau across the Yellow Banks. Their journey would continue through the Berry Islands and then straight across the Gulf Stream to Miami. It wasn't until months later that they mailed us a clipping from the *Miami Herald*. They had successfully completed their two thousand-mile journey and had made it safely back to the USA.

The heat really set in around June. It was doing everyone in. It sapped our energy and required a change of clothes several times a day. Further, the Rain Gods had forgotten Highborne Cay. Rain was a precious commodity in the islands, because fresh water was only attainable by collecting it off the house roofs and storing it in large rainwater tanks or cisterns.

Coupled with the lack of rain and the heat, one day someone had accidentally left the pump running for the main cistern. This error resulted in about twenty-three thousand gallons of rainwater quietly running unnoticed down the back road until the pump ran dry and the cistern was empty. At this time of year, this was a critical mistake. It was frightening to know that what was in our little individual house cisterns was ALL that remained on the island, and if that disappeared, there was no more fresh water, at least until we had a good rainfall.

Life On A Rock

The staff started carting buckets from the well by the horse stable to do their washing. Isaac, along with Arthur, one of several teenagers who worked on the cay, moved several hundred gallons by 'water wagon' from the North House and Guest Cottage cisterns to the staff quarters. This water wagon, as Isaac called it, was merely a fiberglass container on a single-axle trailer that could attach to the back of the tractor and haul water from place to place. We needed the rain desperately, but there just wasn't any in sight. Rain clouds were all around us, but not a drop fell on Highborne Cay. We were careful with showers, toilet flushes and dishwater. We saved the laundry's rinse water for the wash water on the next load. Trying to find ways to conserve was always a challenge.

About this time, I really began to feel the stress of the job and found myself depressed. It was like an abyss—you could never quite reach the top to get a grip and pull yourself out. The job went on and on and on: the lifting, pulling, pushing. We had to use our brains every second of the day to attempt to solve island problems which, if we were in Nassau, wouldn't be a problem at all.

Just when I was feeling really blue, Peter put his back out. One of Peter's physical jobs was to make ice each day by manually filling large plastic bags with water and then carrying them to the freezer. (Mary, the island's owner, didn't want to spend funds on an ice machine which would have made easy work of the job.) It was back-breaking work for Peter. The bags weighed around thirty-five pounds each, and as he filled forty or fifty of these each time, they had to be hand-carried into the freezer at the store. In doing this job, he eventually put his back out so badly that he ended up flat in bed for a few days. That, of course, meant a huge burden on my own workload. As I struggled to pick up the

slack, the final blow was when the mailboat arrived shortly thereafter with over three hundred cases of store goods to unload. It
was about this time it finally hit me: We weren't getting enough
time off the rock. With a long workday, often twelve to fourteen
hours or more, we weren't getting enough time to ourselves to
do some personal things. The Exumas were most beautiful islands, and here we were, working ridiculous hours and not able
to enjoy them. Life sucked.

As we turned the corner into summer, we hoped the
workload would ease. It didn't. Yet, while it was extremely hot
and muggy, and the mosquitoes knew where their next meal
would come from, it didn't discourage our visitors. Word was apparently out that Highborne was the place to be. More and more
vessels were coming from Florida, and day after day the dock
spaces were full. We had worked pretty much 24/7 since our
arrival almost a year ago. All our hard work was paying off for
Mary Smith. Summer was in full swing. The bottom line was
improving, and the clients were happy. Mary was happy, too. That
was the trade-off.

It was late July when a Croatian sailing vessel dropped
anchor in the southwest harbor. We discovered that she was with
a flotilla of vessels that were retracing the route of Columbus.
However, I learned with distress that one of our clients had seen
someone on that boat spear a very large Manta Ray, tie it to the
masthead and haul it up for all to see. I was aghast at this display.
I wondered how they could do such a dastardly deed to such a
beautiful creature.

I soon began to worry about the safety of Highborne's
pet sting ray (a Spotted Eagle Ray). The graceful little ray with
beautiful black spots on the top of her fins, had been coming in
and out of the harbor since early spring, and she seemed com-

fortable with the swimmers and snorkelers in the area. She was always a topic of discussion with new visitors who were fascinated by the animal's beauty and grace. It wasn't until the little ray appeared in the harbor the following day with a spear through her fin that I became angry. Peter, too, was livid. Our little Eagle Ray was injured and fighting for her life. We both wished we could vent our anger on the Croatian vessel, but it would have been pointless. None of them spoke English.

Several days passed. The next time I saw the little ray, the spear was gone, but there was a big hole remaining in her fin. Still, I thought she was over the hump. However, about a week later, Sandy Miles said he saw a shark eating a leopard ray up near the shore of the South Beach, and my heart sunk. We never saw her again after that.

When we took the job in September of last year, we had no idea that the "down season" was only September, October and November. I discovered soon enough that the other nine months were "high season" with a workload that was unbelievable. The guest houses were continually rented and, during this time, Chandra, Ritchie's wife and Pauline, her daughter, had a tough time ensuring these were cleaned and spotless for the next set of visitors. I helped them when I could, but the store's business took most of my time. Also, when the marina became exceptionally busy, I found myself down at Cheap Charlie's helping Peter. In the high season, it really took two people to work the docks, checking boats in and out, pumping fuel, tying yachts up in their assigned slips, reading the electric meters or keeping the status quo with good public relations.

I found it had been a very long year as we came up to our first anniversary on the cay. By the time August rolled around, Peter and I were tired. Bone tired. We found ourselves getting grouchy and knew we were ready for our well-earned vacation in September. However, finding a couple to replace us proved to be a challenge. It had to be people who were familiar with the island and could breeze in and take over for the month we were gone. We finally agreed on Rupert and Patsy, the previous managers. After some convincing on our part, they agreed to come. With the issue now behind us, we were ready for our well-deserved vacation. We knew we could leave the rock, and Rupert and Patsy would be able to hold the status quo until our return.

As we waited at Dock Beach for Rosie's Witch, I looked forward to sleep-ins and slow mornings, long walks in the Adirondacks, a movie now and then, and of course, the business of shopping at the local malls. It was a break in the action that was well deserved.

❦

THE SECOND YEAR

Highborne was now feeling like 'home' to us. Returning from a well-deserved holiday, we were refreshed and recharged and ready to move forward into another year. The bottom line on our past year's work looked much improved over the year before, and we were encouraged. We now fully realized that the job required a great deal of physical and mental effort as well as an enormous amount of patience. It was time to get back to work.

The fall season was now upon us and gave us time to re-group: paint the houses, fix the dock, do all chores and repair work that we never had time to do during the high season.

Sometime in late October, I was again reminded about being very careful not to get hurt out here, because help was so far away. I picked up a transmission from a vessel, *Captain Moxey*, a government mailboat that ran between Andros and Nassau. As I 'copied the mail' on the VHF, people on the *Captain Moxey* were barking back and forth with the Harbor Patrol in Nassau. According to the reports on the VHF, a crew member had been seriously injured while securing a boat which was in tow, and he unknowingly got the tow rope wrapped around his foot.

When the *Captain Moxey* steamed ahead, the slack of the rope unexpectedly tightened around the crewman's foot, dismembering it. The man was bleeding profusely.

At the time, the *Captain Moxey* was sixteen miles south of Nassau, and although she immediately changed course and headed back towards Nassau, she could only make eight knots at best. To return to Nassau to get the man to a hospital would have taken the vessel almost two hours, and by that time he would have bled to death. Luckily, someone had the intelligence to call the D.E.A. emergency number in Nassau, and by the grace of God, the D.E.A. had a helicopter which was leaving Nassau on a routine mission. They were able to divert the chopper out to the boat, air-lift the sailor aboard and fly him back to Nassau. Without the help of the helicopter, the man would have died out there at sea. Luck played a big role—or maybe the people aboard the *Captain Moxey* were praying really hard. In any case, the point was again driven home to me: health services were non-existent out here, so special care needed to be taken at all times to prevent accidents.

We finally got the summons in late October. Peter and I, as well as Tom and Lynn, were expected to appear in the Magistrate's Court in two weeks' time for a preliminary inquiry. Such an inquiry was similar to a grand jury hearing in the U.S. but because The Bahamas was under laws of the Commonwealth, this was held before a magistrate and not a jury.

It had been over a year since the first robbery. The police had finally caught up with the three suspects (after they initially jumped their bail), and we were now required to face them in court. The summons was delivered into Peter's hands at Cheap

Charlie's by the Captain of BDF22, a Defense Force cruiser which happened to be passing Highborne on its way south.

The summons presented another dilemma: Peter and I would *both* be required to leave the island. Never, except for our vacation, had we both left the cay together. Since the island's other employees were not skilled enough, this would require us to find a capable volunteer to replace us for a day or two. (Patsy and Rupert had helped us the month before, so we felt we could not impose on their generosity again.) Brian and Lee Ogilvie were good clients of the cay. They lived in Nassau, and their cruiser, *Fox Hill Gal*, was a frequent visitor to Highborne. Would they be willing to mind the store and the marina for a couple of days while we were off the island? Taking off for a couple of days at the cay sounded like fun to them, and we assured them that their dockage, electricity and any other expenses would be gratis. Thankfully, they were happy to help.

Tom and Lynn's dilemma of the preliminary inquiry was different: They were now 2,000 miles away. Tom headed up a large chain of pharmacies in the suburbs of Detroit, and he and Lynn, too, would have to make arrangements to leave Detroit. They were being summoned to travel back to Nassau and stay in a hotel to await the inquiry. The situation was not an easy one.

The whole issue could have easily disappeared if none of us as witnesses chose to show up in court. The case would have been thrown out, and we could all have gone on our merry ways. But this was not going to happen. Peter and I vowed we would do anything to get our sweet revenge on the three people who had twice disturbed the tranquility and our sanity on the island. Tom and Lynn were also dedicated to bringing justice to the three accused. They said they would do what had to be done to get this job finished.

The day we were to be in court, we met Tom and Lynn for breakfast and hurriedly reviewed the time line and main points of the case before our appearance. It had been over a year since the first robbery, and we all knew there wasn't any evidence or identifications made to warrant any arrests or a trial. The second attempt, though, was a totally different story. We made the assumption that the trial was concerning the second incident: attempted armed robbery. We took time to go over the chain of events to insure everything was fresh in our minds.

Standing outside the courtroom, I could feel the tension. When the prisoners were escorted into court by the officers, I began to feel anxious. The perspiration trickled down the small of my back. I was happy Peter had been called to the stand first. (We were not allowed to be in the courtroom during each others' testimonies.) When Peter came out, he was angry. "Asshole lawyer!" he sneered, as the side of his mouth curled like a growling dog. He had been harassed by the defense lawyer who was trying to get the case thrown out.

Now it was my turn. As I walked toward the front of the courtroom, my eyes kept darting to the back of the heads of the accused as they sat at their table facing the Magistrate. Their expensive three-piece-suit lawyer was seated next to them. Passing their table, I could feel a hint of anger rising in my throat.

The magistrate, a stately brown-skinned lady with red hair, sat at a big, heavy desk at the front of the room, facing me as I entered. There was no air conditioning, and the room was hot. She pointed to the empty chair next to her. A tall policeman in khaki uniform stood next to her desk and smiled as I walked up to the chair and sat down.

As I held my hand on the Bible and took an oath, I looked around the courtroom. I felt a tingling sensation go up the back of my neck; staring directly and intently at me were the three people accused of trying to rob us. I forced myself to return their stares, but it was a real task. In legal jargon these men were being charged with 'Conspiracy for Attempted Armed Robbery.' The sentence for such a charge carries twenty years. Silence hung over the room like the humidity—heavy but invisible. I felt like bolting.

The prosecutor spoke first, asking me to relate what had happened. I told my view of the incident and how we had managed to capture two of the accused. "Thank you. No further questions."

Next, the Defense Attorney, a Mr. Bosfield, slowly sauntered over to my chair and stood close by me; too close. I didn't like it. I wanted to scream. "Mrs. Albury," he began, "I understand you accosted one of the accused outside the low stone wall of your yard. Is that correct?" He was so close, I could feel his breath.

"Yes, that is correct," I answered.

"Mrs. Albury, with that stone wall being your property's border, did it ever occur to you that you had no right to detain a person who was not on your property?"

I began to feel the same contempt I'd felt the day I came face to face with the suspects so many months ago. I felt my hands shake, and I thought I'd scream out my response, but when the words were actually spoken, I was amazed at how calm I sounded. "Sir, I'd like to point out that inside or outside my wall—it makes no difference. The wall is only decorative. Our property does not end at the wall you speak about. The whole island is, in fact, private property. Your client was clearly trespassing and he knew it." I heard my own voice snap with sarcasm.

Mr. Bosfield looked at the judge. "Your Worship, my client wishes to ask a question." This was a surprise. I didn't realize that in a preliminary inquiry, the accused persons were allowed to ask the witnesses anything pertaining to the case. I was shocked when the magistrate nodded to Mr. Bosfield, giving one of the accused the opportunity to question me.

He stood up. "Miss, I wasn't gonna rob ya," he blurted out. "Why you think I was gonna rob ya?"

How dare this person stand up in court and say such a stupid thing! I had a hard time holding back the anger that was welling up inside. I repeated the question sarcastically, "Why did I think you were going to rob me?" I paused. "Tell me, why were a gun, a mask, some gloves, duct tape and a burlap sack found in exactly the same place where you were hiding?" I scowled and paused again. "Were you coming to a Halloween party?" I could feel emotions begin to creep into my testimony, and I fought to hold back the tears. The tension broke as laughter filled the courtroom. Even the magistrate chuckled, but as I sat there, no smile fell across my face. Mr. Bosfield jumped up from behind his desk to do damage control. "No further questions," he said quickly.

After Tom and Lynn had finished their testimony, the magistrate handed down her ruling: The three accused persons would be remanded to Fox Hill Prison. They would be tried at a later date in the Bahamas Supreme Court. Bang! The gavel crashed down like a gunshot. We were done, at least for now. But there would be a time when we would have to return and give testimony in front of a jury in the Supreme Court. When that would happen was only a guess, and I was not looking forward to it. While I wanted to get final closure on these horrific events, it would mean re-living the entire experience again in minute detail.

We said good-by to our new friends, Tom and Lynn, who were returning to Michigan the next day, and we headed to the sea plane ramp where Rosie would be waiting to take us back to Highborne. It has been a stressful few days. I was glad it was over, at least for now.

Because it was late fall and a slower season for us, Peter and I had a little more time to ourselves on the weekends and evenings. This was also a time we could interact with other personalities who lived in the area. Norman's Cay, about seven miles to the south, boasted of a number of unusual personalities, all of whom I grew to love and respect for their various contributions to island society. Most of the people who crossed our path didn't know regular work—some just moved from job to job, while others lived full-time in the islands and bummed year round. This was brought to mind by a party we attended in late October for Ralph's 51st birthday.

Ralph, also known on the VHF radio as 'OK Fine Right,' lived and worked at Pyfrom Cay which sat inside the Norman's Cay archipelago. He, and his dog, Cuda, and his cat who liked to swim and ride in the boat with him, made up the full-time population of Pyfrom Cay. Ralph, who was originally from Philadelphia, was probably one of the few people who could successfully live alone. He was happy with himself, worked relatively hard for his island owner and received a meager wage of about $250 a month, along with a little island cabin, an outside toilet and shower, a fresh water well about 20 feet from the house, and the peace and solitude of living on an isolated island.

Ralph's birthday party was a conglomeration of foods, drinks and people from various walks of life who just happened to drop in to the party. The first couple was Jacqueline and Étienne. Some years back, Jacqueline had been married to one of the big drug cartel bosses from Columbia who ran Norman's Cay in the drug days. She'd been married at an early age and was, I understand, abused and misused. When the drug dealers were arrested by the DEA, she was exonerated and ended up divorcing her husband. In the divorce settlement, he'd given her all his assets so the U.S. Government couldn't seize them. One asset was a house on Norman's Cay.

Jacqueline was really quite a lovely person—quiet, honest, and willing to pay her way in life. Her live-in was a French Canadian named Étienne whom she met in Florida sometime before she returned to Norman's Cay. He agreed to return to the Cay with her—possibly because he didn't have anything better to do with his life—and help her fix up her house which was in complete disrepair when she returned to live there in mid-1992. She was on a "shoestring" budget, so they were very imaginative in their repair work to the house. They had, in fact, done a wonderful job with little money and could be proud of their accomplishment. I might add that Jacqueline made an interesting dish for the party: chicken wrapped in a corn meal pastry and then re-wrapped in a banana leaf, tied gently, and then steamed. It was a recipe she learned in Colombia. Delicious.

Also in attendance were Fritz and Jeri, a couple who were working aboard the yacht, *True Grit,* moored at Highborne on contract for 8 months. We were told Fritz had a bit of a questionable past. (The Highborne grapevine is merciless.) However, we didn't appear to have had any trouble with him at Highborne. Jeri was young and vivacious, and I found her good company at our cay. We liked both of them, even if Fritz was a bit of a braggart and a know-it-all. Their fortune seemed to have turned the corner with his full-time job as captain of *True Grit,* and his life was on a new course.

Life On A Rock

Joanne Pollard was at the party, too. She came from a very wealthy family in the States. Jo used to be a professional horsewoman with great potential but left her past life to live in the Exumas, which she could do because of some trust fund she had. She could always make a person laugh, and that, in itself, was a gift. She was a beautiful girl who knew most of the boat people by first name.

Over the years, Jo had proved to be quite capable of handling Life's blows. She seemed happy with herself, especially after she met Tom Hyler who, in his own right, was another of the mostly unemployed. Tom was a painter, a guitar player and a pilot who flew people around in his little float plane, so he must have managed to bring in some sort of income. However, he worked only when he wanted to, and he loved to sail his little boat, *The Wren,* around the islands on good days. He was, actually, an extremely nice person, and I grew to like him a lot. Everything, according to Tom was "cool" or "hip," and he always reminded me of the flower children of the 60's. Rather than call him a hippie, however, I grew to think of Tom as just another unusual person who had crossed my path in life.

Then there was Jerry Hughes. Jerry and his wife, Bethany, were probably the most similar in their situations to Peter and me. Jerry had taken early retirement from his business in Nassau to live in the Exumas where he and Bethany had bought and refurbished an old house on Norman's Cay. With good social and financial standing, they had packed it away to come here. That's about the closest similarity we had with anyone around!

Jo's friend, John Becker was at the party, too. He took our breath away as he flew over the gathering at just above tree level, doing a barrel roll in his little seaplane before banking around and landing in the lagoon. I had to admit that I had not expected such a thrill. As he taxied up to the beach where everyone was gathered, we all cheered as the pontoons slid up onto the sand. As he stepped from the plane, he was a handsome fellow with salt and pepper hair, a good physique and a bronze tan.

I found John extremely interesting, but like everyone else, he seemed to go from job to job. His last employment, during the summer, was flying as a bush pilot in Alaska. I was fascinated; it isn't every day you meet an Alaskan bush pilot. He was also a certified flying instructor and a plane mechanic, as well.

Lastly, there was one more couple: Karen and Doug. They hailed from Wisconsin. During the summer months they lived in a small cabin in the woods up north, and during the winters they came to Norman's Pond in their little sailboat, *Random*. Rumor had it that Karen was a psychiatrist in another life, a life she had left behind to marry Doug. I found them to be a fun couple and was glad they were anchored in our area. They, too, lived on a shoestring budget but it seemed that most of that budget went towards Bacardi.

So that was the guest list. Peter and I made sure Ralph got a birthday present of Woody's horse manure (in a baggie tied with a red ribbon!) and a carton of smokes. We all got a good laugh over the manure, and I think Ralph really enjoyed his party. One thing I know is true: Peter and I were happy to be able to take two hours off Highborne Cay on a Thursday afternoon to join everyone at Ralph's.

Another autumn plodded onwards towards the high season. Regular clients came and went, and it was early November. The marina was almost empty. Peter and I went about our routine jobs with a new sense of pleasure, since the pressure was off, at least for now. One night I decided to have our good client and friend, Sandy Miles, up for dinner, mainly to give Peter and me a break from looking at each other over the dinner table. Sandy's jokes were always timely, and he kept us in good spirits. One of the most amusing things I found about Sandy was his way of complimenting people. For example, I did a flan for dessert that night—right out of the package—no big deal—it took about five minutes to prepare. Sandy sat at our dinner table, raving about the flan, comparing it to the finest he had ever eaten, comparing it to the best New York restaurants. I always chuckle when I think of that.

It brought to mind the day I did a birthday cake for Rupert and Patsy shortly before we left on holiday. I did the same thing: made the cake out of the package mix and fancied it up by adding a half-bag of chocolate chips to the batter. Patsy, who is just about the best cook in the whole world, raved about my wonderful cake: —how did I make it?—May she have the recipe?—It was so light and moist, etc. etc. I remember telling her I would be happy to give her the recipe, but it was on the back of the cake mix box. Then she said, "Oh, I could never use a package mix! I only bake from scratch." But then, with a pause, she added, "That cake was extraordinary. Was it r-e-a-l-l-y from a mix??"

Cooking on Highborne Cay was always a challenge. Naturally there were no supermarkets on the island (other than our little commissary) to get a pint of sour cream for the baked potatoes or some anchovies for the Caesar Salad. We had to learn to make do with what we had. If we wanted a pizza, we had to make a pizza. There was no hop-in-the-car-to-pizza-hut thing. No sir. If we wanted a pizza, I had to knead the dough from scratch, bake the crust, make the sauce and find something suitable for a topping. Even with all that work, I have to admit, it was always the best damned pizza!

One day Peter came up with the brilliant suggestion of having a pizza party. We agreed on a guest list of three other couples for a make-your-own pizza party. I prepared 4 crusts and set out piles of other ingredients that I had specially ordered from Nassau for the occasion: Mozzarella cheese, fresh mushrooms, fried sausage, julienne green and yellow peppers, and some sliced pepperoni. If guests wanted something unusual on their pizza such as chopped conch or pineapple, they were told to bring it with them. I made up a batch of pizza sauce earlier that day, and each couple was given a crust so they could make their own specialty.

Along with some ice cold beer, the pizza was first-class. Each couple seemed to do something entirely different so everyone got to eat a variety of pizzas. It was a great diversion from our usual routine, even though our time off from the marina and store was limited. Due to our workload and circumstances, little get-togethers such as this were few, so I treasured every moment when it happened.

As far as we were concerned, repeat customers were the best customers. Peter and I got to know them as friends, not just clients of the cay. Capt. Tom Jantz and his family returned to Highborne again and again, even though they had been caught in the middle of the second robbery attempt last year. Tom and his wife, Lynn, on *Damselfish,* were always willing to lend a hand, and they were good company when they were docked at Highborne.

Tom loved to fish and Lynn loved to dive, so between them, there was always enough fish in their freezer and ours. One evening they invited us aboard *Damselfish* for a fish dinner so Lynn could try a new recipe. Suddenly, as we were all enjoying our meal at the dinner table, Tom grabbed a piece of bread, stuffed it in his mouth and quickly drank a glass of water. In a voice that was hoarse and husky, he said, "Trouble here. I got a bone in my throat. Take a look." With a small flashlight stuffed in the side of Tom's mouth, neither Lynn nor Peter could spot the bone, but he assured us it was there.

Because it was after dark, it was impossible for a seaplane to land near Highborne to take Tom to Nassau. In addition, this was not a life-threatening situation, so the Coast Guard chopper refused to come to our aid. It was Peter who finally made a brilliant suggestion: telephone the emergency room at Doctor's Hospital in Nassau to find out what *we* should do.

The physician on duty gave his assurance that Tom's throat wouldn't close up, at least not before morning. "Try to get him into Nassau early tomorrow," the doctor told Peter.

Sure enough, the next morning dawned with the bone still stuck in Tom's throat. Lynn called for a seaplane which flew directly into our harbor to pick them up. I went along as well to facilitate the hospital check-in and later, to make a bank deposit. In addition, Peter called a friend who had connections at the hospital to make arrangements for Tom to be quickly admitted.

All turned out well. Under a short-acting anesthetic, Tom had the bone removed, and we were back at Highborne by 6 pm. I was thankful it wasn't more serious.

Coincidentally, about two weeks later the *Lady Jan* was at the dock with Capt. Mike and DJ, a crew member. There was an almost identical repeat of the scenario we had with Tom. This time it was Mike who got a fish bone stuck in his throat at dinner. Like Tom, he ended up chartering a seaplane the next day. Again, I ended up in the waiting room at Doctors' Hospital with our client. For a second time in two weeks, the situation turned out o.k., but I began to wonder what would happen if a serious medical emergency was to occur at the cay.

Unbelievably, three weeks after that, it happened.

One of the Rotary Clubs from Nassau was holding a weekend fishing tournament at Highborne, and everyone was having a great time. After the first day's fishing, all the Rotarians enjoyed a beach barbeque and, of course, lots of booze and wine were flowing. There was much bragging and back slapping. I was convinced; this was a male-bonding weekend. Peter and I were invited to join the group for dinner, no doubt because of Peter's long-standing relationship with his Rotary Club in Nassau.

Around ten pm, Jake West, one of the Rotarians, went to do a routine evening check on his little boat, a twenty-five-foot vessel with a small cabin and galley. Jake always joked that his boat was a 'leaker;' He always found water accumulating in the bottom of the hull. To counteract the leak that he never seemed to locate, he had installed a bilge pump to siphon out the water. That night, he had, as usual, tripped the switch for his bilge pump, and in a split second, there was a huge explosion that could be heard for miles. Apparently, there were gas fumes in the bilge, and a spark from the breaker must have set off the blast. Jake was projected through the air—from the cockpit, out and over the stern of his boat, into the water about eight feet away.

Jake was in bad shape by the time we fetched him from the water. He had terrible burns over his arms, and the skin looked exactly like he had worn a pair of latex gloves and turned them inside out, with the ends of his fingers clinging to the fingers of the glove. It was serious.

Someone had enough foresight to loose the burning boat from its ties at the dock and push it into the middle of the harbor to avoid catching the nearby boats afire, not to mention the entire dock. We watched, horrified, as Jake's boat burned to the water line. I thanked God that no one was killed and that the whole marina didn't go up in smoke.

We were able to get a helicopter here by midnight to air-lift Jake to the hospital in Nassau. In the meantime, there was a guest aboard *The Other Ten* who was a doctor. With his medical bag in hand, he arrived quickly after the accident, willing to do what he could to help. He assessed the situation and gave Jake an injection of Morphine to ease the intense pain. The doctor also gave instructions how to cover Jake's burns with wet towels after several of the other Rotarians gently laid him on the ground near Cheap Charlie's. We tried to make him as comfortable as possible with a pillow and blankets until the chopper arrived, but what he really needed was a hospital. During the two-hour wait for the helicopter, Jake kept requesting water, glasses and glasses of it. The doctor assured us this was good as burns cause tremendous evaporation of body fluids through the open wounds. The more fluids he drank, the better. Jake would have lots of scarring, but at least he was still alive.

The chopper came thumping in about midnight and chose to land in the middle of the road going towards Coral Point. Although it would have been better for Jake if the pilot could have landed on the dock beach, the beach was a place that helicopters preferred not to land. The blades always threw sand everywhere as the chopper descended, creating a type of cyclone that sucked the blowing sand up into the mechanism. So, the pilot elected the road as his heliport. This was the best alternate open space we had to offer, but it was still a difficult and dangerous landing since telephone wires ran along one side of the road and loose debris such as small stones and rocks covered the ground.

We picked up the paramedics in the truck and drove them down to the marina where Jake still lay near Cheap Charlie's. As the paramedics loaded him onto the stretcher, the incident reinforced my feelings that we really needed a proper landing place for a chopper in future emergencies. It was that very night that Peter and I decided on a goal: to make a suitable clearing near the south end of the island which would be a safe place to land a chopper in the event that we ever needed one again. The space would have to be clear of all bush and loose rubble, and away from any communication wires. Peter had a perfect place in mind about two hundred yards from Coral Point. We'd work on it. But for now, bed sounded like a grand idea.

As we became an integral part of Highborne Cay and its community, Peter and I learned, little by little, about the symbiotic relationships that existed between the island and some of its guests. A good example of such a relationship was Highborne Cay and Bill Marshall. Bill was president of a bank in Florida and was a very hard-working and successful businessman. However, he loved Highborne and had been a personal friend of the island's former owner for many years. Bill would arrange all of his spare time so he could be at the cay. He owned his own twin-engine Cherokee and found he could fly directly from Homestead, Florida to Norman's Cay airstrip with only a short customs stop at Andros on the way.

Norman's Cay was one of the toughest airstrips in the whole Bahamas. This local landing strip was not only short; it hadn't been repaved in almost 50 years. The toughest aerodynamic issue, however, was the tall stand of casuarina trees that lined the runway. These trees blocked the strong cross winds that came off the Atlantic, so when the pilot dropped his plane beneath the level of the trees, there was an instantaneous void in air current that often created a steering issue for the plane. To watch any plane land at Norman's Cay would take my breath away. The wings would always bobble as the plane came beneath the level of the trees. But Bill was an expert pilot; Landing at Norman's Cay was no problem for him. He'd do a fly-over at the marina to let us know he'd arrived, and Pete would take *Bookalukus* to Norman's Cay to meet him on the beach there.

Bill frequently transported items from Florida to Highborne Cay for our staff and neighboring Norman's Cay residents. He was always thinking about things that could benefit Highborne. Even though he was in Florida most of the time, his heart was at the cay. His thoughtfulness proved this fact. After the bank had repossessed a nice second-hand tractor, Bill earmarked this needed piece of machinery for Highborne Cay. He was very familiar with our old Farmall Tractor and knew it was on borrowed time. He arranged for the new machinery to be shipped from the USA and took care of all the incidental expenses.

Several years after that, Bill felt that we needed a better vehicle in which to transport customers to and from the store. He found a Ford van that would be suitable, and once again, he gave it to Highborne at no charge to the cay.

In return for his favors, he always requested the North House, our premium rental unit, when he visited the cay. No rent ever exchanged hands. The North House was his, as long as it wasn't rented to paying clients, or unless Mary and her entourage were here.

Each time Bill arrived at the cay, his arms were always full. One time it was a satellite dish for a staff member; another time it was a computer for a resident of Norman's Cay. Christmas time meant fresh strawberries from farmers in his area. Easter meant fresh corn. Bill's kindness didn't stop with us. Every boat in the marina always got a portion of Bill's strawberries and corn. He was one of our guests who always wore a halo, and if Highborne Hill was not available, he was always welcome to stay with us.

We were well into our second winter. The island economy continued to grow. More and more boats arrived, and business was booming. The rental houses were always full, and Becky, Isaac's wife, was doing a great business with her "catering." She was not on the Highborne payroll, but she had a little catering service that she worked from her house. She cooked for any guests at the marina or in the guest houses who were willing to pay the premium dollar, and in this way, she made extra money to help defray the added expense of their two children.

Most of the clients found her charming, but for those of us who lived on the cay, she was often moody and wore a chip on her shoulder. She found it hard to smile, did not mingle well with the other staff, and had a particularly difficult time with me. In the early days at Highborne, I just blew it off and figured it would take a while before we became friends. That never happened, even though I always treated her with respect. The bottom line, though, were our clients. They loved having their meals cooked and brought to their yachts or guest houses. Since keeping the clients happy was *our* job, I had to ignore the personality differences and continue to recommend her service.

❦

With another busy winter season upon us, Peter and I began to realize we were, once again, on 'overload.' At the marina, Peter was always there by seven-thirty a.m., and although he always attempted to close Cheap Charlie's around five p.m., it was often six-thirty a.m. or seven p.m. by the time he had tied up his final boat for the evening and balanced his cash. That routinely made a twelve-hour workday for him. In addition, it was often past closing when the Shell tanker made a late fuel delivery to the island. And, of course, there was always the mailboat.

As for me, my days seemed to get longer as well. The weather report on the VHF always started my day early, and it was now the norm to find me in the office late in the evenings making up orders for the next mailboat, balancing the weekly accounts, doing payroll, bank deposits, paying bills and any other record-keeping practices that were necessary. By the second year, I took the leap of faith and personally purchased a computer and printer, hoping to make the work somewhat easier. However, it was more often the norm that I would get to bed after midnight. The long days and lack of sleep began to show; I was tired all the time.

And the cay became busier.

One day we received a VHF call from a boat that had been anchored at Allen's Cay, a small island north of us which had a snug little harbor, but where the ocean rollers never ceased to find their way inside. "Highborne Cay, this is *Waypoint*. This is *Waypoint*. We're tired of rockin' and rollin' here at Allen's. Do you have a mooring available?" (To take a mooring rather than a slip or berth at the dock usually meant the boat was on a budget.)

"We have one mooring left, *Waypoint*," answered Peter. "It's yours. Come on in."

Within half an hour, the little trawler appeared through the cut. She was about forty-two feet in size and appeared to be a Marine Trader. I could see she was U.S.-registered as she flew a U.S. flag from her stern. She swung by mooring #2 and easily picked up the rope that would hold her secure. Not long after that, a tall, lanky man in an inflatable dinghy arrived at the dock. He sauntered into Cheap Charlie's, and warmly extended his hand to Peter. "Hi, I'm Don," he said with a smile. He and Pete chatted for a while. Don and his wife, Leslie, had both recently retired from the military service and had bought their little trawler in Florida to cruise through the Bahamas and further south. This was as far as they had come in a month.

Eight days later, they were still on mooring #2.

As their stay continued, Don would regularly frequent Cheap Charlie's. He was good company for Peter, and in the course of conversation, Peter learned that Don was a top-notch mechanic who could fix anything. He was bright, quick, and had a personality that seemed to meld with Peter's.

I began to develop a fledging friendship with Leslie that grew as time passed. We started to walk the island each morning after my weather report, and I found her to be excellent company during our two-mile hike that always culminated at Cheap Charlie's.

It wasn't long before Peter and I had the same idea. Might this couple be just the people who could lend us a hand here? It was too early to tell, but we would quietly give it further consideration.

Our second Christmas came and went without incident. The marina had been chock full of boats for the holiday, and Mary Smith and her family had paid us a visit for a week after Christmas. Things were just beginning to slow down a little.

Two weeks after the holidays however, a crisis arose with a trawler which had been lying aground at Allen's Cay, about two miles north of us. The winds had been howling at about fifty mph a few days after Christmas when this trawler, which was anchored at Allen's Cay, came loose from her anchors and ended up laying on her port side on the beach. There she sat for several days while her captain waited for a salvage expert to arrive from Sampson Cay to survey the vessel.

No VHF radio transmissions are private, so everyone in the general radius of about twenty-five miles was able to pick up the radio transmissions between the salvage vessel and the trawler in distress. Any normal person would consider this eavesdropping, but on the VHF, 'copying the mail' was a normal occurrence.

The salvage vessel reached Allan's Cay and gave the skipper a quote to pull the trawler off the sand and out of danger. The skipper turned them down flat. The amount was more than he wanted to spend. "I'll try and move the trawler myself," he told the salvage vessel. "I'm going to use a block-and-tackle and a shovel to dig her out of this predicament."

Shortly thereafter, the skipper arrived by dinghy at Cheap Charlie's seeking to borrow the necessary equipment. We gave him the shovels and block-and-tackle, and off he went to attempt to re-float his boat. However, after much digging over the next few hours, he unfortunately managed to change the list of the boat; Now, instead of listing toward the shore, she was leaning toward the sea. Consequently, as tide rose, the water began to wash over the gunnels and into the main salon. The captain radioed for help and got a good response.

From Highborne, Isaac and Peter answered the call and hurried to Allen's Cay, along with other boaters in the area, to help the vulnerable captain dig his boat from its firm position in the sand. I worked the big VHF radio in the kitchen, trying to find a new salvage professional, while Peter, Isaac and others were working on the boat. My job was to keep everyone in touch and help in the operation by making phone calls and relaying the messages back and forth. By the time evening came, I had located another salvage vessel which was now on its way to Allen's Cay. Four hours was a long time to be standing by the radio. I was drained.

The minute I signed off the radio, the phone rang. It was Becky. She was her usual bitchy self plus more. She, too, had been 'copying the mail.' "What the hell you referrin' to my husband as a black guy for?" she asked, without hiding her anger.

"Huh?" I didn't understand what she was so angry about.

"Why you callin' my husband a black guy?" she repeated. "I don't like that….you callin' him a black guy."

I was stunned. "Becky, listen. That's the only way I could identify Pete and Isaac to nearby cruisers who wanted to go and help them!"

"Well," she began to raise her voice, "you had no business calling my husband a black man!"

I tried to make her understand. "Becky, black and white are terms of description— not terms of slander. You heard me say 'the tall black guy and the white guy with a beard.' Nothing was meant by that!" Now *my* voice was getting louder.

Becky didn't get the picture as she continued her tirade. I finally asked her what the hell she wanted me to call him—a Negro? That finally shut her up. She hung up in my ear.

I've never been racially prejudiced, so her call upset me. With Pete, Isaac and others, I had worked long hours to help people save the trawler. As tired as he was, when Peter walked in the house and found me upset, he quietly walked over and put his arms around me and kissed my forehead. "Don't mind her. You did a fine job." I rested my head on his broad shoulder. We had all done our best and had worked long hours to save the trawler. I had put my heart and soul into manning the radio to assist with the salvage. As the last light of day faded, the salvage vessel could be seen passing Highborne's west cut. As it motored northward, it would be aiding the trawler within the hour, and I knew all would end well now at Allen's Cay.

However, the incident with Becky left a bad taste in my mouth. Isaac apologized for his wife the next day, but nothing ever came from Becky. This was another experience of out-island living in a small community. On the surface, I tried to forget the incident, at least until the next time; However, I filed her outburst in the deepest memories of my mind.

Early January found me with some sort of eye problem. I knew I wasn't seeing well out of my right eye, but I didn't know why. I found the eye sensitive to light, and I was continuously plagued with an abnormal feeling of irritation. I decided to catch a ride to Nassau with Rosie and get the eye checked.

The trip to the doctor was made difficult because as Rosie's plane approached Nassau, the weather turned bad with gusty winds and heavy rain. The Nassau Air Traffic Controller told Rosie she couldn't land. But, Rosie was a tough chick. "I have to land! I have a medical emergency!" she said into her headset mike.

The Controller replied, "OK, but within twenty-four hours I want to see a doctor's certificate on this medical emergency on my desk!"

I looked over at Rosie with her headset on and tapped her shoulder. She freed up one ear in order to listen above the noise of the engines. "Rosie," I said, nearly yelling so she could hear. "My eye isn't an emergency."

"I know," she replied with a grin, "but I need to go shopping." There was a short pause as she smiled. "Can you get the medical certificate?" she asked in a casual tone.

I shrugged. "Hopefully," I said, raising my eyebrows. She deftly put the little plane's pontoons down on Lake Cunningham, a freshwater lake near the Nassau airport. We landed in a thunderstorm and pouring rain. I like to fly, but this particular episode had been less than fun.

Lake Cunningham was a great place for a sea plane to land because it was so protected by the surrounding Mangrove bushes. The brackish waters were usually calm and there was plenty of approach room for a sea plane. However, there was no passenger terminal. Only a small dock and a dirt road met each passenger. As Rosie tied her plane up to the dock cleats, I was able to cajole her into letting me catch a ride to the mall with her where I could then catch a bus to the doctor's office.

For me, the end result was a corneal infection caused by a septic contact lens, and the doctor told me in no uncertain terms that this corneal infection could have ended on a very serious note. (That fact made it easy to get the medical certificate Rosie needed to get out of hot water with the controller at the airport.) Situations such as the problem with my eye reminded me once again that on an isolated island where there are no medical facilities, we have to be extra careful about ourselves and take care of our health.

While in Nassau with my eye issue, I had a couple of hours to kill before returning to the seaplane. My good friend, Angie Brown, had some little Jack Russell puppies for sale, so on the return trip to the lake, I had the cab make an extra stop (10 miles out of our way) just to take a peek at the litter. There were four left, but one in particular caught my eye. The brown and white pup was tiny, the runt of the litter, but she came right up to me, wagging her docked tail as if to say she was the one I should choose.

Without considering the consequences, I sat right there at Angie's kitchen table and wrote out the check. This must have been what people refer to as 'impulse buying'; I had absolutely no intentions of purchasing a puppy when I originally walked through Angie's door an hour before. Now, with the little puppy in my arms, I began to doubt my judgment. Peter liked Labs, Setters, Danes—any dog that was good-sized. He did *not* like small dogs. As the cab drove me back to the lake to catch Rosie's ride home, I hoped I hadn't made a big mistake.

When I returned to the cay that evening, Pete was trying to close out the books at Cheap Charlie's for the day. As he stood preoccupied behind the counter, the cash laid out in front of him, I was nervous to show him my purchase. The little brown and white spotted puppy sat quietly in my big cloth shoulder bag, waiting to be introduced. After all the preliminary discussions about my eye, I finally dug up the courage to make the introduction. "Oh, by the way," I began as casually as I could.

"I found something really cute for you while I was in Nassau." I hesitated.

Peter continued counting the cash. "Oh?" he answered absently.

"Yes," I replied, not quite getting his full attention. "She's a real cute little gal." His head popped up. He said nothing but tilted his head slightly as he tried to take his attention from his present chore and focus on me.

I slowly and gently reached into my shoulder sac and out she came. She was so darling and so tiny she fit right in my hand. I held my breath and waited. A huge grin spread across Peter's face. As I passed her over to him to hold, I could tell it was love at first sight.

He tagged her 'Little Spottie' or Little, for short. She was so full of life, bouncing around and happy about everything. She held her own with the big dogs and easily became an integral part of the island pack in just a few days. At night, I could always find her sound asleep on the bed next to Peter. Another canine had become part of our family, and, while we probably wouldn't admit the fact, she'd soon become the favorite.

Around the middle of the winter season, Peter and I had been seriously discussing the fact that we might not be able to last much longer in the job. We began to admit to ourselves that we were getting 'rock fever.' The 24/7 schedule was pulling us down. Highborne was now a very popular cruising stop, and the high season was, yet again, in full swing. The work, both mentally and physically, was taxing, and the small stipend we were earning certainly wasn't commensurate with the job. The novelty of working on an island for high responsibility and low pay had begun to wear off. And, while we had seven other staff members, none of these employees could give us needed assistance with such things as store inventories, price lists, customer check outs, fax replies, phone reservations and more. They were not literate enough to help us in our managerial work, thus creating a void in needed assistance.

We composed a letter to Mary Smith with a proposal: we'd continue as her managers if she would agree to let us hire another couple on a part-time basis to help us. In her recent visits, she had seen for herself how busy Highborne had become, but it was still a hard sell. Discussion went back and forth. At one point we were asked to write a "why-we-need-help" letter, and I saw Peter begin to run out of patience. It took almost four weeks of heavy negotiations before we finally got Mary's reluctant O.K.

Around the middle of February, Don and Leslie were still on mooring #2. They appeared to love Highborne. We were getting to know them better and found them to be an honest and hard-working couple. Don and Les had both retired from U.S. military service and were on pension from the government for long service.

Don's knowledge and creativity in the mechanical field amazed us. He could fix anything, and if he didn't have the right part to fix something, he'd make it. For example, when *Waypoint* was on the mooring, she would sway and swing on her anchor line depending on the wind and the tide. This would mean that the little satellite dish they had purchased for good TV reception was totally useless, since the satellite dish depends on a steady location for a good signal. However, Don was not discouraged.

For several days we didn't see him; Leslie said he was working on his 'project.' Finally he emerged from *Waypoint* with a big grin on his face. He had managed to design a base for his satellite dish that was comprised of, among other things, a gyro, a small electric motor and a compass. Now, as his boat swung in different directions while at anchor, his little electric invention would cause the dish to rotate to keep aligned at all times. His creativity impressed everyone.

Leslie also had worked in the Air Force. She had, however, been forced into early retirement because of breast cancer. She was a self-starter and highly motivated, and liked nothing more than to pluck her guitar strings, sing off key and enjoy a local brew. She and I had started walking together each morning almost two months ago, and I found this daily walk helped reduce the stress of my own job. We yakked and laughed as we walked the east beach, and southwards to Coral Point. When we reached Coral Point, we would make a circle at the base of the driveway and head north again, ending up at the marina. Part of the walk was always done on the East Beach in the early morning with the sun breaking the horizon. The blue hues, mixed with the orange of a new morning, reflected on the ocean's surface in whatever mood it happened to be in that particular day. If it was rough and high tide, the sand at the top of the dune would be loose and difficult to negotiate without filling our sneakers. If tide was low and it was calm, we could walk the water's edge where the sand met the sea, and the walking was as easy and firm as a concrete sidewalk. I absolutely loved walking at this time of day. The sea took on a whole new appearance, and whatever the day had planned for me, I knew I could meet the challenge after such a walk. Leslie and I soon became good friends.

Life On A Rock

The East Beach at low tide, Fritz Shantz photo

After Peter finally got Mary's o.k. to hire extra help, we decided to try the idea that we had been formulating for a number of weeks—to ask Don and Les if they would be interested in a job. Peter put forth the proposal: For no charge, *Waypoint* could come in to the dock and hook up to electric power if Don and Les would agree to work the marina half day on Wednesday and all day Sunday. That way, Peter and I would have some needed time off.

With this proposal came one glitch. The Bahamas government required all foreigners to hold a valid work permit, and obtaining such a work permit required months of red tape. To circumvent this issue, we were careful to tell people that Don and Les were just 'helping out' and not salaried. We weren't actually paying them a monetary salary, but rather giving them free dockage in return for their service. This fact would come back to haunt us later.

Don and Les were a welcome relief. Having some down time was a real luxury. A half day in the middle of the week, plus all day Sunday meant that Peter and I could start to enjoy the beautiful Exumas. We could spend our 'free' time fishing, shelling, or spend the night with *Bookalukus* on the hook at Hawksbill Cay, about fifteen miles south. Our occasional time off meant that Peter could watch sports on Sunday afternoons; I could take Woody on a leisurely ride down the beach. Life was grand once again.

Mary and her entourage were due to arrive in early March. We had some work to do on Highborne Hill, the largest house on the island. When she visited over Christmas, she had brought to my attention several items that needed work, and Peter and I wanted to be sure these were done by the time she returned in February. Peter put Ritchie to work on this project. However, as the days progressed, it seemed as though we were treading water.

Ritchie had been working for almost two weeks to touch up the exterior paint and trim. I had ordered the same paint that we had previously used, and this had arrived on an earlier mailboat delivery. But, once Ritchie started, he and I could both see that the new paint on the first patched area didn't quite match the rest of the house. This created a predicament. Ritchie couldn't paint the rest of the house because we'd run short of paint. Yet, if he patched the spots, it would be an obvious blunder. Knowing there wasn't another mailboat due for two weeks, Ritchie and I agreed we'd have to be creative.

After some discussion, we came up with what we thought was the only solution: We would paint the one side of the house that had required patching, but we would end the painting at the outside corners of that side. Hopefully no one would notice the slight difference in paint from one side to the other. As he worked, I gave the nod. We could get away with it, at least for now. It would be our secret.

The following two days were set aside for Ritchie to apply the "sealer" to hold the color of the paint. Unfortunately, the weather would not cooperate and it poured with rain. That put our deadline further back in time.

While struggling with the painting and sealing, Ritchie found a rotten timber in the porch roof. When he went to change that beam, he found the entire fascia board needed replacing, as well. Another two days down the tube. Then, as he was working on the fascia board, he noticed the boxing under the roof on the west side of the house was warped, so he had to replace that board. I found some further rot in the main beams around the south porch; Ritchie had to excise the rotten part and replace it with good lumber. By this time I was convinced; we were not dealing with rot. It was an invasion of termites, and I shuddered to think of Highborne Hill being slowly but methodically consumed by these destructive pests. We would have to be meticulous in checking for such damage in the future.

While Ritchie was gallantly struggling with the exterior, Isaac came to install the new vanity and sink in the guest bathroom, only to find that the hardware store which sent the vanity assembly had forgotten to include the hardware to put it all together. It would be another two weeks before the mailboat again made a stop at the cay.

It seemed as though the Highborne Hill project was destined never to end, but time marched on. Ritchie had steadfastly worked through the job. Isaac had arranged for a yacht, leaving Nassau and destined for Highborne, to bring the parts he needed for the sink and vanity. Mary arrived as planned just a few days after the last piece of lumber had been planked. All ended well, but the previous few weeks had been a close race against time.

After Mary's visit, we learned *Emmett & Cephas* was up on dry dock for a month, and the store and machine shop were desperately in need of supplies. The only way we could solve this issue was for Peter and Don to take *Bookalukus* into Nassau for supplies. This was not the norm; *Bookus* was an expensive boat to run. The thirty-five-mile trip into Nassau and return would cost the cay about forty-five gallons in fuel. But, in a pinch, *Bookus* filled a necessary gap. She was thirty-one feet in length, and with her protected cabin, Peter and Don could pack her with plenty of supplies for the trip back to the cay. She was powered with twin 225 outboards and could make the thirty-five-mile trip from Highborne to Nassau in ninety minutes with an empty load. The return run, with a boatload of freight, took longer.

Peter's Bookalukus

Peter and Don left the cay on a Wednesday afternoon, to spend two days in Nassau taking on supplies. Leslie and I could easily manage everything, we were sure. All went well for the remainder of Wednesday. We took care of the marina and store and balanced the cash at the end of the day. Leslie invited me for dinner on *Waypoint* that evening, and after a few rum and cokes and a full stomach, I headed home to bed.

Early the next morning, I was startled from a deep sleep by a banging on my front door. The sky was still pitch black. Glancing at the clock, it was 4:45 am. The dogs were starting to bark furiously and my heart pounded. I knew I couldn't handle another robbery alone. There was more banging. I jumped into a pair of shorts and hesitated just a moment as my brain began the instructions: Get the gun. Get the gun. Get the gun.

I picked up the Winchester, chambered a shell, and slowly walked through the house to the front door. The banging continued. Taking a deep breath, and with the stock of the gun at my shoulder, I reached for the tattered brass door knob and gradually opened the door. There under the porch light stood a small black man, peering not at me but at the gun I was holding. "What do you want?" I asked in a stern voice.

"Mammy, we got trouble." He trembled. "We got plenty trouble," he repeated, never taking his eyes off my Winchester. This was no employee of ours. This was a Haitian. I could catch the thick Creole accent. In his broken English he told me he was sailing from Haiti to America and the rudder on his boat had broken.

"Is dis Miami?" he asked.

I shook my head. "How big your boat?" I asked, imitating his broken English.

"Thirty-one," he replied.

So, it was a small vessel. I quizzed him further. "How many people on boat?"

Raising his head to look directly into my face, he answered, "One hun'red one." He pointed in the direction of the west beach. "Plenty trouble now."

I stood in the doorway in disbelief, trying to picture a thirty-one-foot vessel with over a hundred souls clinging for their lives by standing on the gunwales or anywhere they could find a foothold to give them a ride to freedom from the ravages of their Haitian homeland.

I took a moment to gather my thoughts, anxious and pondering what to do. This little man looked so bedraggled and scared. He obviously had no idea on what island he had landed, or what his chances might be of getting out of his predicament. This now presented a crisis in human smuggling and desperate people trying to leave their homeland for a better life. And, here I was, by myself, with the problem right in my lap. Peter wasn't here. I had no back-up. Once again, I felt helpless out in the middle of nowhere.

Dawn was breaking as the man's silhouette now blocked a portion of the dark grey sky behind him. I told him to return to his people and the boat, and I would be down to the beach shortly. Then, I called Les on the VHF. This was not her day to work, so I woke her up. "Les, we got ourselves a little situation up here. Bring the truck and drive up to the house. I could sure use your help."

In the meantime, I racked my Winchester on the dashboard of the car and drove past Woody's stable towards the west lagoon. As I came around a blind turn in the road and rounded the corner of the cove, I gasped. There stood a sea of Haitians, mingling closely together, confused and frightened. I had been told there were a hundred people, but I never imagined this dramatic scene.

I needed to find my little man who had come to the house. I didn't want to leave the car with the gun resting on the dashboard; Yet, I knew if I carried the Winchester, people would panic. So, I stood up on the edge of the door frame and peered into the crowd, my eyes scanning the faces. After finally locating him, I flagged him over. "You tell people," I tried to say in broken English and sign language, "I try help your people." He nodded an acknowledgment. As I drove back to the house, however, I was not feeling comfortable about the situation.

Leslie arrived around 7 am, and we had a quick cup of coffee and a little meeting. "Les, there's no doubt about it: We have to give these poor people food and water before we do anything else."

Leslie was quiet for a moment. Then she asked, "Are these people agitated or peaceful?"

"They're peaceful at the moment, but I feel uneasy with a hundred illegals on our doorstep."

Carrying my Winchester with us, we headed for the store where we both loaded bottles of water and granola bars in the car, and then we drove back down to the cove. As the little car rounded the last corner, she saw the scene for the first time. "Holy crap!" she exclaimed. Reality was now setting in. We recognized the seriousness of the problem we now faced: What would we do with these hundred illegal immigrants?

As we handed out the supplies, each person crowded the next, desperate to reach the bottles of water we were handing out. It broke my heart to see the destitution in these people. Most looked frightened, tired and impoverished. They wore their few pieces of clothing in layers on their bodies since there was no room on the little boat for suitcases. As they needed a clean shirt, they just peeled their dirty one off the top layer. It was so distressing.

I again located my little man and explained, both in broken English and sign language, that they must build some sort of latrine in the bush for their people. Leslie found a couple of shovels in the barn while I trudged up into the bush to find a suitable place. Once this chore was established, the men went to work. I returned to find Leslie working behind Woody's barn to set up a make-shift shower using Woody's watering hose so the people could bathe. We felt we had to treat these Haitians with respect; After all, they were human beings.

As Leslie and I headed towards the house, Isaac met us on the road near the barn. We discussed the situation and we all agreed: it was time to call the Bahamas Defense Force. There was a pit in my stomach and my emotions ran high when I dialed the number for the Defense Force in Nassau. I felt I was betraying these people whose only purpose was to get a better life; But, I had to do it. When I told the duty officer about our predicament, he said a Bahamas Defense Force vessel was about 4 hours away and would be immediately dispatched to Highborne Cay. As I hung up the receiver, I couldn't help but feel a wave of guilt.

It was now way past opening time, so Leslie returned to the marina to open Cheap Charlie's for business. In the meantime, I went back to the house to prepare some food for our 'refugees.' Ten pounds of rice and fifteen cans of black-eyed peas, along with 10 cans of tomatoes, onion, green pepper and celery boiled up in a huge pot with some spices seemed like a good choice. Leslie was right; Meat would have upset their stomachs. Beans would be a good source of fiber and protein, and the rice would act as a filler. When the concoction was finally cooked about mid-day, Leslie returned to help me cart the whole meal down to the barn to feed the hungry Haitians. Everyone got a plate of hot rice covered with the peas-and-tomato sauce and a large can of juice. It was the best we could do. I began to realize if I couldn't keep these people placated, we could end up with unrest or even a riot on our hands. In this sense it was disconcerting, and I could only hope that things stayed status quo until the Defense Force arrived.

By now the weather was beginning to change. I heard low rolls of thunder in the distance and could see the rain clouds forming. Nasty weather was coming in, and I began to worry about the Haitians.

Isaac arrived at the machine shop. "Why don't I move the tractor from the barn so all those people can move inside to keep dry, just in case we get some rain," he suggested. It was a good idea, because shortly after he relocated the tractor, the heavens opened up and it poured. I know our illegal visitors were very thankful for a temporary shelter and for such acts of kindness.

It was at this moment I realized I had not been alone with the Haitian problem; I had Leslie's and Isaac's help, especially at a time when Peter wasn't there. I was grateful.

About mid-afternoon the Defense Force steamed into the harbor. I had felt so uncomfortable calling them, after hearing some awful stories about Haitian refugees getting mistreated. I was pleasantly surprised. Their personnel were courteous, soft-spoken, and compassionate. When I asked them why they wore medical masks and latex gloves, one of the officers told me that tuberculosis was very prevalent in Haiti, so orders had been given to take proper precautions. Other than that, our Defense Force personnel treated the people with dignity and respect.

That night, the Haitians were allowed to remain in the shelter of the red barn, and the cook on BDF-45 Patrol Boat, now docked at the marina, had made them all a hot dinner. Leslie and I collected the food from the marina and took it to the barn where the Haitians would spend the night.

The next morning, in the grey light of the pre-dawn, as I stood at my VHF radio in the kitchen awaiting the early morning weather reports, I saw the Haitians quietly walking in single file, as they were escorted to the dock by the Defense Force personnel. The profound sadness that I felt at that time weighed heavily on my heart all day.

It was late that afternoon when I made contact with a vessel that had been anchored on the west side of the island, near the grounded Haitian vessel. "*Bar Girl, Bar Girl,* this is Highborne. Are you still at anchor on our west side?" I asked.

"Hi. Yes, we're still anchored here," replied the captain.

I continued, "Can you give us an update on the Haitian vessel that was beached there since early yesterday?" (I had assumed the patrol boat would load the illegals on board and take them back to Nassau for processing, leaving the beached Haitian vessel where it had landed—on our west beach.)

The captain chuckled. "Well," he began, "from what we could see, it appears the Defense Force people and the Haitians teamed up and got that derelict boat to float again."

I was surprised. "Did the patrol boat tow it back to Nassau with them?" I asked, still puzzled.

"Hell no," replied *Bar Girl.* "From our vantage point, it appeared the Haitians re-boarded that little boat and sailed westward towards Andros. Looks like the Defense Force vessel was headed back to Nassau."

Then I remembered a comment the Defense Force commander had made the day before. The Bahamas had some sort of treaty with America to let such immigrants through our waters so they could proceed to the United States as refugees. True or not, I secretly hoped our Haitians would make it, and Les and I had a hell of a story to tell Peter and Don when they returned to the cay the next day.

Life On A Rock

❦

Winter was the season for the little birds. Banana Quits, Indigo and Painted Buntings abound throughout our islands in the winter months, so it only seemed fitting to have some bird feeders around. Peter had heard recently about bird feeders made out of coconuts, and it sounded like a great idea. There were several coconut trees at the north end of the island that were always bearing fruit. So, one of the boys went up there to collect several green nuts and return them to Cheap Charlie's where Pete waited with his machete to begin husking.

Husking a coconut was an art in itself. Natives could take a green coconut and a sharp machete, and in seven or eight minutes have the entire husk cut off, exposing the hard inner nut. Cracking this extremely hard part of the coconut was a little more difficult, but with skill and a good hit with the machete, it would split open to reveal the silky white coconut meat that was encased inside.

Peter, however, made this even more challenging as he specifically wanted to remove only one-quarter of the coconut, leaving the other three-quarters in tact. Once he had taken off the outside husk, he used a band saw to cut away only that part of the nut which he wanted exposed for his feeder's interior. Along the way, he almost took off his index finger, so there was a break in the action to mend that mess. However, he finally had his finished product, and I had to admit, it was an interesting feeder. Whether or not it would be successful was yet to be seen. He drilled a small hole through the top of the nut and threaded fishing line through it. After he hung the feeder, he filled the hollow interior with sugar.

Everyone was into the project as Peter worked on his coconuts: the boat captains who came to Cheap Charlie's to settle their accounts, the sailboat people who stopped by to drop off
130

a bag of garbage, and the fishermen who came in for a six-pack. Peter got directions on what tools to use, where to drill the holes to be most effective or what feed to put in the coconut hollow. It was fun to see everyone getting into his act!

The first feeder Peter made was hung under the thatch roof of Cheap Charlie's. It was a busy place. People were constantly coming and going to pay their bill, buy some smokes or use the public telephone. There was always noise and movement around there, but that didn't stop the success of the bird feeder. The tiny Banana Quits loved it! With their bright yellow breasts and black band around their throats, they were a beautiful sight on the feeders. Within two days they were flying under the thatched roof of Cheap Charlie's, oblivious of all the other activity going on around them. They would chirp to each other, have little fights over who got the best perch, and generally were an interesting sideshow. People would come to Cheap Charlie's just to watch the birds. Buying a Coke or a beer was merely an afterthought.

Banana Quit eating out of Peter's bird feeder

Life On A Rock

The Painted Buntings were totally different. These were very shy little birds. With their vibrant colors of indigo, red and chartreuse, most avid bird watchers were thrilled to see one. Peter wanted to find a place for their feeder that was protected by foliage, but still able to be seen. He finally settled on a large bougainvillea bush near the back patio of our house. He could easily watch the birds through the sliding glass doors.

It took several weeks. Peter was discouraged. Only the tobacco doves and mourning doves had found this feeder, and they were hogs with the food. He began to think the big doves were causing the little birds to turn away. So, he found a piece of chicken wire in the machine shop and wrapped it once around this feeder. It was the strangest thing I had ever seen. Surely this would scare off everything!

Several more weeks went by without much action. Then, one day, Peter was home for lunch and walked by the sliding glass door. There on his feeder, was a Painted Bunting in all its amazing colors of red, blue, purple and green. The bird was small enough to get through the wire and onto his feeder. Soon after that, the feeder was full of buntings of all colors. They easily managed to squeeze in and out between the wires and yet the big tobacco doves could not. Pete was ecstatic. His coconut feeders had now proved to be a good idea that, when modified, had turned into a great success.

Each winter thereafter, we hung the feeders for the little migratory birds, and each winter their population on Highborne grew. The birds became our company, both at the house and down at the marina. Even a pelican befriended us for a short time. We managed to feed him by hand from morsels that had been discarded at the fish-cleaning station. Also, a pair of osprey hawks nested in one of the casuarina trees at the beach, and occasionally they would attract attention as they brought their kill home to their fledglings. A one-footed seagull, raucous yet tame, seemed to like hanging around the marina and came in each evening to say hello. His left foot was gone, and a short length of fishing line that dangled from the short stump gave every indication that he had tangled with a fisherman somewhere along his route.

Peter had never been an animal lover when we were married. For the past twenty-five years he had put up with stray kittens, puppies, and even an adopted pony during our marriage. Our kids had picked up my love of animals, too. So, majority ruled in our house and over the years, Peter had finally mellowed. He even picked the name of our home in Nassau: Summerland Farms. By the time we moved to Highborne, he was now entrenched in the world of animals and actually was beginning to love it. This was a wonderful trait I now saw in Peter because Nature was part of Highborne, and we both could appreciate it.

Spring was fast approaching when weather was always so volatile. The fronts seemed to pass through several times a week, bringing gusty winds and rainy weather from the north. The ocean could be flat-calm one day and then, in only a few hours, turn into a rage with six or eight-foot seas. Listening for weather reports became an important pastime and topic of conversation for boaters who wanted to be sure they arrived at their destination without incident.

It was one of these spring days that Don was on duty at Cheap Charlie's. Peter had just begun to enjoy his half day planting a vegetable garden up near Woody's stable. His portable VHF was clipped to his belt. I was using my half-day off to bake some cookies for a group of kids on *Terre des Hommes,* a sailboat whose owners were great clients of the cay. I was ignoring the usual chatter of the VHF in the kitchen as I worked, when suddenly there was a hail-and-distress call for Highborne. Now with full attention on the radio, I could hear Don pick up the call from Cheap Charlie's. I was sure Peter had picked up this transmission as well.

"This is *Oden*, this is *Oden*. We have a mayday, mayday!" hailed the captain. "We've lost both engines just outside the south cut. It looks like we're headed for the rocks!" This was a treacherous place to be in a bad sea. The strong current through the southern cut ran fast, and a boat without power would be at the mercy of the wind and sea.

Don answered in a serious tone, "This is Highborne. Stand by! I'll see if we can get out there to help."

"Please hurry!" the captain replied. "We're getting close to the rocks!"

Peter had heard the conversation and whipped the little VHF off his belt. "Don!" he interjected, "I'll be right there for *Bookalukus*. Stand by!" With that, he came running up to the house, grabbed his keys and I heard the screech of tires as he pulled away in the truck. Now, the only thing I could do was be at the radio if they needed any help from shore.

From our kitchen window I saw *Bookalukus* racing out of the harbor with Don and Peter. I knew they were going to have a rough time of it. Winds were out of the east at twenty-five knots, and the Nassau weather office has posted a small craft advisory earlier in the day.

Peter in *Bookalukus* and I in my kitchen both switched to channel fourteen, our working channel, so we could keep in constant touch. As *Bookalukus* rounded the southern tip of Highborne, Peter and Don saw that they had to deal with high waves crashing through the cut, as well as *Oden*, wallowing helplessly.

And, there were the rocks themselves—black, jagged coral about two hundred yards off shore, jutting fifteen feet straight up out of the ocean. As the waves violently crashed over and around these rocks, the relentless winds continued to push *Oden* directly towards them. The two occupants were waving for help but soon realized they needed to abandon ship in order to get out of grave danger. Soon an inflatable dinghy appeared over the stern, and as the next large wave approached, they pushed the dinghy into the water and jumped for their lives. The following wave that struck the vessel banged her starboard side into the rocks. Now, with each subsequent wave that broke over the shoal, the *Oden* was again picked up and thrown against the rock face. To make matters worse, as each wave receded, the *Oden* slammed down onto her keel and running gear.

The crashing waves made a rescue or salvage attempt extremely dangerous. Both Peter and Don knew this risk. *Bookalukus*, herself, could end up on the rocks in such a rescue, not to mention the fact that either Don or Peter could be hurt or even killed in their attempts to salvage the cruiser.

"Peter!" I screamed into the mike. "Don't do it! Please! It's too dangerous!"

"We're gonna try it! I've got a good boat and a good crew! I think we can do it!" He sounded as though he was on an adrenaline high. The only thing I could do was worry and pray. As I held the mike, I knew luck would have to play a big part.

With the waves as their enemy, Don worked the ropes as Peter deftly maneuvered *Bookalukus* up next to the rocks and into position. On the next swell, Don would have to be fast and accurate to get a tow line over the bow cleat of the *Oden* without falling overboard, and Peter would need expert timing to avoid putting everyone on the rocks. Miraculously they were successful, and with the other end of the rope tied to *Bookalukus'* bow cleat, Peter threw *Bookalukus* into reverse, narrowly missing the rocks as he crashed through the waves that broke over the stern and threatened to stall his engines.

As Don tied off the line, Peter realized he was now in very shallow water in breaking seas. With about sixty feet of tow line out between the two vessels, Don and Pete waited for the next wave. As it struck, the bow of the *Oden* was raised off the rocks enough so Peter could rev the engines of *Bookalukus,* take the slack out of the tow rope, and swing the *Oden* away from the rock face and into deeper water. Don quickly moved the tow line to the stern cleat of *Bookalukus,* and with *Oden* securely in tow, Peter revved his engines once more to start the long pull back to the dock. As I listened on the VHF, I said a little prayer of thanks. Leslie had also been following the radio conversations, and she, too, breathed a sigh of relief. By the grace of God, both our boys were now coming home intact, boat and all. I was very proud of both of them, but it had been a big risk.

I drove the golf cart to the marina, and by the time I arrived at Cheap Charlie's, I was happy to see the two occupants in the dinghy had made it safely back to our dock. Another twenty minutes later, *Bookalukus,* with *Oden* in tow, rounded the end of the island and headed towards the marina. *Oden* was heavy in the water, and I knew for the next few hours, Peter, Don, Isaac and the owner of *Oden* would be working hard to keep the cruiser afloat until we could get a salvage vessel into Highborne to take over.

All in all, it had been quite a day…not my idea of a peaceful half-day off, but then, nothing around the cay ever seemed to go according to plan.

As time wore on, I had come to love our little house up on the hill. I remember when I first arrived how I hated it: it was dark, dingy and depressing. With a little work over the past eighteen months, the house had become transformed. While we did nothing to the beautiful stone exterior, we did quite a few things to lighten up the interior: re-cover furniture, change the paneling, and add some island art work to the bare walls. We even pulled up the entire living and dining room rug and sent it to the dump. It was beyond cleaning, and looked stained and disgusting; But this meant for the time being, we would have to get used to a grey cement floor until I could get into Nassau to choose some new tile. Amazing as it seemed, with several throw rugs in various places, this cement floor became almost un-noticeable, at least to us.

As we began to make this residence our 'home,' Peter was using most of his time off to improve the surrounding yard. The little garden at the side of the house began to flourish with bougainvillea, bromeliads and sea lettuce, adding a swatch of color here and there. However, across the road in front of the house, there was still very dense bush. While this vegetation grew no more than six feet tall and followed the contour of the land from our house to the beach, the wild vines and prickly bush formed an extremely dense barrier that could not be penetrated. Unless a person knew the specific areas to find access to and from the beach, there was no way anyone could wander through the bushes to get there.

Sometime during the early months of summer, I was walking the dogs in the yard at the front of the house. Clapping my hands to get the dogs' attention, I suddenly and distinctly heard a man's voice say, "Help?" I looked around but no one was there.

That was odd. The dogs continued to play at their games, sniffing and peeing—the usual stuff. They weren't disturbed in any way.

Shortly, however, I heard a woman's voice in almost a whisper. "Hello? Help us." Still I saw nobody! (I actually thought it might be another load of Haitians in the bush somewhere.)

Finally, I heard both voices plead, "Please help us!"

"Wh–Where are you?" I asked, turning a full circle and perplexed at not seeing anyone.

"Here, in the bushes..."

What a quandary! Where the hell were they? I couldn't see beyond the first twelve inches of the thick vegetation.

"Please keep talking so I can find you," I replied with a chuckle that I tried unsuccessfully to disguise. What a strange situation!

"Over here, over here, we're over here," they repeated several times. I was finally able to follow the voices and sure enough, caught in the heavy bush outside our house were two people. I could barely see them; they were totally surrounded by the vegetation. They couldn't move one way or another. They were completely entangled in the vines. Bush prisoners—how else could I describe them!

As I pulled at the vines, trying to help make some sort of escape, I asked, "How in the world did you get into this predicament?"

From their position in the prickly bush, the woman explained. "Our dinghy capsized on the east side of your island, and we swam to the beach."

The man now spoke. "I saw your telephone tower above the bushes, so we headed straight for that, hoping to find someone to help us."

"Yeah, you sure did," I quipped as I worked with little success to burst the prison they were now in.

138

By this time, the vines had begun to cut my hands. I figured there was no way I could pull these bushes apart without proper equipment. This was a job for Pete and Don. "I'll go and get help," I told my two detainees, and I hustled back to the house to call Cheap Charlie's.

In front of the big radio, I wondered how to put out the call for help. It would certainly sound ridiculous to say there were some people trapped in the bushes up here. And, of course, everyone within twenty-five miles would be copying the mail, so I made the call as vague as possible. "Cheap Charlie's, Cheap Charlie's. Please switch and answer channel One-Four." I waited until Don answered. "Hey, can you guys make a run up to the house? I need you to bring a couple of machetes a.s.a.p."

Don answered with a question. "What's going on?" He obviously wanted to know what was so important that he needed to leave the marina. And, bring a machete?

"Trust me on this one, Don. You and Pete just get on up here and bring a machete….and don't dawdle."

Once they arrived on the scene and were briefed, quiet grins spread across their faces. This was not their usual rescue. Hacking away with the machetes, they tore at the vegetation for at least ten minutes before they finally were able to cut a makeshift path, freeing the bush prisoners.

Once out of the entanglement, the two people thanked us profusely and were ever so grateful that someone had heard their cries and come to their rescue. But, I had noticed as our detainees emerged from their incarceration, they were bare-foot and bare-backed during their long walk up the hill through the bush. This was not a good omen. Aside from the usual scratches and cuts from the vegetation, I knew in a couple of days they would be covered in a poison bush rash. Pete and Don drove them back to the Marina where their big boat was anchored, but

I was sure they'd be back in a few days for the Benadryl ointment that sat on the shelf in the store.

By now Don and Les had become an integral part of the cay life; As time wore on, Peter and I asked for their help more and more. Six months after our original offer, they were working three full days a week alongside the two of us. We continued to give them special perks to entice them to stay, without paying out a proper salary, in order to avoid any confrontation with the Bahamas Immigration Department.

Peter was working at Cheap Charlie's when the phone rang. "Highborne Cay," he answered in his usual way. "This is Peter."

A male voice at the other end of the line asked, "Do you have someone there on a boat, working?" He spoke with a Bahamian accent.

Peter's brow furrowed. "Uh, I don't understand," he replied. There was a brief pause.

Rewording his question, the unidentified voice asked, "Do you have someone staying at your marina who is working at the cay?"

Up went the red flag for Peter. "If you're referring to Mr. and Mrs. Berkley on *Waypoint*," he responded curtly, "you should know that they're guests at the marina. Although they help out occasionally, they're not receiving a salary for their work." There was a note of anger starting in Peter's voice. "Who is this anyway?" he asked sternly.

The unidentified voice on the other end of the phone replied, "This is the Immigration Department." Peter knew this wasn't Immigration. The call didn't sound official, and nobody identified themselves at the beginning of the call. But, who the hell was this? And why would they even bother to make a prank call?

After they hung up, Peter went looking for Don who was hard at work setting up the new water maker (which we had finally cajoled Mary Smith into buying.) "Don, I just got a prank call which makes me nervous. It's about you and Les...and Immigration."

Don pulled his torso out of the housing he and Peter had constructed for the new equipment. "What d'ya mean?" he asked, standing up and looking at Peter.

Peter rubbed his chin, deep in thought. "Might be a local issue. I don't know. Could be someone wants your job." He paused. "But, whatever, I don't like it."

"Hey," said Don, shrugging his shoulders, "we aren't doing anything illegal. We're merely helping you guys. No money is changing hands." Then he laughed. "Who the hell would want *our* jobs, anyway?"

Peter thought a few moments. The fact was that remuneration could come in many forms. The call could mean trouble.

I stewed about that phone call for several days. Why would someone make such a call? Was an employee upset that we had started to integrate Don and Leslie into the business of the cay? Was someone down-island thinking they should be considered for such a job here on the cay?

Several evenings later while we were having dinner, Peter broached the idea of trying to get Don a proper work permit from the Bahamas Immigration Department. If we agreed, it would cost Highborne Cay $3000 a year for the actual permit. However, it would also cost another $1000 to have the cay's Nassau lawyer do all the paperwork to accomplish this. Mary would balk at the costs, I was sure. Peter, on the other hand, had further considered the strange phone call of the previous week and now felt it was time to make Don legal under the Immigration laws. His thinking was that if we could obtain a permit for Don, then Leslie could be segued under the first permit. It would also help eliminate the risks of deportation, should Immigration come to Highborne Cay on a tip from any disgruntled person.

However, we knew that if we secured a permit for Don, we would have to hire him on a full-time basis, thereby increasing the payroll and decreasing profits.

We discussed these issues well into the night. Ever the bookkeeper, I couldn't help but ask the real question. "Will Don be able to cover our outlay in funds with his expertise?" We were working so hard to stay in the black. Another payroll packet would stress the numbers.

He thought for a moment. "I think it's worth a try, if only we can get Mary on board with the idea." Spottie jumped up in his lap and nuzzled his hand. With a far-away look, he stroked her absently as he thought further on alternative solutions. "Otherwise, maybe we could go to a Plan B: Say, if Mary doesn't agree to pay the cost, what would you think about trying to scrape the money together, ourselves?"

"You mean pay his wage out of *our* meager salary?"

"Yeah," he mused, "here's my thinking: Right now we are working ourselves to death on the rock. The way I see it, our sanity has become a priority over our money…what little we make."

I saw his point, but couldn't see how Plan B would work. "Let me give it a try with Mary. Let's not even go into any other 'plan' until I've exhausted that option," I said.

Now we had some preliminary thoughts. It was late and I was dead tired. We headed to bed, thinking of the distinct possibility of moving forward with Don's application.

The VHF had been barking all morning. I was in the store doing my favorite job—green grocer. At the time, I was sorting through some lettuce that had seen better days. I liked working alone in the store. When I ignored the sounds of the VHF, it was a good time for contemplation. As I worked that morning, I reflected on our past two years at the cay which had given me new insights. Peter and I were learning about so many things: nature, the sea, and living in the islands. We were learning about being ambassadors for the cay and about keeping up good public relations, meeting new people. In addition, the job at Highborne Cay was helping me to learn about myself. I was learning about courage, about fortitude, about stick-ability. I was learning patience.

My mom would have been proud; she was such a patient lady. Before I came to the cay, I was just the opposite—always so independent and impatient, always thinking I could do everything on my own in a nanosecond. I guess that was my dad's personality which served me well in most instances—probably helped me in those other high-powered jobs. Yes, I was always a free thinker, but on the rock, it was different. I had come to learn that out here, you had to depend on other people to help you reach a goal. Patience was the key. Out here, I was learning that the wheels turned slower.

In addition, Highborne was teaching me about love and its endless boundaries. Peter and I had been married for many years and had two wonderful daughters. As the years passed, even in our stressful times, it seemed that our love continued to strengthen. In such isolation from general society here at Highborne, we were not only lovers; we were best friends. He was my confidant, my sounding board, my business partner. We had worked together some years before, so when the opportunity to work at Highborne presented itself, we knew we could be happy doing so again. At Highborne, we complemented each other because we did different jobs and had different responsibilities. Yet, we combined our knowledge and skills easily to share in solving problems and challenges as they were presented to us. We were very much as one.

As I reached for the next case of lettuce to trim up, I asked myself the hard question: what was keeping us at this job? The pay was terrible, the hours were extreme, and the responsibilities were great. I was always tired. The heat, together with the workload and too little sleep, all played a part in the balance of things. I took vitamins to boost my energy level, but the pills didn't seem to help. I also started having some sort of heart arrhythmias, or 'thumps' as I eventually named them.

Peter, too, became drained after working in the hot sun all the time. Often, after lunch, he found he had to lie down for fifteen or twenty minutes in the air conditioning of the bedroom in order to re-charge for the afternoon's work. In the heat, working on Highborne in any type of physical capacity was difficult. Sunscreen was a must, but it was often forgotten in the rush of the day; our skin began to weather. I was always nagging Peter about wearing a cap, since sunburn and sun exposure were ripe grounds for melanoma. "Yes, Dear," was always his sarcastic reply when my nagging started to annoy him.

So, what was the magnet of Highborne Cay? It was the love of the outdoors and the challenges that always confronted us: challenges that continually made us show to ourselves and to others that we were capable—capable in the job and capable in life. It was as if we were being tested all the time and were always trying to prove something. Highborne Cay was like an addiction.

"Hello? Anyone in the store?" I heard the door squeak as a customer entered.

"Be right with you," I answered from the storeroom.

The store, Fritz Shantz photo

As I rose to assist the customer, I reflected that another vacation loomed close at hand. It wouldn't be long before Peter and I headed for Upstate New York to get respite from the scorching heat of late summer and to rest our weary bodies from the last few months' heavy workload. As my customer headed out the door with several bags of groceries, my thoughts reverted to the fact that September was nearing, and the cay's business would slow down for the next three months.

We were anxious to secure Don's work permit so he and Leslie could run the cay during our four weeks away. But, the wheels of Government turn slowly with its usual red tape. We had no other back-up personnel this year. No one wanted to take on the job for a month, and because of literacy issues, we couldn't leave the job to any local employee. I headed back to the case of lettuce I was trimming, still musing about the fact that we might have to cancel a needed holiday.

We had started Don's work permit process back in May. In the beginning, it had taken several months to persuade Mary to approve the idea. Finally we were given the go ahead, and we started the wheels in motion. The paperwork was submitted. We waited a month. We pestered the lawyers to seek information on the progress of the permit. We waited another month. Finally, after a nail-biting week just before we were supposed to leave, the phone call came. Don's permit had finally been approved.

I quietly said a little prayer of thanks. The island had been teaching me patience again. Peter grabbed a bottle of champagne from the store liquor supply, and we went down to *Waypoint* to break the good news to Don and Leslie. All four of us were ecstatic. Pete gave a toast, and we clinked glasses with the new assistant manager of Highborne Cay. This would be, we were sure, a turning point in our job. Finally Don would be legally employed by the cay, and we would get the full-time assistance we badly needed. The next step would be a permit for Leslie, but for now, we were thankful that our vacation was the top item on our agenda.

THE THIRD YEAR

Mid-autumn had arrived by the time we returned from New York. We were overjoyed to find that things had gone well in our absence. The Berkleys had done a great job in keeping the status quo.

Not more than two weeks later, however, the weather began to change. The barometer was headed toward the basement, and the weather reports I had been collecting over the past week in late October had not been good. There was a tropical storm brewing in the southern Caribbean. Peter wriggled through the crawl space of the attic, dusting off the cobwebs as he located our magnetic hurricane tracking map in one of the unpacked boxes. It was time to start tracking the storm. For the past two years we had been lucky. There were no threats so we had become complacent. This year was different.

Hurricanes were commonplace in the Caribbean. Those of us who lived and worked in this geographical area were used to the idea. We knew how dangerous these storms could be, and we knew how to prepare for them. Storm shutters should be in easy access. Canned goods should be purchased. A good supply of bottled water is needed. Bathtubs need to be filled with tap water for emergency use in the event that the water supply is disrupted or destroyed. Extra batteries, flashlights and a radio are all standard equipment. If you live in the Bahamas, this is all too familiar. As native Bahamians, we knew the drill.

However, living on a small island such as Highborne, we soon came to the realization that, surrounded by the ocean, we were totally exposed to all the quadrants of the compass. On a small island, hurricanes created a more serious threat. No matter which way the winds came, there would always be a high risk of damage since there was nothing to break the force of the wind— no tree lines, no mountains, just low scrub brush.

The marina posed a further problem. Multi-ton vessels tied to the dock were hazardous to each other and to the pier, itself. High velocity winds, coupled with a storm surge and high tide could push a fifty-foot boat up and out of the water onto dry land, smashing anything in its way. Therefore, it was a policy of the cay that, three days prior to a possible hurricane, all boats were required to go elsewhere to find a protected area or harbor.

By the time this storm had left the southern Caribbean and was on its way up the pike, we went to work. It was now a full blown hurricane with winds up to ninety miles per hour, and a name: Hurricane Gordon. While the rest of us began preparing the cay for the storm, Peter went to the marina to cajole, beg and finally demand that our good clients leave the cay so the marina's dock could be empty before the storm. For our customers, he worked to find alternate docking arrangements in Nassau where an excellent harbor offered good protection. Everyone prayed the storm would go another way. I was now doing 'hurricane updates' over the radio every six hours.

The sky, normally a deep blue with snow-white clouds of cotton, had begun to turn an ominous grey. The winds were puffy and the barometer dropped another 3 points. About midmorning, Peter mustered the staff to begin shuttering the houses. It wasn't until then that we discovered a crucial mistake: In our past two years at the cay, we had assumed from the previous managers that the hurricane protection was in order. Now we found ourselves in a real predicament. The pile of heavy shutters that had lain in the corner of the machine shop since we arrived two years ago had neither been labeled nor stacked in any order. The reality was we had absolutely no idea which shutters went with which house. It took our whole team three times as long to do the closing up. At the end of two very long days with rising winds, Peter and I promised each other we would never be so disorganized with hurricane protection again. I volunteered to take the responsibility to label every shutter of every house before we took them down after the storm.

As the hurricane approached, the winds began to increase. From the present course of the storm, we were now about twenty-four hours away from a direct hit. The TV was constantly tuned to the weather channel as we watched the projected path of the storm. The last boat had left the marina, and Pete and Don went down to secure their own boats in preparation for the big blow. When they finished, *Waypoint* and *Bookalukus* looked like a giant spider web. Ropes went back and forth, crisscrossing from the dock to the shore and back again. Anchors were set, antennas pulled down, and anything that could blow out of the boats was secured.

The VHF was noisy with news about the pending storm as boats in the area either made a run for Nassau or tried to find safe harbor in the Exumas. We were slowly but surely getting ready.

In a severe blow of over a hundred and fifty miles per hour, we knew everyone on the cay could seek safe shelter in one of the empty rainwater cisterns. We sat in front of the TV late into the night, watching each update on the projected path of the storm. By morning, the winds were howling around the house, and I found myself yelling to be heard above the wind. Over the past six hours, the hurricane had veered slightly westward and it looked like a direct hit on Highborne would be avoided. However, it was still too close to call.

The driving rain tinkled sharply against the west windows as I wedged a towel under the front door where water was seeping in. We could peek at the digital display of the weather equipment on the wall in the kitchen each time we passed through the house. The needle on the wind gauge crept higher and higher until it finally leveled out at a steady eighty-five mph, although we did see it bounce between ninety-five and a hundred for short gusts. We knew this storm was giving us just a glancing blow. The storm's center actually passed about thirty miles to our west, but the howling winds continued well into the next night, causing large branches and loose debris such as coconuts to fly through the air, occasionally hitting the house with a bang. We didn't sleep well until it was over.

Finally, the rain and winds began to subside. The following afternoon Peter donned his foul weather gear and went to meet Isaac and Don to assess any damage. There was brush and debris everywhere. As they motored around the island, it was difficult to see where the road began and ended as a carpet of green leaves lay across the truck's path. A coconut tree had fallen in Chandra and Ritchie's yard, just barely missing their roof. The screen porch at Coral Point at the south end of the island had not fared well. A large coconut limb acting as a missile went through the screen, tearing one whole side from the frame. This was minor, however, in comparison to what they found when they arrived at Highborne Hill. The roof had suffered heavy damage. Shingles were strewn everywhere, the tar paper was ripped to shreds, and flapped in the wind. Upon closer inspection, there were places where the interior ceiling was actually open to the sky where the plywood had been lifted off in an updraft. I wondered what curved ball God would throw us next.

In any normal suburb or town, a telephone call to a qualified roofer would start the process of repairing the roof. On our cay, however, the process started with a measuring tape, and several phone calls to knowledgeable people. The next event was the ordering process: how many sheets of ply, how many rolls of tar paper (and what weight), how many squares of shingles, how many boxes of roofing nails, when was the next mailboat? I was tired before I began! Shingling a roof was going to be another new challenge.

At some time in his past, Don had helped to shingle a roof or two. Since he was the only one with any knowledge of the task at hand, he was immediately promoted to Supervisor. Peter took up the position of tractor driver and commandeered Ted as his partner. Their job was to collect all of the trash materials that accumulated as the roof project progressed and take each load to the dump. Meanwhile, Leslie, Isaac, Arthur and Ritchie were up on the roof with hammer and nails under the watchful eye of Don. As for me, I was given the task of running the marina and store for the next week, and taking refreshments to all those "worker bees" while Mary's house was re-roofed.

That entire week I prayed no one would fall while they hammered the plywood, tar paper and finally the shingles. In the end, I saw the result of a real team effort. The job was finished in time for Mary's next visit, the house got a needed facelift, and Peter gave everyone a bonus in their pay packets. I looked back at the job and smiled. We proved again that working in an island environment was challenging, diverse and educational, even though Roofing 101 was not a course I would have chosen in school.

Mary and her family had scheduled a visit shortly after the hurricane. The roof repairs had been completed and everything was in order, but this visit was the first time I felt some tension. She was in a bad mood when she arrived. Her travel plans had been delayed because of the storm, so by the time she arrived at the cay with her family, she was tired and unhappy.

By the next day, she had made a good start on a to-do list. As she began to read this list to Peter, she complained, "There's paint drops on the porch screens, Peter. Can't someone on this island paint properly?" Peter could sense she was clearly annoyed. It was best to play mute.

"The color of the spotlights in the garden is awful," she continued, briefly looking at her list, "and, I don't like the garbage container at the base of the driveway." This list went on and on. As her eyes moved from her list, to Peter, and back to the list, she read down the items with a whine in her voice. Peter's blood pressure rose, but he remained stoic as he stood and listened to Mary's complaints. "I want another air conditioner in my bedroom," she continued, "I'm tired of sleeping with the clatter. And, the kitchen faucet needs a replacement." Peter discreetly shook his head, thinking she was finished, but she took a breath and went on. "There are ants in the bathroom, and we don't have enough videos to watch in the evening."

My husband was a smart cookie. He nodded a good-by, turned and left before he exploded. Mary had no idea what we had done to be ready for her visit! As he related his tale to me that evening and showed me the list, I jumped up from my chair and threw my arms up.

"Geezus, we worked our butts off to get her house in order after the hurricane. Could she be this ungrateful?" Peter decided to take some time to think about her 'list' of things; maybe he'd cool down. Not me. I stewed about it all night.

The next morning I went to see her. That was probably my first mistake. She met me at the door. She began to tell me that she wanted more money out of the cay; the profits were not to her expectations. She intimated that we were not keeping her interests in mind.

I tried to reason with her. I explained that more business meant more profits. "Let me print you up a copy of the P&L for the past couple of years," I offered, "so you can—"

She interrupted. "I shouldn't have to remind you that one of the major expenses of the cay is the taxes, and they don't even cross your desk or enter your silly little P&L!" She was almost yelling. "*I* pay those property taxes!" She was right, of course, but at that moment, she sparked my adrenaline, and I could feel myself getting ready for a fight. I should have turned and walked away. Instead, I blew my cork. That was my second mistake.

My tirade began with a higher pitch than hers. "We're working our asses off for your precious cay, Mary! We're understaffed, underpaid and unappreciated!" I took a quick breath. "You're giving us 'lists' of frivolous items to complete as if we're school kids with nothing better to do with our time." I took another breath. "I'm sick and tired of working a fourteen-hour day for a small stipend, and I don't appreciate being bullied."

I knew I was in pretty deep now. "I suggest you stick around for another thirty days and see, first-hand, what we do for you at Highborne Cay! It'd be a real eye-opener!" I was now fuming, but the outburst was not quite over. "And," I added as an afterthought, "if you don't consider us for a substantial raise within the next few weeks, Peter and I will contemplate leaving."

Mary's mouth dropped, but before another word came from her, I was out the door and headed for my golf cart with my heart pounding and my hands shaking.

Of course, once behind the wheel, I suddenly realized the magnitude of what I had just done. I had put our jobs in jeopardy. I was still angry, but now I was also angry at myself. What a stupid blunder. As I drove back to the marina, I was wondering what I would tell Peter—because of my big mouth, I had put his job on the line, too.

About four hours later, Mary found me in the store, stocking shelves, which I'd found to be a great stress reliever in the past. By this time I'd cooled off and was feeling considerably guilty for losing my temper. As she approached, I straightened up, about to apologize for my earlier outburst, but she put her hand up to stop me. "I like nothing more than a straight shooter," she said with a straight face. "Let's start our conversation from the beginning and give each other the respect we deserve."

From that day forward, Mary and I could sit and discuss almost any issue at hand without either of us having to take an anger management course. Peter, on the other hand, had an elephant's memory, and he continued to have doubts on the status quo. In addition, he had taken the brunt of Mary's wrath a second time earlier in the day when he made the mistake of trimming the casuarina trees near the marina as a mosquito control method. Mary was very unhappy about that and minced no words in telling him so, in front of the entire marina.

We took bets on the prospects of a raise. Either way, we knew our plan: a raise, we'd stay. No raise, we'd be gone by December.

Shark fishing from the marina docks and piers was off limits to guests. Obviously, sharks and rays were constantly patrolling the fish-cleaning area where they were always the recipients of tidbits as people cleaned their fish. However, a beautiful white sand beach, known as Dock Beach, ran parallel to our little harbor, and we didn't want to encourage these big fish to come near the shore.

Dock Beach was exceptional for swimming. The soft, white sand bottom gradually deepened into azure blue, and the clients loved it. They were close to their boats in the marina and could take their drink or a sandwich in hand and enjoy the water, lie in the hammock or sit under the shade of the casuarina trees. So, when a ten-foot Hammerhead Shark was found swimming off Dock Beach, people became nervous. After the shark was spotted coming near the shore a second and third time, Peter and his friend, Dudley, the captain of a client's yacht, decided it was time to do something to help protect the swimmers.

The shark was again seen around five pm that evening, lolling back and forth in an easy manner about fifty yards off shore. Dudley rigged a shark line with a steel cable and six-inch hook and baited it with a whole Blue Runner Jackfish. He swung the whole rig round and round over his head like a cowboy with a lariat, and then hurled the bait out into the deep water where it hit with a splash. Peter took the other end of this cable and made several turns around one of the dock pilings to make the improvised fishing line secure. They didn't have long to wait.

The shark took the bait just a few feet from the fish-cleaning station. It thrashed and splashed with every ounce of energy it had, the Jackfish held tight in its mouth, as salt water flew through the air in all directions. For the first twenty minutes,

155

Life On A Rock

Peter and Dudley took turns fighting the Hammerhead. Then, as a crowd began to gather, it became a free-for-all to see who could subdue this giant fish. In the beginning, the fish had the upper hand, so the cable would jerk and snap, knocking anyone off balance who was trying their best to bring the creature in. As the spectators became more boisterous, the air crackled with excitement. I hoped nobody would fall off the dock into the water that swirled and splashed beneath. Finally, the fishermen were able to pull the giant shark into the shallow water of Dock Beach. The shark, still unhappy about the whole situation, made his final effort at escape and mistakenly launched himself onto the beach within a few feet of Dudley. The crowd gasped and backed away. This was a very big fish with a very big mouth.

"Step back!" Dudley yelled as he pulled a pistol from its holster. The shark, now a bulky weight out of water, banged his head from side to side, his eyes protruding on each side of the margins of his wide head. Finally, several shots rang out and the crowd quietly momentarily, as if the fever of excitement surrounding the kill had ended. (I wondered how Dudley would explain the missing bullets to Customs when his boat returned to the states, since the gun and each round of ammunition were all listed on the boat's cruising permit.)

Now, as the dead shark lay on the beach, from where I stood, it seemed as though the men were in some sort of male bonding session. Peter, Dudley, Don, Sandy, Bill and many other men crowded around the big shark which now lay dead on the beach. From a distance, I heard someone exclaim, "Shark's jaw!" and that was enough incentive for Don. He jogged over to *Waypoint*, grabbed his bowie knife and headed back to the beach to do the work.

It was a huge shark, and I agree it was disconcerting to see it swimming so close to our beach area, but actually I felt bad for the fish. Sharks are one of the oldest creatures in the sea, having evolved millions of years. To see the killing of this shark in such a manner disturbed me. "Hey," said Leslie, seeing that I was somewhat distressed, "let's go back to my boat, pop some popcorn and open a bottle of wine."

"Yeah," I answered solemnly. "The guys can deal with this one."

It was now November. We were well into our third year with Mary Smith and her island. After several months of negotiation, we had finally received a modest raise in salary. Peter was content in his job as long as Mary wasn't breathing down his neck, so it looked like we were into the job for at least another year. I couldn't make up my mind: Was that a good thing or not? It seemed as though I never got a break to leave the cay unless it was to go to Nassau for a dentist appointment or medical emergency. I tried to blow off the feelings of imprisonment. I kept telling myself that I could ride my horse anywhere I liked on the island, or I could take a long walk on the beautiful east beach. But, I couldn't shake the feeling; I was fenced in. My job WAS the island, but when I wasn't working, I couldn't get away from it. Peter had Bookalukus, a thirty-one-foot Morgan powered by twin 225-horsepower outboard engines. She was a wonderful boat with a little cabin which included a V-berth, a small galley and a head. I loved the boat almost as much as Peter did. The problem was, she was too big for me to handle, or at least that's what Peter said. That meant I was trapped on Highborne Cay, a prisoner in my own job.

I happened to be returning from the store with several customers and overheard a client at Cheap Charlie's say to Peter,

"Do ya know anybody who might wanna buy my Mako?" He went on to describe his Mako as a nineteen-foot runabout that was powered by twin 90 hp outboards. It was a great little open boat with a center console, Bimini top and teak trim. My ears were flapping! This could be my ticket out of prison!

I took a few minutes to casually walk down the dock and have a look. She was a beauty, and I fell in love with her at first sight. Her teak was clean and bright, the chrome was polished and the upholstery looked new. She had a place to store a couple of fishing rods, and a fish box with a teak lid, a good place to store fish after they were caught. The canvas top was big enough for adequate sun protection, and I liked the idea of two engines: in case one broke down, I'd never be stranded.

Before lunch, I reasoned it out: back in Nassau, Peter and I always had two cars. Out here, we should have two boats—one for him, one for me. This would be my general approach. I waited for Peter to come for lunch. Then, I made an initial attempt.

"Pete," I started. "Have you ever considered getting another boat?"

"What?" he replied through a mouthful of ham sandwich. "You know I would never sell *Bookalukus*."

"Yeah, I know," I tried to answer as casually as possible without blurting out my whole idea in one sentence. "I was thinking. If we had a second boat, one that was smaller than *Bookus*, we could save on fuel, especially for small jobs like picking up clients at the Norman's Cay airstrip."

He took another bite of sandwich. No comment.

I pressed on. "And, we could use it to run up to Ship Channel Cay when we need to collect items sent from Nassau." I waited. Still no comment.

"...and it would be a great boat for me to have." There, I said it, adding, "kinda like having two cars in Nassau."

Peter looked up. "I really don't want another boat to look after," he answered with a shake of his head.

This was my cue: "Oh, *I* could look after it. You know, keep it clean, keep the teak bright. *I* could do all that." I was on a roll. "Just think," I added, "I could do all the short runs for you, save you the time."

He thought for a minute. "Well," he said, "Harry has a little Mako he wants to sell. Maybe that would work."

Bingo! I was ecstatic. My own boat. Now I could get the heck off this island once in a while, maybe get my hair done in Nassau. Maybe I could take some time to go down-island and see Rosie. The possibilities now seemed endless.

Peter bought the little boat for me that same afternoon. We named her *MFWIC*. Sandy used to call me that as a nickname. It's an army acronym for a person in charge. Peter flipped me the keys and promised me a docking lesson on the weekend. I could hardly wait.

October and November were always slow at the cay. Summer vacations had ended for many people. The hurricane season was at its peak in September and October, and often the threat of a storm would keep the boats in home ports. Christmas was just around the corner, and it seemed most people wanted to stay close to home to get organized for the Christmas season.

For Peter and me, it was our breathing space—a time for repair and renewal on the cay. That fall, Peter and Ritchie re-planked the dock and re-screened Harborside, ensuring that, from that time forward, no mosquitoes could get into the porch through the floor slats. Ted and Arthur were busy re-painting the bedrooms in Highborne Hill under Ritchie's supervision. Isaac and Don were overhauling the small generator and had the whole thing spread out on the machine shop floor. My project was to refurnish the living room at Coral Point on a tight budget. I also planted a vegetable garden down near Woody's stable. This was my favorite time of the year.

On a particular morning, as usual, Peter awoke around 5:45 am to let the dogs out. As he opened the front door, he was startled to see a young Caucasian man standing under the porch light. We didn't hear him knock.

He looked at Peter with pleading eyes. "Please. I need help," he begged. "My boat sank." With that, his lips began to quiver and in a nanosecond, he broke down in tears as he stood there bare-chested in a pair of cut-off jeans. He was a pitiful sight: his feet were covered with sand and his pants were soaking wet.

I walked up to join Peter on the porch. Through his sobs, the man began to tell his story. He recounted how he had been sailing that night without any light from the moon. His charts showed a cut between Long Cay and Highborne, a small channel that gives access from the Atlantic Ocean on the East side of Highborne to the Yellow Banks on the West side. (It was the same cut where Don and Peter had salvaged the *Oden.*) He decided to sail through this channel from the ocean to continue his journey to Nassau. In reality, however, he was off course by some 200 yards, and because the night was so pitch black, he failed to see, until it was too late, that he was headed smack into the coral rock on the ocean side of Long Cay. His sailboat, a twenty-three-foot Morgan, violently crashed into the rough coral, tearing into the side of his vessel. The man described how he had tried to tow his sailboat off the treacherous rocks by using his dinghy, but the ocean surge that night had thwarted his efforts. When his dinghy finally ran out of gas, he realized his efforts were futile. He ultimately had to abandon his little sailboat and row the dinghy several hours to safe refuge—Highborne's beach. The man's name was Aaron.

"Please come in!" I told him as I stepped inside the house. "I'll fix you some hot tea." He followed behind as I walked to the linen cupboard in the hallway and pulled out two beach towels. "Here, wrap yourself up, Aaron. I'm Kate and this is Peter." That was the best introduction I could muster under the circumstances.

"We'll try to help you as best we can," added Peter.

When dawn broke, Pete and Don took Aaron in *Book-alukus* to search for the sailboat. Thirty minutes later, Peter called on the VHF. "It's gone, Kate. It's smashed into little pieces. There's nothing left." I felt like crying. The little sailboat and all of Aaron's belongings were now scattered on the coral rocks of Long Cay, along with his dream of sailing through the Caribbean.

While they had gone to look for the remains of Aaron's vessel, I scurried around to find some clothes for the young man. I shuffled through Peter's closet and found a pair of knit shorts I thought he could wear, along with a tee shirt I pulled from the shelf of the store. I had an extra pair of flip-flops and a sweatshirt to donate. When Leslie learned what had happened, she found an old pair of Don's chinos, as well. At least Aaron now had some clothes to wear. However, the big question was: what were we going to do with Aaron now that he had no boat, no money and no way to get back home to the States? Lady Luck finally showed her face: As I gave the weather report the next morning, I learned there was a salvage boat that was working down-island. After explaining the situation, the captain agreed to take Aaron on as "temporary crew." In a few days, the salvage vessel would be heading to Ft. Lauderdale, and the captain agreed to stop in at Highborne to pick up Aaron. That way, the captain of the salvage vessel would have an extra able-bodied person to assist him, and Aaron would have a way of getting back to the States. To solve his financial situation, we purchased Aaron's Avon dinghy and 5 hp Johnson outboard motor. We really didn't need the dinghy and engine, but Peter knew it was the best way he could help the young man. Aaron now had some money and a ride to Fort Lauderdale. When the salvage vessel came in to pick him up and we said our good-bys, I couldn't help but think how life out here in the islands could change in a flash. Aaron had lost everything he owned. Luckily, he hadn't lost his life. Now he would have to make a new start, and I didn't envy him.

As the cool weather finally began to creep in after the sweltering days of summer, we were grateful. Usually, by early November, we could feel a difference. The winds picked up and began to come from the North instead of the South. The weather was now more unpredictable as the fronts began to blow in from the North, bringing cooler temperatures and sometimes rain.

Even the animals could feel it. Woody was frisky when I rode him, and in the cool, windy weather, he liked nothing more than to put in a hefty buck as we trotted down the beach. The dogs were back to rough-housing again, romping and rolling over each other, being more comfortable with the weather. Spottie, especially, was more active. She was not a year old yet, but very interested in everything, including chasing seagulls and shearwaters on the beach. I began to notice that she and Isaac's dog, Jumpy, a medium-sized mutt with the colors of a Doberman and a body like a Greyhound, were together much of the time. When I walked the beach with Spottie, Jumpy would always follow so the two of them could chase the birds and dig for crabs. When Spottie went to the marina with Peter in the truck, Jumpy would usually hop in the back behind the cab and catch a ride, his nose in the air and his ears flapping in the breeze.

Spottie also loved the golf carts. She would quietly jump in and go to sleep on the seat, no matter where a golf cart was parked. One day I couldn't find her anywhere, and finally someone saw her in a golf cart, parked behind the store for repair. Shortly after that, I lost her again, only to find her on a golf cart that was parked in the machine shop for a battery charge.

On another occasion, I found she had walked down to the marina by herself, probably following one of the marina guests. She was small, and Peter and I worried that she could make a good meal for an Osprey Hawk who could easily swoop down and lift her away in its talons. With this in the back of my mind, I would panic when I lost her.

One day in particular, she was nowhere to be seen. It was after five pm, and I checked all the usual spots. I paced the house, waiting for her to come home. Pete arrived from the marina around six pm. She had not been there, either. We both walked down the road on foot, looking for her, whistling and calling her name. It was dusk now, and the red and orange light of sunset was fading. Still no Spottie. We called and called. No Spottie. I could tell in Peter's face that he, too, was worried. I had seen the Osprey circling around and prayed the bird hadn't spotted the little dog for its next meal. It was almost dark and she had now been gone over two hours. We returned to the house, not knowing what else we could do.

Finally, a little while later, with the night closing in, I glanced out of my kitchen window and who should I see?

Life On A Rock

There, trotting up from the dump road was Spottie and her able companion, Jumpy, tongues hanging out and looking plumb tuckered out. Peter's blood pressure skyrocketed. He opened up the kitchen door and his voice boomed out, "Jumpy, you son-of-a-bitch!" Then, he looked over at me, as if to explain the whole fiasco. "He took Spottie down to the dump to chase rats!!" Both dogs heard his unpleasant outburst and reacted to the tone in his voice. Jumpy galloped off for his house, and Spottie, head down, ears back, came hurrying up the hill. Peter was not happy that some ragamuffin dog had convinced his sweet little girl to go on a wayward walk. I, on the other hand, was so thankful our little Spot had returned home and that no hawk had captured her.

As the months wore on, Jumpy and Spottie became good companions for each other. In fact, the two dogs were almost inseparable. Often Jumpy would spend the night by the kitchen door on an old bedspread I had relinquished to him. Julia and KG accepted him as part of the 'pack' although they never joined in the rat hunts at the dump. As time wore on, I became very fond of Jumpy and secretly wished he was my dog. But, the reality was, Jumpy belonged to Isaac, and I would have to keep that fact in mind unless I wanted to face another of Becky's tirades.

Christmas came and the season went from slow to fast in a heartbeat. To save some time, I had put the little Christmas tree in the attic last year without removing the decorations. All the ribbons, lights and small glass balls still hung from the little branches exactly as I had left it last year. I had gently covered the entire tree with a plastic garbage bag, hoping I could be successful in having one again this year without spending time with the lights or making and hanging decorations.

Carefully, I brought the little tree down the ladder and set it up in its usual place in the living room on an old rickety chest of drawers. I held my breath and plugged it in. Bingo! Instant tree. All the lights still worked, and most of the decorations had stayed in place despite the jiggling of the move. All in all, it took about 10 minutes—just the right amount of time that I could spend on the project this year. The marina had started to fill with boats around mid-December. It was going to be a busy holiday.

Christmas should be a time for families. For the last two Christmases, behind my façade of happiness in the season, I pined about not having our two daughters spend some time with us over a nice turkey dinner on Christmas Day. Both Kelly and Victoria had made their way into the work force after college. Kelly was living in Florida and working for a large travel agency; Victoria had remained in Nassau and joined an underwriting firm in the insurance industry. They were both on their own in the big world now.

I had often thought about having a family Christmas, but it just seemed too difficult to plan here on the cay. Aside from the geographic issues which were complicated between Florida, Nassau and Highborne, I couldn't see how we could have a traditional family holiday gathering. Peter and I were on call all the time, the marina was full, and Mary Smith was due here shortly after Christmas. We were just too busy. I had visions of having to leave the family in the middle of carving the turkey to tend to some pressing task for the cay. I admitted with regret that we wouldn't have the time to spend with the two girls, once they were here. Yet, not being with them over the holidays for three years in a row was a hard pill to swallow.

The day before Christmas, a Nassau sport fishing yacht, *Contigo*, called for a space at the marina. The owners were long-time

165

clients of the cay and usually visited us around the holidays. I was in the store, stocking the shelves.

"Highborne Cay, Highborne Cay, this is *Contigo,*" the Captain radioed. "We have an important package for you." I picked up the Mike.

"This is Highborne," I answered. "I'll be at the marina shortly. Thanks, Jorge."

I hopped into the golf cart and headed to the marina. As I came down the hill towards Cheap Charlie's, there was my 'package' waving to me from the dock. Our two girls stood there, next to Peter, laughing and hugging each other. Secretly he had arranged for them to come for Christmas via *Contigo*. I was at a loss for words as tears welled up and spilled down my cheeks along with most of my mascara. "Don't cry, Mum," Kelly chuckled as she planted a kiss on my cheek.

It had been months since I had seen either Kelly or Victoria. How I had missed them both! Victoria, tall and blond, was an eye-catching figure in her designer slacks and trendy shoes. Kelly, the older of the two, was also striking with beautiful curls that fell to her shoulders as she stood there in an oversized sweater with a big purse slung at her side.

It dawned on me; Peter had planned and executed this whole event. He was always the thoughtful husband, but this? This was the best Christmas present he could have given me. I gently put my hands on his cheeks and looked up at him. "Thank you," I whispered. "You're a great mind reader."

He kissed me lovingly, and, with a wink, quietly said, "I took the turkey out to thaw." This was going to be a really special Christmas.

❦

Living on the rock meant living the job. Early mornings. Late evenings. The sun was always sapping our energy. Peter and I were tired much of the time and had to be mindful that the love we shared together should never be taken for granted. We were each other's best friend, confidant, co-worker and lover. Most of this we took at face value. But the lover role was something which needed special attention. We often found ourselves so tired from the day's events that to get fired up for a wild love-making session just wasn't going to happen. Peter might kiss the back of my neck while I was clearing up the dinner dishes, and I would be so tired that the only thing I wanted to do in our bed that night was sleep. Or, another evening when I'd felt romantic and had a little extra time to fix a special dinner with wine and candlelight, Peter would fall asleep in his recliner. That's where the little red pillow came in.

The small red throw cushion caught my eye in a furnishing store on a trip to Nassau one Valentine's Day. I brought it back to the cay with a purpose: The little red cushion would have a place in the corner of the kitchen counter; But, if, at some point during the day, the cushion was moved to the bedroom, this would be the signal to save some energy for the evening! Since both of us returned to the house several times a day, this quiet signal gave us time to look forward to the coming evening and not to expend all our energy at our job! Never did I think in our life we'd have to make an appointment to make love, but at Highborne, nothing was quite what it seemed, and if an appointment was necessary, so be it. We had a strong marriage, but the little red cushion helped to keep us focused on our love and our special time together.

Life On A Rock

A week after Christmas, another major crisis arose. (I actually began to wonder what this job would be like without one crisis after another.) On a Friday evening, the Bahamas Defense Force cruiser BDF45 arrived at Highborne and tied up. I met Chief Petty Officer Hudson as he stepped off the ship. He was, I noted, the same person who had helped me with the Haitian situation several years ago. We shook hands again with the usual pleasantries. He explained that he was here with two Bahamas Customs agents to do a routine check of motor vessels and sailing yachts in the Exumas. Several hours prior to arriving, he had called on the VHF for a room reservation for the two customs agents. I booked them into Harborside for the night.

By the time they arrived, the marina was almost at full occupancy with sailboats, cruisers and luxury yachts. The two plain-clothes customs agents systematically began to check each vessel's documentation to be sure all was in order. I watched the procedure, puzzled. No spot checks had ever been done before as long as *we* had been here. Finally, Agent Deleveaux, the lead customs officer, told Peter the necessary documentation for all vessels appeared to be in good order. I breathed a sigh of relief.

After all the inspections, both agents then boarded the Defense Force's BDF45 for dinner, and subsequently retired for the evening at Harborside.

The next morning, Leslie was pounding on our kitchen door at 7 am. "Kate! Kate!" She was frantic. "They boarded our boat this morning! They want $5,100 or they're going to confiscate *Waypoint!*" she blurted out, her voice breaking.

"What are you talking about, girl?" I asked, grabbing a Kleenex for her.

She paused, took a deep breath and tried to compose herself. "Don asked him why, and Deleveaux told him a person on a work permit was required to follow the same customs laws as a Bahamian citizen." Another pause. "We should have paid duty on the boat." Leslie could hold her emotions in check no longer. As she stood at the door, sobs now wracked her body, as she shook her head. "We didn't know….we didn't know!"

I grabbed her hands and looked into her face. "O.K., O.K. Look, we'll get this thing figured out." I said it, but at that point I had no idea how; On their salaries, Don and Leslie would not be able to make such a payment. That also meant that Don's U.S. registered vessel, *Waypoint*, was now in Bahamian waters illegally, since no duties had been paid on the boat after his permit had been approved.

Leslie sniffled and tried to continue. "Don asked the agent if Customs could wait until Monday so he could arrange for the money to be transferred from our savings in the States." She blew her nose. "The guy said no! Can you believe it? He told Don that if he didn't get the full amount of $5,100 by 9:00 am this very morning, *Waypoint* would be seized and towed to Nassau!"

I looked at my watch. It was now 8:10 am. We didn't have much time to solve this crisis. "Let's get the hell back down to the dock," I said as we ran out to the golf cart. "We're on the clock!"

We arrived at Cheap Charlie's to find Peter already in conversation with Agent Deleveaux. Don stood quietly next to Peter. "Mr. Deleveaux," I heard Peter say as we walked up, "why are you doing this right now, so these people only have a few minutes to get things straight?"

"Mr. Albury, I have my instructions." Deleveaux wasn't moved.

I jumped into the discussion. "You were here yesterday. Why didn't you do this yesterday, a weekday, so at least we could have made some financial arrangements? Now it's Saturday, with no banks or offices open and no way to get this money."

Agent Deleveaux repeated the same answer. "Mrs. Albury, I have my instructions." This young man, probably in his twenties, was flexing his authority. Now I was starting to fume.

"Deleveaux, who gave you these instructions? How can you treat these people this way? They've tried to do everything legally. They've checked in properly with Immigration and Customs. There has obviously been an oversight, but now you're giving them only twenty minutes. TWENTY MINUTES? To get this whole thing sorted out?" I had a hard time being civil.

Deleveaux, his face stoic, answered a third time exactly the same way: "Mrs. Albury, I have my instructions."

My frustration was evident. "On whose instructions are you acting, Deleveaux?"

The agent made direct eye contact when he answered me. "I am acting on instructions from my superior."

Was the customs agent not prepared to even discuss the matter? Peter saw I was getting irate. He gently touched my arm and said, "Pay the duty for Don with Highborne Cay funds." We could work out the logistics later. Right now, we needed to be rid of these agents.

I took the golf cart back to the house, picked up the checkbook and returned to the marina. As I stood in Cheap Charlie's preparing the check for $5,100, Deleveaux pointed at the check. "I can't take a personal check unless you have a security bond with the Comptroller of Customs." I detected a sneer in his tone.

"What?" I replied, my voice getting louder. "What do you mean, Deleveaux? Why didn't you tell me that? Do you actually have to be paid in cash?" Now my anger was obvious. Don and Leslie had been nervously standing there for most of the conversation. Don put his hands to his head as if in disbelief. I slammed the checkbook closed, picked it up and walked briskly past the agent. "I'll find the damned cash for you," I mumbled as I walked out.

Back at the house, I managed to put together $5,100 in Bahamian and U.S. notes which was part of our vacation savings and part of the island's payroll for the coming week. After the robbery several years ago, we tried not to keep much money on the cay, with the exception of payroll.

Again, I drove back to the marina. I took the cash out of the envelope and began to count it for Deleveaux. He shook his head. "I'm not allowed to accept any U.S. $100 bills."

"Deleveaux, for Christ's sake, this is all we have!" I think I was yelling. The agent was impossible to satisfy, no matter how hard we tried. I lost any composure that was left. "The Haitians that got picked up here a few months ago got better treatment than this!! This looks like a set up, Deleveaux!"

"Take a walk," whispered Peter, resting his hand on my shoulder. "Let me run this dog-and-pony show now."

I could feel the tension in every muscle of my body. Peter was right. I needed to step away from this before I did any more damage to the situation. I walked over to the dock beach and resolutely did some deep breathing. I was so frustrated at the cloak-and-dagger affair created by the customs agent that I had blown a fuse. Our friends were being treated like criminals, and I wasn't able to do anything about it because I couldn't keep my cool.

Without saying a word to Deleveaux, Peter went to the phone and dialed the number of the Cay's attorney, Rory Le-Robin, who had helped secure Don's work permit. Luckily Peter was able to contact him at home, since it was a weekend. Rory, in turn, called a well-connected person in Bahamas Customs, and, within thirty minutes, secured a customs bond that would cover the $5,100 until Monday when his law firm would replace the bond with a check.

Now, with the bond in place, an official at Customs called Peter back to say all the requirements for Don's boat had been satisfied. Without another word, Peter handed the phone to Agent Deleveaux. It was sweet revenge to see the agent's facial expression change as the customs official in Nassau took control of the situation. Now there was nothing Deleveaux could do but get back aboard BDF45 and leave. To me, this was a victory, and I would have liked nothing better than to shoot the finger at this jerk that had caused chaos for the past several hours. But, I had regained my composure and knew that would surely have made matters worse.

Now what to do? Rory's law firm would have to be re-paid $5,100. How much of this cost was the Cay prepared to pay? After all, who thought about duty on *Waypoint?* Don and Leslie didn't, Peter and I didn't, and Rory didn't when he secured the work permit. That $5,100 represented a big portion of a year's salary for Don. If we all had known this fact, Don and Leslie's decision to work here might have been altered. I started mulling over how I would approach Mary Smith on this one.

The other troublesome fact was my growing paranoia about our staff. Woman's intuition told me they had caused this to happen. I didn't yet know how, but I just felt it. This was no random incident. Peter agreed. "Things are beginning to tie in. Think back to the strange 'immigration' phone call several months before."

"I think you're right, Peter. At the moment, we have no concrete proof, but we *will* eventually get to the bottom of this issue. That I can promise."

We sat at the dinner table until well after midnight, talking at length about the happenings of the day. I called Mary Smith in Philadelphia to bring her up to speed on the situation. She wasn't pleased about the issue, so I very much doubted that we would get anything out of her by way of financial restitution. Mary was basically of the opinion that Peter and Don should have been aware of this angle long ago. It appeared we were on our own with this one.

It was late when Peter finally came up with what he thought would be a fair and considerate way to handle the matter. The most important thing was to repay the $5,100 to Rory's law firm; To do this, Peter and I mutually decided to stand for that money. We would send the $5,100 from our personal savings account in Nassau to Rory's law firm. Then, to repay us, Don could give us $1,600 that he was due to receive on a small salvage job he did recently. Next, we could place Don on a retainer (which we arbitrarily valued at $2,000) for Don to keep our two boats in good running order for the next two years. Lastly, Don and Les could give us an IOU for the remaining $1,500 to be paid back over the next year.

However, Peter and I discussed another solution as well: I would continue to plead our case with Mary Smith for financial help. If I could convince Mary to allow the cay to pay that last $1,500, we'd all be winners. This would release Don of any IOU, Don and Leslie would have the duty paid on their boat, Pete and I would have a great mechanic on call for a year or two, and Mary would show that she was compassionate towards the fate of her hard-working staff. It was going to be my job to convince her. Until then, Peter and I would not tell our alternate plan to Don and Les, just in case it didn't come to fruition. We didn't want any more disappointments.

As the months went by, I began to realize the job at Highborne was more diverse than I had ever imagined. We had captured burglars, wrapped a dead body in ice, helped with illegal immigrants, salvaged boats on the rocks and attempted work in the medical profession, just to name a few. It was now late in January. Don and Peter were working well together, and Leslie and I effectively split the store work. I continued to do the bookkeeping in the evenings. Peter and I felt good about our assistant managers: Although we still carried a heavy workload, the job had become tolerable and at times, even fun.

One morning in particular Don was in Cheap Charlie's and took a call on the VHF. He switched to the working channel and answered into the mike, "This is Highborne, go ahead."

"Highborne, this is Capt. Walker. I'm eight miles northeast of Highborne Cay and in need of assistance. I have a twenty-three-foot vessel with six people on board who need to get to Saddleback Cay for a photo shoot, but my boat has lost an engine and is taking on water." (Saddleback Cay is several miles south of Highborne.)

"Are you in danger?" Don asked.

"No sir, but my passengers have only a limited time to do this photo shoot. Can you help?"

It was quite rough on the Yellow Banks between Nassau and Highborne that day, so Don and Peter elected to take *Bookalukus* to make the rescue. As usual, I manned Cheap Charlie's in their absence, and Leslie took responsibility for the store.

By the time *Bookalukus* arrived on the scene, the people had become extremely nervous about seeing water sloshing about on the floor of the cockpit. They were bailing with any container they could find, including cocktail glasses.

As Peter maneuvered *Bookalukus* alongside the crippled vessel, Don reassured everyone that they weren't sinking. "Don't worry, we'll get you all to Saddleback."

Peter helped the passengers offload onto *Bookalukus*, and Don jumped aboard the other boat to help the captain take her back to the marina for repair.

Peter then continued to Saddleback Cay so his passengers could do their photo shoot. Naturally, he was delighted to do this as several of his passengers were gorgeous models!

At the end of the afternoon, the Captain thanked everyone for their help, tipped Peter for his time and the use of his boat and tipped Don for his mechanical work to put their boat back into running order. Everyone was happy with the day's events as the photo crew and models headed for Nassau. However, it wasn't until a short time later that we learned Peter was the happiest; the photo shoot turned out to be a porn movie! Now we all understood why Peter returned to Highborne with a grin from ear to ear. Even the make-up was interesting, he reflected with his eyes rolling. There were tattoos in the oddest places. He must have been paying particular attention. We all chuckled and remarked about the diversity of jobs here on the rock—and, according to Peter, it was another beautiful day in Paradise.

One of the most important things in cruising through the Exumas, and throughout the Bahamas was always to have a good set of charts for guidance. The islands are made of coral rock and shifting sands, and anyone who cruised without a set of charts was asking for disaster.

A captain needed to know how to 'read the waters." This meant that the person at the helm had to be aware of the depth of water in which he found himself. An experienced captain could estimate the depth merely by the color of the water: cobalt blue water was over a hundred feet deep, dark aqua water was between thirty and one hundred feet, light aqua meant a depth of between ten and thirty feet with a sandy bottom, and aqua-white was shallow at under ten feet with a sandy bottom. The water is crystal clear and on a calm, sunny day, a person can see from the surface down thirty feet with ease. Therefore, dark patches could mean a reef or shoal, and a hue of brown usually meant sea grass or a rough marl bottom. Aside from knowing how to read the charts, knowing how to 'read the waters' was a necessity.

Highborne had several shoals and coral reefs around sections of its perimeter. One shoal lay just off the entrance to the harbor. This was clearly marked with a large white barrel that was anchored to the shoal and bobbed around for all to see. Seldom did people go aground on this coral head. There were also large coral rocks off the southern end of the island, but these, too, were shown on the charts and were easy to spot unless traveling at night.

A less-conspicuous problem area was a hard rocky bar that lay about a mile to the southwest of the harbor's entrance. This treacherous bar, known as "Tea Table Bar," had a reputation for claiming yachts on a regular basis. (It was rumored that even the editor of one of those fancy boating magazines had gone aground on this bar a few years ago.) Coming from the south, a captain would be at full throttle, thinking all was clear since the water for miles around was good. Then, without warning, the boat would find herself on top of the bar, usually with a hole in her hull.

Such was the case with *Huntress*, a 46' Bertram. She was coming from Sampson Cay at dusk, when the water at that time of day was hard to read, since the sun was low and the reflections on top of the water made it difficult to judge the depth. The captain, Frank, and his wife, Sally, were cruising by sight alone and not using the charts. When they hit, the yacht came directly up onto Tea Table Bar and crunched to a quick stop. Frank was definitely shook up by the time he radioed Highborne for help.

Little did we know this was going to be a personal rescue effort. Frank and Sally were Don's good friends from Clearwater. They had been cruising for two weeks through the Exuma Cays and were bound for Highborne when the accident occurred.

It was almost six pm when Peter, Don and Isaac answered the May Day call and took their boats to the rescue. Isaac loaded his whaler with a large water pump and tools. Pete and Don found some old pillows to stuff any thru-hull holes to keep Huntress afloat. As usual, Leslie and I remained at Cheap Charlie's to work the VHF and coordinate the operation.

It was eight pm and getting dark. Isaac called back on the VHF to let us know the extent of the damage. "There's a large hole in the bottom of the cruiser. She's torn off a rudder and seriously damaged both shafts. She's dug into the rocky bottom pretty good, so luckily, when tide went down, she's stayed relatively upright." None of this information sounded good.

"We'll need Marcus. Can you call him?" added Isaac. "We'll try to do some damage control right now, but *Huntress* needs to get back to the dock where it'll be easier to keep her afloat."

The men worked on *Huntress* until well after midnight. Leslie and I were both bone-tired, but we couldn't leave Cheap Charlie's until everyone had safely returned to the cay. *Victoria*, the salvage vessel, was now steaming towards Highborne from her home port in Sampson Cay. This salvage vessel, and her captain, Marcus Mitchell, had a variety of methods to get a crippled ship into safe port, temporarily seal the holes in the bottom, and then tow her to the States for repair. We anxiously awaited her arrival.

Life On A Rock

It was after one a.m. before *Victoria* arrived. Marcus and his crew would have to work the remainder of the night to make *Huntress* seaworthy enough to be towed into Highborne. Shortly after two a.m., Peter, Isaac and Don returned to the marina. They looked beat. Thankfully, Marcus and his crew had taken over. It was time for bed.

Frank and Sally were, of course, devastated with their costly mistake. Tea Table Bar had claimed yet another casualty. As *Huntress* sat at the dock the next morning, the salvage crew rigged her up for towing to Florida. The beautiful Hatteras was now a mess, her hull scratched and marred, the bow rail bent, not to mention the serious damage that had been done by the shoal. Frank and Sally decided they could watch no longer. Early that morning they chartered Rosie to fly them to Nassau where they caught a flight home to Clearwater.

The whole episode seemed to depress me for the rest of the day. Peter and I had now been on the island almost three years and had seen our share of wrecks, but each time it happened, I seemed to get into a funk of gloom and doom. I found Highborne did this to me: up and down. My emotions were like a roller-coaster most of the time. And, when I was down in the dumps, I always wondered if this was really the job for me–if I should be here. Then, when I climbed out of the funk, things would go back to being ok, once again. It was a real carnival ride.

It took almost three years before I finally got the whole picture. Out here in the beautiful Exumas with wonderful clients and employees, there were still deceitful and dishonest people, and somehow, one or two of them ended up at Highborne Cay.

Jenson James, along with his Border Collie, Gypsy, had been at Highborne for several weeks on his big sailboat, *Sir Galahad*. During this time, I finally came to realize we were meeting some really strange people here during our tenure. Jenson was one of these. While he never actually stated that he was a undercover person, Peter and Don always had inclinations that this was so. Jenson was also a braggart. He said he could procure information about people from government bureaus and financial institutions. He suggested that he had rubbed shoulders with politicians and other important people in high places in Washington D.C. He said he had worked for the 'government' on projects in various areas but was never specific about his former jobs.

I found Jenson to be manipulative and shifty, and I seldom believed what he told me. What annoyed me most was how he tried, first one way, then another, to make us reduce our rates for his dockage. Anyone can ask for reduced rates, but this guy was a real pest about it. His conversations always started out as generic but eventually turned to dockage fees; he constantly nagged about the price. At one point, he said he wanted to call our boss to get a reduced rate, but neither Don nor Peter would give him Mary's number.

The following Tuesday, when Don was doing some work on a broken pipe at the marina, the doors at Cheap Charlie's had been left unattended for a few minutes. That afternoon we couldn't find the Highborne Cay phone book, a loose-leaf binder with over three hundred clients' names, addresses and phone numbers. Don, Les and Peter searched all the drawers and cabinets, but the phone book was missing.

The next day, the book miraculously appeared on the countertop in Cheap Charlie's. No one knew how it had disappeared, and no one knew how it had re-appeared. Upon inspection, however, Peter brought something strange to our attention.

179

"All the pages have been inserted in the exact reverse order, with the 'Z' on the top and the 'A' at the bottom. Take a look," he said to Don. Sure enough, the pages had been neatly inserted in reverse alphabetic order between the dividers.

"Looks like someone took the whole thing apart, page by page," said Don.

Later, after I arrived from a store run, they showed me the book. Then it hit me: Only a few days prior to this, in a casual conversation, Jenson had joked he was dyslexic. Now seeing the loose leaf binder in its backward order sent up a red flag.

The clincher was the next day when Mary Smith called Peter. "A client called me yesterday, requesting special dockage rates," she told Peter. "I don't deal with the clients; you do. How did he get my number?" she asked curtly. Peter explained the situation: The only way Jenson could have obtained Mary's number was by consulting the cay's client book.

Jenson had taken the book, gleaned the phone number and then probably made a copy of the entire book. With a copy of our client list, Jenson could sell this private information to anyone for the right price. I was hopping mad. So was Peter.

The next thing I knew Pete was marching down the dock to *Sir Galahad*. Running after him, I grabbed the back of his shirt to stop him from confronting Jenson. He turned on me. "What?" he scowled angrily.

"Let it go, honey," I pleaded. "He's a jerk, and he could make trouble, which is one thing we don't need."

"So, what the hell do you want me to do?"

I paused for a moment. I hated conflict. "Why don't you just ask him to leave in the morning?" I suggested. I was thinking this would give Peter time to cool down, and it might save some nasty public argument on the dock.

"No Way!" Peter dug his heels in. "He can carry his ass out of my marina now." He turned and stormed down the dock toward *Sir Galahad*.

I never knew what had happened between Jenson and Peter, and I never asked. I thought it was probably better that way. That was the last time we had Jenson and his boat in the marina, but I always worried about the list of clients' information that I was sure went with him when he left.

Around the same time as the phone book incident, our mistrust in the staff was on the rise. Ted, one of the younger staff members, was my mole. He was always spreading sip-sip, a Bahamian colloquialism for 'gossip.'

Some of the sip-sip, I might add, was helpful. We had recently hired a new boy from Black Point. The new lad's name was Sully, and I assumed he got his nickname because he was so moody. He did his job satisfactorily, however, so we paid no mind to his mood swings. He bunked in with Ted, and Ted didn't complain.

Sully had been with us about three months when Ted provided some sip-sip that our newest employee had been quietly growing marijuana in a clearing he had made in the bushes behind Woody's stable. When I reported this news to Peter, we chuckled together. Neither of us had any idea what a marijuana plant looked like. We had smoked it once or twice when we were younger, but that had been long ago. To identify a growing marijuana plant was something we couldn't do. Don and Leslie, however, were of a younger generation, and we knew they would be able to make the identification. Later that day, Peter and Don headed towards Woody's stable to check out the 'ganja garden.'

"That's the stuff." Don pointed to several rows of green, healthy looking plants. "Pretty nice lookin', too," he added with a chuckle.

Early the next morning, Peter staked his position out of sight in the bushes near the plot of ganja. It was daybreak and the mosquitoes nearly carried him away, but he toughed it out, waiting for Sully to arrive to tend his crop. The wait proved fruitful. Just before six a.m., Sully arrived with his watering pail. Peter watched, unnoticed, as Sully gave each tender plant a drink. When Peter finally stood up and Sully spotted him, Sully couldn't find the words to make up any excuse. He had been caught, and Peter fired him on the spot. We hoped we could keep the incident under wraps.

As Ted continued to tattle about the staff, some of his gossip generated more mistrust of other staff members. What finally clinched my feelings happened a week later. Ted had caught me alone in the store to tell me about a call that he knew had been made by a staff member. A few months ago, the Commissioner at Black Point had been asked to do an 'immigration' check on Don and Leslie. I learned to my dismay it had been Chandra who had made that call; Chandra, whom I trusted, who worked in my house, who worked alongside me every day. I was shocked.

Last year when the 'immigration' call had come in, I had been fairly sure it was a staff member who had stirred the pot. Now, however, this fact was being confirmed; it was Chandra who had set up the bogus phone call. I was really angry. How could I have been so trusting and naïve? Ted expounded on his little tidbit of information: The staff apparently thought that Isaac, not Don, should have been the assistant manager.

I sighed with disappointment and thanked Ted for his candid revelation. Of course I could say nothing about this or my informer would be revealed; I needed to keep the lines of communication open between Ted and me. As I stood there, stunned by what I had just heard, I kept asking myself how Peter and I could have missed this. Were we too trusting, too naïve? How could we have let our island staff make us look like fools? Wouldn't I be better off back in Nassau on a regular 9-5 job with little hassle? Even my weekends would be free. What the heck was I doing here, anyway?

I loved spring. The weather was still cool (under 80 degrees) but the winter winds began to diminish; they blew from the south, now—gentle Trade Winds.

On one particular day Peter was taking a cigarette inventory in Cheap Charlie's when he received a phone call from a surveyor in Nassau. After the usual greetings, he cut to the chase. "Peter, I've been hired to survey the cay."

"Really? How come?" Peter was puzzled.

"I have no idea. Mrs. Smith has requested a topographical survey, but she gave me no further information. This'll probably take me and my men about a week. Is there some place we can stay?"

Still puzzled, Peter replied, "Sure. I'll get my wife to give you a call to arrange things."

When Peter arrived home for lunch, he relayed the information. "Somethin's up but I don't know what it is."

Within a month after the surveyors' job was completed, another call came through. I took the call at my desk. It was Ken Adderley, a well-known realtor in Nassau. After a few pleasantries, he got down to the crux of his call. "Kate, Mary Smith is now actively marketing the cay for sale." I was totally taken aback, and there was a long pause.

"Wow, Ken. That's pretty big news," I managed to say in the coolest tone I could muster. How could Mary do this without at least letting us know her intentions!

"Sorry, I thought you knew." Ken sounded embarrassed. "Listen, I'll always call you or Peter before I bring a prospective buyer to see the property. Will that be OK?"

Somehow I managed a reply. "OK, thanks for letting us know. Will you keep us in the loop on this, Ken? After all, we have our employees to think about."

"Sure," he replied. "Will you guys be all right with this?" he added sheepishly. I didn't know what to say. I felt a sick feeling in the pit of my stomach.

"Yep, we'll be fine. Don't worry."

I waited for Peter to come home for lunch to drop the bombshell. What about our jobs? The employees? What was going to happen to the cay? I could feel I was getting wound up by the minute.

When Peter arrived, I was noticeably distraught. We sat down, and I relayed the information from the realtor. While I spoke, Peter listened quietly until I was done. There was a short silence before his hand came down as he banged his fist on the table. "Christ!" he exclaimed. "We break our backs to do a good job here, get the business into the black, and all we get is a slap in the face!" His thoughts were the same as mine: What was going to happen? Would we have to leave if the island sold? Could this beautiful island be chopped up into a development? We both agreed nobody should be told about this until we could ascertain the full picture. The thoughts of Mary selling the island were hard to shake. That evening I found it difficult to concentrate on my other tasks. At bedtime, sleep was a long time in coming.

Within twenty-four hours after the realtor's call, we finally received a call from Mary, most apologetic for not phoning sooner. (Maybe she found out someone had spilled the beans about the sale.) Peter answered the phone and immediately addressed the issue.

"Listen," she said. "You knew the island was for sale before you took the job." He gave me a look and rolled his eyes. "Don't worry, your jobs are secure, Peter. If anyone buys the island, they're going to need good managers to run it."

That was little consolation for Peter. After what seemed like an eternity, she finally hung up, and he was left holding the phone, not knowing much more than he did before.

As time passed, Peter and I continued to keep this information secret. We surely didn't want everyone in panic stations, since we didn't know any further details; Discussing this with any of the employees wouldn't be prudent at this stage.

Several weeks later, Mary called again. She had hired a production company to have a movie filmed about her island. A team would be arriving in a couple of weeks, and she asked us to help them as much as possible. Sure enough, the production manager phoned several days later and made arrangements for pick up of the crew and their equipment from the Norman's Cay Airstrip and for the rental of two houses for a week.

I told the staff about the movie-making project but nothing more. Everyone seemed thrilled to help. "What's the movie for?" asked Leslie casually. She was a person who was very intuitive. I knew what she was thinking. She had seen the surveyor come and go. She was a smart chick. She knew something was happening.

"Mary says she wants a movie to promote Highborne Cay," I replied. "She even says if it turns out well, we can sell copies of the tape in the store." Heck, that sounded like a good idea to me and a diversion from where the conversation might be headed.

Life On A Rock

When the crew arrived, I could see we would be comfortable working with them. The four crew members were jovial, respectful and skillful. I set them up in the North House and guest cottage so each person could have his own private room. Peter arranged for Becky to cook for them each night, and the store was free game for their breakfast and lunch.

They were no trouble at all. Each afternoon after their filming, they would meet with Peter to inform him what they would be doing the next day in order not to conflict with other guests. They filmed the harbor with yachts coming and going. They even filmed the birds and the natural habitat. They spent time at each guest house, filming the house, the views and trying to catch the ambiance of each.

Finally, the supervisor, Mark, asked Peter if there was some way he could get a shot of someone catching a fish. Peter, of course, lit up. He explained to Mark that we had two boats, one of which could be the fishing vessel and the other the filming vessel. While he and Mark went to check out our two boats, I was given instructions to find two or three guests who'd like to have a free half-day charter to fish on *Bookalukus*. Once this was coordinated, we were ready to go. Peter would captain *Bookalukus*. Don would act as mate. Dee and Bob, guests aboard a sailboat at the marina, were thrilled to be asked to fish for half a day, and volunteered immediately. I was commandeered to drive *MFWIC* with Mark and the rest of the filming crew. Leslie drew the shortest straw. She had to stay at Cheap Charlie's and run the show while we were gone. Everyone agreed to keep in touch by VHF radios.

Once out of the harbor, Mark asked Peter and *Bookus* to make a couple of runs across our bow so he could film the boat at full throttle. I'd never looked at *Bookalukus* in such a way. She was a beautiful boat, but under full steam, she was outstanding.

Her bow sliced through the sea throwing white water far on each side. Her bow rails gleamed as they caught the morning sun. With her outriggers swaying, she was a picture of a fishing machine. Mark's cameras rolled. After several "takes" we now followed Peter out to the ocean through Highborne's southern cut.

It was a perfect day. On the surface, the ocean was tranquil and serene as the cobalt colors met the sparkles of light which danced off millions of tiny ripples. The sky was cloudless. There'd be no shade today. We couldn't have asked for better weather. As we sped through the southern cut, however, I was reminded again about the *Odin* affair and the day Don and Pete put their lives on the line to save the sinking vessel. I steered well clear of those rocks.

It was now time to let the fishing begin! Don worked to be sure the lines were baited, and his fishermen strapped themselves into the fishing chairs while Peter worked *Bookalukus* back and forth in the ocean. Mark and his two crew members on *MFWIC* filmed various scenes to catch the excitement. We cut across the bow of *Bookalukus* to get special shots of the fishermen. We filmed the captain and the mate, working hard at the task at hand. We got sunburned. Where the hell were the fish? We made close cuts in front of the bow and behind the stern of *Bookus*. I knew these maneuvers were risky but *MFWIC* met each challenge. We all worked hard for ninety minutes. Take a break, Mark said.

Bookalukus remained out in the ocean, trying desperately to catch some fish for Dee and Bob. *MFWIC*, on the other hand, returned to the marina so Mark could have his crew check the work already done. Shortly after tying up, Mark came back to *MFWIC* shaking his head. I was busy cleaning off the boat, but his expression caught my attention. "We're in trouble." He paused and looked around, exasperated. "The tape we used for all those shots was faulty."

"Oh crap." That's the first reply I could muster. "Do we have to do the whole thing again?"

Mark thought a moment. "We need those shots to give character to the film. Yep, we have to go back out," he said, nodding to himself.

So, back out we went. By this time, Peter's half-day charter had caught a big thirty-pound barracuda, but of course we had missed the shot. However, Don came up with a brilliant idea: to use the Barracuda as a 'stunt' fish. The fishing volunteers were happy to play this one to the hilt. First, Don re-attached the hook and leader to the dead Barracuda and then to Dee's rod. Then he threw the dead fish over the stern. The rod bent with the weight of the dead fish, and it all looked very real. Roll 'em! Action: Don sets the hook. Don gives the rod and "fighting fish" to Dee. Dee fights the fish. The rod bends. Dee works the fish like a pro. Dee gets the fish close to the boat. Don gaffs the fish and heaves it realistically into the boat. Dee claps her hands and kisses her husband. "Cut! Great segment!" Mark yelled. Now that was fun.

Returning to the marina, Mark commented they still had further to go before the project reached completion. There was editing to do, creating the graphics, and adding the commentary and background sounds such as splashing water or singing birds. Mary would have to approve or change the draft, but generally speaking, our work was finished. As they began to pack up their gear, I asked Mark if we might have a few copies for promotional and marketing purposes. He promised to mention this request to Mary.

Several months passed and finally one evening, the mail-boat delivered, along with our regular supplies, a large box which bore a return address: Tremalino Productions. Peter grabbed the box from the mailboat captain and immediately began to cut the heavy tape that secured the contents. He raised the lid. Mark hadn't forgotten us. There, packed tightly against each other, were at least a hundred VHS tapes, all labeled 'Highborne Cay.'

It was late when we finished unloading the mailboat that night, but we couldn't wait until morning; We had to see the video. Don and Leslie came back to our house around midnight and as tired as we were from the mailboat work, we broke open a bottle of wine and sat down in front of the TV to see the film we had helped to make....and it was everything we hoped it would be. The tapes had been carefully and skillfully edited to produce an interesting, informative video of the island, complete with the great fishing segment.

In my heart, however, I knew that the video would only enhance the chances of the island's sale. It was a bittersweet feeling. I also knew it was time to tell Don, Leslie and the rest of the staff that the island was actively on the market.

⚜

As we moved into our third summer, Highborne was as busy as ever. Leslie and I kept up our morning walks before each day got started, and that seemed to help somewhat with the stress levels, but I felt I needed a break from the busy routine. During one of our morning walks, I confided in Leslie.

"I want to go solo, Les."

She glanced over at me as we headed down the east beach. "What do you mean?"

"Well," I said, "I want to get a decent hair cut." She didn't bite, so I continued. "I think it's time for me to make my first solo run into Nassau in *MFWIC*." Leslie stopped dead in her tracks and turned to look directly at me.

"The run is thirty-five miles over open waters, Kate; a ninety-minute run each way if all goes well," Les said.

"I can do it, Les," I stated emphatically, as we continued our walk down the east beach. In my heart, however, I knew the trip would be daunting, especially for the first time alone. But, I needed to make the trip, not only to get my hair cut, but more to prove to myself that I *could* do it—to complete the round-trip journey successfully on my own. The trip would be my first real taste of independence since my arrival three years ago. As we finished our walk, I told Leslie, "Once inside Nassau's harbor, I'll dock *MFWIC* at a marina near the base of the Paradise Island Bridge and then walk to the hairdresser's place, which is less than three blocks away. I'll be back at Highborne by early afternoon."

Our walk ended at Cheap Charlie's. I could tell by the way he sucked air through his teeth that Peter didn't think much of the idea, either. But, he kept his thoughts to himself.

The next day the weather seemed suitable for the trip. "Kate," Pete told me, "keep your radio on at all times and I'll stay in touch." I knew he was concerned. But as I left the harbor, I felt comfortable in my *MFWIC*. Over the past few months I had become quite adept at captaining her. My docking had really improved, and I had learned to handle her in a rough sea. I had sanded and re-stained the teak and had put a new canvas cover over the helmsman's station. She looked fantastic.

It was a beautiful morning when I left Highborne and crossed the Yellow Banks to Nassau. A Danforth Compass sat on the dashboard, and that was all I needed. *MFWIC* had been motoring along at a good clip and although I liked this thought of being independent and going to Nassau by myself, at some point in the trip, there was thirty minutes when *MFWIC* and I were totally out of sight of land. It was just me, my boat and the ocean.

I was glad when I finally saw the hotels on Paradise Island come into view along the horizon.

In Nassau, all had gone well. I now sported a new haircut and even had time to stop at the supermarket for some precious items such as capers, water chestnuts and dog biscuits. Walking back to the marina where *MFWIC* was tied, I again asked myself, was this what I wanted—this style of living and working on a rock in the out islands? Another one and one-half hour's boat ride to return home seemed a long trek just to get a hair cut.

On the other hand, Highborne had no traffic issues, no stoplights and no confusion of a metropolis like Nassau. Yes, it was often inconvenient, and yes, we were working far too hard, but it was a trade-off. We had the ocean at our doorstep, and the trade winds blowing through the windows of our house, high on the hill.

As I untied *MFWIC* and fired up the two outboards, I knew at some point the scales would weight the other direction. But for now, the trade-off was still good. I was ready to get back to the island.

I was halfway across the banks when the rain clouds came. They had been building up in the south since leaving Nassau, and I knew I had to go through them to get home. I didn't like thunder and lightning at the best of times, but out on the ocean, it was troubling to see the purple clouds just waiting to engulf *MFWIC*. I slowed down just long enough to drop the outriggers along the gunwales and radio Highborne to let them know the weather had changed. Of course there was nothing anyone could do to help me; I had to go through the storm to get home. It was as simple as that.

The rain pelted *MFWIC's* canvas and stung my face like needles. I winced each time the lightning cracked and the thunder rolled, as the little boat bounced around like a cork in the rough seas. But I had to push on through the storm. My compass

191

was very important now; Visibility was poor with the heavy rain. However, the rainstorm had mercifully calmed the ocean so I asked *MFWIC* for a little more speed. Thankfully, twenty minutes later, the rain suddenly stopped and the sun appeared. This was typical tropical weather, and I gave a sigh of relief. The groceries were wet, and my new hair-do looked a mess, but the storm had passed. Now I was anxious to get home. It had taken most of the day just to get my hair cut. As I picked up Highborne on the horizon, the thought of a trade-off began to creep into my mind again. Was this all worth it? Was this still fun? I pushed those thoughts from my mind quickly as I pulled into the Harbor.

We were into late July when Eric and Darnelle arrived for their semi-annual visit. "Highborne Cay, Highborne Cay, this is *Steppin' Up* calling." We always looked forward to having them at the marina. Both Eric and Darnelle were divers from Spanish Wells, a small settlement on the island of Eleuthera about sixty-five miles north of Highborne. They came to Highborne several times a year for two to three weeks at a time to spear for fish and lobster and eke out a meager living. "Got any space for us for the next couple of weeks?" Darnelle boomed into the radio.

Don picked up the call from Cheap Charlie's. "C'mon in. We'll fix you up."

Steppin' Up was twenty-seven feet long, a home-made affair with a tiny cabin that served their purposes with two bunks and space for a small stove, sink and a head (toilet) and a precious VCR. Everything that needed refrigeration was kept in a cooler that sat in the outside cockpit behind the cabin. Their catch of fish and lobster were stored in a chest freezer next to the cooler.

In the Bahamas, it has always been against the law to use any scuba gear or spear guns to capture fish or lobster. Divers must 'free-dive,' meaning they can use goggles, flippers and a snorkel to dive and spear their catch with a wooden sling and spear. People who have done this for a living will tell anyone that spear-fishing is physically challenging work. It requires stamina to hold the breath for long dives down thirty feet or more, be accurate with a spear and sling, retrieve the spear once it has been shot from the sling, and be resourceful with one's energy to insure enough oxygen is left for the journey up to the surface. Diving is a tough way to earn a living.

Eric had a bad leg as a result of a motorcycle accident many years ago, and the constant diving in salt water had not been kind to his injury. He had developed osteomyelitis (an infection in the bone) in his left leg which always plagued him with pain, and he walked with a limp. Eric's resolution of this issue was Tom on *Damselfish*.

Tom's expertise was in critical wound care, so he was in the best position to help. When Tom and Lynn came to visit, they always brought special bandages and a 'boot' for Eric to help heal his leg.

Darnelle, a tall, hefty gal, usually drove *Steppin' Up*'s dinghy while Eric did the spearing. When their day was done, it was fascinating to watch her clean the fish. She could clean a snapper in about thirty seconds flat. In the evenings after supper, she would often be found sitting on the dock with her crochet needles and yarn, making items to sell back home.

We loved Eric and Darnelle. They were down-to-earth people who had taken life's whacks and were never disheartened. It was our custom always to give them free dock space and reduced electric rates as they eked out a difficult existence in our area.

Life On A Rock

Peter, Don and I were all working near Cheap Charlie's when Eric and Darnelle motored into the harbor on that hot day in August. Eric waved at all of us to come over to his boat as they tied up. Excitement was in his voice. "There's a huge whale—beached itself up at Ship Channel," he told us. He and Darnelle had seen the animal flailing around in the shallow waters near the beach at Ship Channel Cay, a few miles north of us. "Ain't never seen nothin' like it," he added, shaking his head.

"Don't think nobody else seen this kind o' thing," Darnelle added. "What could've made that big creature swim in from the ocean, go through the cut at Ship Channel, and then turn itself right 'round and swim up onto the beach? It's a sad sight, if you ask me."

"Hey, let's take *MFWIC* and run up there," I said. Peter and Don couldn't go because the docks were busy that day, but Darnelle, Leslie and I decided to have a closer look. In *MFWIC* it was about a twenty-minute run.

When we arrived, we were shocked at the scene. "Holy crap, that's a monster!" exclaimed Leslie, as the three of us gazed at the beach. Lying in the shallows with half of its body out of water was a huge thirty-five foot Sperm Whale who was almost at life's end. Its tail splashed the water without gusto, and its struggling had obviously diminished since Eric and Darnelle had spotted it an hour before.

"Geezus, this is a pitiful sight," I said, "to see this beautiful ocean creature like this—in such a helpless predicament."

Leslie pointed to the big shadows in the water. "Hey, take a look at those buggers." Enormous tiger sharks were all around, waiting like vultures to attack. They were black as the ace of spades, and up to nine feet in length, as they slowly swam back and forth. As we got closer to the whale, we also got nearer to the sharks. One tiger shark swam without fear directly under *MFWIC*'s hull.

194

My mouth dropped as I saw him slither beneath us; The shark's body spanned both sides of the boat. These were big and dangerous fish. "Don't anyone fall overboard," Darnelle warned.

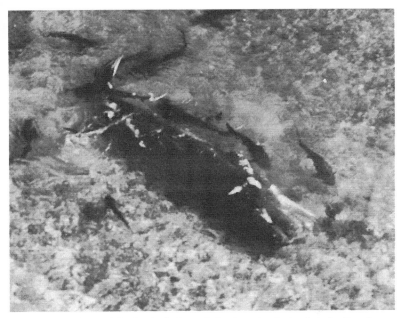

Aerial photo of the dead whale and the tiger sharks in their feeding frenzy.

We motored around for about an hour, watching to see if this big whale could possibly get itself turned around and back out to sea. It wasn't happening. Finally, one of the big tiger sharks could wait no longer. He streaked in at full throttle, mouth wide, and rammed his teeth into the whale's side. His jaws violently shook from side to side trying to free the flesh he now had securely in his jaw. There was much splashing, both from the shark and the whale. Once the feeding started, however, it turned into a frenzy. All the sharks now became agitated as blood seeped out into the water. It wasn't long before they were all feeding off the whale. There was nothing we could do. The animal was too big to move. We had to sit and watch nature take its course.

Life On A Rock

When we returned to Highborne to report our findings, Peter, Don and Eric decided they would make a trip up there the next day. They were thinking they'd each like to have a whale's tooth. Peter thought we should notify the Exuma Cays Land & Sea Park headquarters, based at Waderick Wells about thirty miles south of us. This national park was the only underwater sea park in the world. Its existence, development and purpose fell under the responsibility of the Bahamas National Trust and focused on the preservation of the environment. Peter called Ray Darville, the Park Warden, who wanted to come and have a look, so everyone decided to wait for the warden's arrival and then make a proper excursion for whales' teeth.

Unfortunately, however, the Warden was two days late in arriving. By the time the excursion took place, the whale had been dead for several days and the stench was beyond belief. The water shimmered with whale oil and half the whale's body had been torn away by the ruthless sharks. The men quickly returned to Highborne for a couple of hacksaws, a bowie knife and some Vicks to stick under their noses to cut the smell.

The second time they left the marina, they were gone three hours. We couldn't understand how cutting out three whale's teeth could take so long. Little did we know that Ray was cutting out the whale's entire jawbone—for research purposes. Finally, when the job was done, it took all four men to lift the jawbone into Ray's seventeen-foot Boston Whaler where the sheer weight of the bone promptly put a hole in the bottom of his boat. As the men towed the Whaler (and the jaw bone) back to Highborne, Peter, Don, Ray and Eric were ecstatic. Peter and Don each got two teeth and Eric took three. Ray, of course, was still trying to figure out how he and his disabled vessel could get back to the Exuma Land & Sea Park, thirty miles south, with the jaw bones intact but protruding through the bottom of his boat.

The whale's jawbone

When they arrived at the marina, we could smell them! Their clothing, their shoes, even their hats held the stench. The whale oil in the water had coated the sides of *Bookalukus* with slick debris so she, too, smelled worse than a hot day behind a garbage truck. Their project had been disgusting work because not only did the whale reek, but the oil in the water had another stench, and it was hard not to get this oil onto their clothes as they worked around the big mammal. All in all, however, they were excited with their prizes, and they said the effort was worth the time and trouble.

Later, as the scent wafted behind, I carried Peter's clothes at arm's length between my thumb and forefinger and deposited them in the trash. The whale's teeth, however, were put on steps of the back patio so the ants could finish Peter's work. Soon they would be given a final cleaning and placed in the safety of the knick-knack shelves in the living room.

However, the question of the whale still haunted everyone. After Eric made some telephone and VHF radio inquiries, he learned that the U.S. Navy had been conducting special operations in Exuma Sound. The sound waves created by these tests may have disoriented the whale, causing it to go through the cut at Ship Channel and mistakenly turn into shallow water. We'll never know for sure, but I prayed I wouldn't see another episode.

As the third anniversary of our move to Highborne was approaching, Peter and I were finding that, with Don and Les to help us, the stress of the work had lightened from the burn-out job it had been over the past several years to a workload that was acceptable. I was still very tired at night; that never changed because of the physical and mental effort required in the job. But I began to sleep better, more soundly, and woke up quietly, without the jump-start which was usual when Peter and I were handling the cay alone. In fact, we could actually divert our thoughts occasionally from work to pleasure which helped me mentally to stay on a more even keel.

MFWIC was one of those diversions, although keeping the teak clean, the bottom scrubbed and the engines oiled was always a work in progress. She was a great little boat, and I continued to improve my boating skills. After my one solo trip to Nassau, I never got the urge to repeat the scenario; But, I did enjoy making the trip occasionally with Leslie as my navigator.

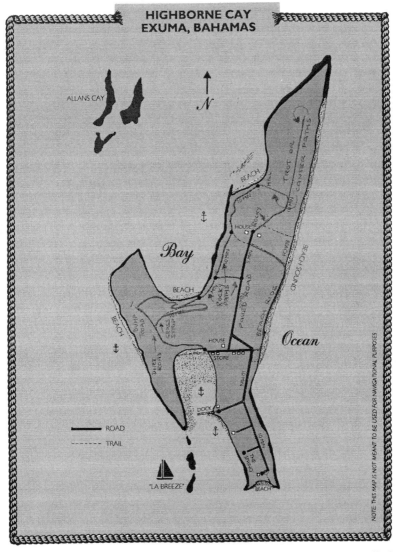

Map of Highborne showing riding trails. Courtesy Highborne Plantations Ltd.

Life On A Rock

Another diversion was my early morning walks. Further, over the past several years, we found that many of our clients enjoyed hiking. So, Peter decided to once again open up a variety of these old trails for our visitors to enjoy. Ted and our new hire, Christopher, were sent with their machetes and rakes each morning for almost a month to make the old paths wider and more accessible. They battled the mosquitoes as they chopped back the underbrush and pulled down the wild vines that were choking the trails. They raked up the debris and moved any rocks that blocked the pathways. They loved this job for one reason: anyone within a mile of their work area could hear their boom-box as it jammed with Reggae.

Soon the trails began to take a life of their own. Of course I was delighted as well, since those very trails proved to be suitable for Woody and me. Because I had some quality time off each week, I now had the opportunity to enjoy riding again. I could easily ride from Woody's stable, down the dump road, and connect with the newly made trails that now ran parallel to Horseshoe Beach and end up at the north end of the island.

This new part of the ride was an obstacle course with shrubbery and scrub brush poking out of the hard sand, but I was eventually able to set some rudimentary jumps along the route which I carefully marked out with red strips of material tied to nearby bushes. Although Woody had left his show-jumping career many years ago, his ears would prick up at the sight of each little obstacle, and he always appeared to enjoy his outing.

As we rolled into summer, the man who had been dating Victoria, asked Peter for her hand in marriage. Bill and Victoria had been dating since we left Nassau three years ago. Peter and I both loved Bill. We were thrilled with the engagement.

The wedding, itself, was another story. "Tor," I asked, "how can we organize your wedding when we're here at the cay? Weddings take a great deal of time and planning, and there's no way I can help while employed by Highborne."

"No problem, Mum," Victoria replied. "I've thought it through. I'll have a really small wedding, and I'd like to have it at Highborne."

I gulped. Could we do justice to her wedding out *here*? Would Mary consent? I could picture Peter rolling his eyes when I told him.

"I know you can't help much to organize it," Victoria said, "but I'll do everything from this end. Just give me a budget and I'll run with it."

Unbelievably, over the next few weeks, the wedding plans actually began to take shape. Victoria was true to her word. She had done the organizing. She and Bill set a date for late September. She had sent out the invitations, bought the wedding dress, found a priest to do the ceremony, hired the caterer (who was conveniently a member of the wedding party) and found a couple of musicians who would be willing to give up their weekend gig to have a trip to Highborne. She had secured a small luxury cruise vessel, *Ballymena*, for the wedding weekend that had ten luxurious staterooms and enough space to transport all the guests, the wedding party, the food, the champagne, the cake, and the musicians to Highborne. The priest was to be flown to the cay in Rosie's seaplane and then returned to Nassau shortly after the ceremony. Plan A was for the wedding to take place on a Saturday afternoon, the reception dinner would be that night on the lawn at Highborne Hill, and the boat would then return everyone to Nassau on Sunday. There was no Plan B if the wind arose or the seas became rough.

One of my jobs was to contact Mary Smith to see if we could 'rent' her island for the weekend. We needed every house on the island for those guests who were not going to sleep aboard the cruise vessel, and we wanted to close the marina that weekend so all of our attention could be focused on the wedding ceremony and the guests. I caught up with her by phone a few days later.

"No," she said, "you can't *rent* Highborne Cay." There was a nanosecond when my heart sank. "Instead," she went on, "I'll *give* you the island for your daughter's wedding weekend. That'll be my wedding gift to her." I was practically speechless. When I got my wits back, I thanked her profusely and told her how grateful we were for this opportunity. Before hanging up she added, "Don't forget to send pictures."

My other responsibility was to fix some sort of continental breakfast for all the guests for the next morning. I was to set this up on board the *Ballymena* so people could have something to eat before they returned to Nassau the next day. The breakfast was to include bloody marys and mimosas in five-gallon pump bottles, home-made honey buns, mango bread, cinnamon rolls and banana muffins to go with the fruit salad which I was going to prepare the night before the wedding.

Peter ordered a hundred boxes of last year's Christmas lights which came on the mailboat a month prior to the big day. On his days off, he took the job of creating a fairyland of lights on the coconut trees around the lawn at Highborne Hill where the reception was to take place. Then one evening at dusk, a few days before the wedding, I was invited to the official lighting of the coconut trees. As Peter flipped the switch, the sight took my breath away. I marveled at the magical appearance of the garden when several thousand little lights came on. It was perfect.

Due to limited accommodations, the guest list was tight; Only forty-eight people could be invited. Twenty would stay in the cruise vessel's cabins, seven would go to Coral Point, six would sleep at Harborside, four would be in the Guest Cottage and Highborne Hill would house the would-be bride and groom, along with the best man, maid of honor and two other chosen guests. Our house would hold another three guests, and the remaining two hearty souls would have to sleep on *Bookalukus* with the mosquitoes.

Victoria and her bridesmaids arrived the day before the wedding. It was cloudy and windy, and the forecast wasn't good. Peter and I listened to the weather report; a nor'wester was predicted to move into the Exumas in the morning. It was then I started to panic. Without an alternative plan, I had no idea what we'd do if it rained. The tables for the reception had all been set up on the lawn of Highborne Hill. Little did I know that was the least of my worries.

True to the weatherman's report, Saturday morning I awoke to thirty-knot winds and threatening skies. Luckily, Victoria and her bridesmaids were on the island to help. We had a big meeting in our living room that morning, and I was the only one crying! Tor, always on a even keel like her dad, didn't seem too worried. "Buck up, Mum. We've got a lot of work to do in only a couple of hours, and I need *you* to help."

She and her bridesmaids drove to Highborne Hill to move all the tables inside the house. How they were going to do it, I hadn't a clue. My job was to call the dock master's office in Nassau and find out if *Ballymena* could still come (with all the guests) in this bad weather.

I spoke to the Captain, Luther Smith. "Don't worry," he told me in a quiet tone. "We'll get there. It'll be rough, but these are Bahamians, not tourists. We'll make it. See you around two o'clock this afternoon." My nightmare was easing. We might be able to pull the whole thing off, after all.

Leslie brought me a Bloody Mary which she had concocted aboard *Waypoint*. "Here," she smiled, handing me the glass. "Have one on me and stay calm."

Ballymena arrived as Capt. Luther promised, and as we offloaded everyone and took them to their various houses, I couldn't help but think that God had intervened. Then I got the phone call. It was the priest. Rosie couldn't land in thirty-knot winds. That meant there would be no priest, and no ceremony.

Leslie brought me another Bloody Mary. "Why don't you let Captain Luther marry them?" she suggested. "Not sure it would be legal, as the boat isn't on the high sea, but it might do, under the circumstances."

I looked straight at her. "What a brainstorm, Les! Thank God *someone* is thinking in this outfit!" We hugged, and I went to find Tor to give her the alternative plan. She was actually going to have a wedding after all!

The skies were spitting that afternoon, and the wind blew, but nothing could stop Peter from walking his daughter down the dock and onto the boat to give her away in marriage. The main deck of the boat was under cover and proved to be the perfect place for the 'ceremony.' (Even though this was a temporary fix in lieu of the priest, the priest would make it official when the boat returned to Nassau the next day.)

Capt. Luther did a fine job under the circumstances. However, there were a few chuckles as he continued reading *all* the ceremony vows, until Victoria gently tapped his arm. "Captain, I think I'm supposed to say that part," she told him quietly with a smile.

Capt. Luther gave a big grin and replied with a wink, "I never did this before…"

Peter and Victoria walk down the aisle (dock).

After the ceremony, the guests were loaded into the backs of the trucks (where Ritchie, the week before, had built benches), and everyone was transported by truckload to Highborne Hill. The girls had done a great job of arranging the tables inside the living and dining area, and the food tables, filled with fancy dishes and flower arrangements, lined the hallways. They had set up the bar on the outside porch and the musicians played from the doorway. The wind howled outside, but nobody seemed to care. This was a night to remember—who'd ever thought there'd be a wedding on Highborne Cay?

Life On A Rock

The next day, I bounded out of bed with the sun and went to set up breakfast on the boat for everyone. Most people were still asleep. A few were nursing bad hangovers. By the time I had finished, the table looked like another gala buffet. I had stolen some of the flowers from the celebration the night before, and these now decorated the platters of breakfast goodies.

By ten, everyone was back on board, and *Ballymena* prepared to cast off lines. The next wedding would be dockside in Nassau several hours later where the priest promised he would meet the boat and do the official ceremony. Unfortunately, Peter and I could not be there, but we wished Tor and Bill well and gave them a hug. As the vessel pulled out of the harbor, we stood together waving good-by. I knew everyone had a great time at this most unusual wedding which would be remembered for a long time, if not by everyone else, at least by us.

Our vacation time was fast approaching when Leslie developed a back problem that could not be ignored. Don wanted her to see a specialist in the U.S. During mid-September, they took a week of their own holiday and flew to Florida to see a back specialist and have a few days of R&R before they dug in for the month Peter and I would be away. So, we were on our own once again, at least for a short time.

The day after Don and Les left, a familiar face appeared at Cheap Charlie's: Mr. Deleveaux from Customs. He arrived unobtrusively, and I saw no Defense Force vessel this time. But, he was just as rude and demanding as the time he came to confiscate *Waypoint*. This time he wanted to see the customs duty entries on the red truck and the beige van. The red truck was over ten years old and the van had been on the cay over a year. I could not understand why he would come all the way from Nassau to inspect such old vehicles. I would have given anything to say 'Deleveaux, fuck off!' But, I held my tongue and quietly drove back to the house to check through all the files to find the proper documentation. I actually surprised myself that I even found these papers as the red truck's documentation went back seven years before we had arrived. I felt on the edge of another victory as I handed Deleveaux the papers.

Deleveaux stood at the door to Cheap Charlie's, thumbing through the documents. No telling what he might ask for next. Finally satisfied, he passed these papers back to Peter, waved to a small boat which came and picked him up from the end of the pier, and he was gone as quickly as he had arrived. Never said thank you. Never said good by. Peter turned to me. "That guy is a problem waiting to happen." I couldn't have agreed more. Now we felt the staff was stirring the pot again; We had to be ready for anything.

That night my heart palpitations were bad; the stress of the day had brought on the arrhythmia. I knew it was time to see a cardiologist, but I hoped our vacation might solve the issue. I decided to wait. As soon as Don and Leslie returned, we would pack and leave for our little cottage in upstate New York. I was looking forward to a change in temperature and to see the fall colors once again. I found it hard to believe that three years had passed since we had moved to Highborne Cay, and I had to keep reminding myself to 'appreciate each day.' For now, however, our only concern centered on our vacation and time away from the cay.

❦

THE FOURTH YEAR

Rested and rejuvenated, we returned to the island at the end of October to learn that some prospective buyers had visited the cay. Our employees were starting to fret, and gossip was rampant. Even our clients were asking: What's going to happen to Highborne Cay? Why's Mary selling the island? How much would a five hundred-acre private island command in price?

We didn't know much, ourselves, until one afternoon, while I was at the house doing office work, there was a knock at the screen door. Standing on the front porch was an elderly gentleman in a fine pair of Bermuda shorts, a plaid linen shirt and leather walking shoes. I extended my hand, and gave him my name. After the usual pleasantries about the beautiful weather and enjoying his walk, he asked, "Are you and your husband the managers here?"

"Yes, we are. How can I help you? Do you need to go to the store?"

"Oh no," he replied. "I'm just walking about. This is such a beautiful island, and I want to take it all in! I'm not planning to change anything here. I want to leave it just the way it is." He waved his arm across his body in a wide swing as he said it. "I am a happy man, now," he added quietly. "I hope my wife will be happy, too."

I stood there with my mouth gaping, unable to utter any words. He shook my hand, I somehow managed a smile, and off he went to continue his walk over 'his' island. I felt like I had been hit with a bowling ball. The sale was reality and we were out of the loop.

Without missing a beat, I picked up the phone and called Mary.

After the usual greetings, I asked, "What the hell is happening, Mary?" She must have picked up on the change of tone.

"What do you mean?" she replied.

"Well," I told her, "we have a man walking the island who intimates he owns it. Maybe you can shed some light on this fact." My concern was evident. "This is a shocker, Mary. You promised you'd keep us in the loop." I could hear the whine in my voice. "Who is this dude, anyway?"

She stammered. I caught her off guard. "Uh…well…. The man is Henry Oxmoor." I could hear the embarrassment in her voice. "I'm really sorry this happened, Kate. The sale isn't consummated yet. I had no idea…." She paused, and then added, "I need to contact the realtor." She paused briefly. "Look," she continued, trying to placate me, "you knew the island was for sale. There *are* definite prospects. But, nothing has been finalized."

It was time to get serious. "OK," I began, "but we need to be more involved, Mary. I'd be grateful if you'd put Peter and me in touch with your lawyer. Are you using Rory?"

"Yes, I am," she replied.

I chose my words carefully. "Good," I said. "Any transition will need to be as seamless as possible. Aside from us, you have nine staff members here, some of whom have given you more than thirty-five years of service." I let the words hang there. If Mary didn't get the picture before, she did now. "Anyway," I said, "please keep in touch."

Little did I know that at the same time I was on the phone to Mary, Mr. Oxmoor had walked back to the marina and cornered Peter in Cheap Charlie's to ask questions about 'his' island. By the time I had taken the golf cart from the house to the marina, Peter, who also had been taken off guard, had been quizzed about work, island operations, life on the cay and the staff. By the time I reached Cheap Charlie's, Peter was standing at the doorway, looking quite bewildered. "Hey, what the hell is going on?" he asked. "I got asked a whole bunch of questions by some guy who says he owns the cay."

I filled Peter in on my own experience with Mr. Oxmoor and my subsequent phone call to Mary. "Peter, I think you'd better call Rory," I concluded. "We're going to have to tell the staff pretty soon, and we want to be sure we get the correct story."

That afternoon Ken, the realtor, called. I was back in the office at the house, so the call was private. "There's a consortium of wealthy businessmen in Nassau who were planning to form a group to buy Highborne Cay." Ken paused. I knew he wasn't prepared to give out names yet, but I asked anyway. He responded with the usual beat-around-the-bush skills that professional people often have. "The group hasn't been finalized. You know, I am sensitive to your situation and specifically concerned for your jobs. How do you feel about the prospect of a sale?" he asked me.

He was fishing. What he probably wanted to know was: Were we prepared to stay on, or would we take off for other parts after the sale.

I hesitated, not really knowing what to say. "I dunno, Ken. We'd probably come back to Nassau if things go south. But, we both love it here. We'll have to wait and see." I paused. "One thing is sure; Peter and I want to be sure the staff is taken care of, so we'll give Rory a call shortly." My mind jumped back to thoughts of the staff and the things they'd done to thwart our trust; but I couldn't overlook the fact that they'd been here long before us, and they deserved some sort of remuneration if the cay changed hands.

Before hanging up, Ken made a point of saying we would be kept fully informed from that moment on. I knew Peter and I would have to make sure that happened. So, every few days, Peter had regular discussions with both Rory and Ken about the sale of the cay. There was much buzz, but nothing had finalized. We had to play the waiting game along with everyone else.

However, one important fact emerged: In the Bahamas, when a business is sold, it is customary procedure to fire all the employees. The new owners then have the opportunity to re-hire if they so choose. Peter told me he would talk to Rory about encouraging Mary to pay exit bonuses to all the staff upon consummation of the sale. Those employees with long tenures would, of course, receive the best benefits. Now all we could do was continue with our work as if nothing was different, and keep our ears open to the 'jungle drums' for any news.

Finally, in late November, Peter got the call. Highborne Cay had finally been sold. The consortium which had been negotiating with Mary to buy the island had finally prevailed. Ken phoned Peter with the news. There would be five people in the group, and he proceeded to rattle off the names of well-known individuals from Nassau. Not long after, Rory called. Everyone was ready to close.

Life On A Rock

A meeting with the staff was scheduled for the following week. Rory had agreed to fly in to talk to everyone and give them their exit bonuses. One of the new owners, Alfred Daily, was also going to accompany Rory in order to re-hire all of us. As I went about my job that day, I couldn't decide if I was happy or sad; it was as if I was in limbo.

The following week seemed endless, but the day finally arrived. Everything went smoothly. The staff was ecstatic about their exit bonuses; we had purposely not told them about this aspect of the sale that Peter and Rory had worked so tirelessly to secure for them. Mary had finally agreed to the terms; each person's bonus was based on their position and their time under her employment. This fact, along with the accompanying check had left a good feeling with each employee and set the stage for a fresh beginning with our new owners. After each person's private meeting with Rory, Alfred Daily was there to shake their hands and welcome them back into employment with Highborne Cay under the new leadership.

The whole procedure was mere formality, but the employees loved the individual attention and the assurance that their jobs were secure. Peter and I were the last ones to step into the office for our checks. We shook hands with Rory and thanked him for representing the cay. He had given the cay some expert legal assistance during our tenure, and we chuckled as he reminded us about the situations with Bahamas Customs and Immigration; he thanked us for putting some excitement into *his* work.

We had a good chance, also, to talk with Alfred about the island's new ownership. He was very forthcoming with the information. The Cay was now owned by five wealthy individuals, all of whom lived in Nassau: some we knew; others we did not. The price they paid for the island was hefty, and they had plans to upgrade the marina docks and electricity as soon as possible, since their goal was to make the island more profitable. I wasn't sure how things would evolve, now that we had five owners instead of one, but we would take one day at a time, and hope for the best.

This year the winter weather came early. November was a rough month. Aside from the sale of the cay, we lost our good friend, Sandy Miles, to a heart condition. Sandy hadn't been feeling well for some time. He secretly carried his nitro pills and never complained, but I noticed on his last visit that he was more pensive than I'd ever seen him. Finally, he told us he'd be having heart surgery shortly after returning to South Carolina. He was apprehensive.

Just before Rosie flew in to pick him up for his flight to Nassau and ultimately back to Myrtle Beach, I poked my head inside the main salon of *The Other Ten*. He was sitting on the couch and beckoned me in. "Sandy," I said as I stepped inside, "I've come to see if you'd like to have a prayer with me before you leave." I'll never know what made me ask that question because Sandy always gave the impression that he was definitely not a religious person. But, he nodded and patted the seat next to him. I sat down beside him, and took his hand in mine. The words just flowed from my heart as I prayed for Sandy's courage, steadfastness and healing; for his wife, for the doctors who would attend to him, and for God to cover him with His love. When I finished, I looked up at Sandy and the tears that had welled up in his eyes quietly spilled down his cheeks. We stood, and I hugged him and told him to hurry back; I promised the fishing would be good. As he stepped into Rosie's sea plane, I waved, hoping it wouldn't be long before he returned. But, he never did.

For Peter, the loss was especially hard. Sandy had befriended him since the first time *The Other Ten* cruised into the marina. They shared stories, meals, recipes, and jokes. Their personalities were so much alike that they were almost kindred spirits. Their friendship for each other became a special meld of their personalities, and I was lucky to be a part of it all. Together, Peter and I had known both Sandy and his wife, not only as wonderful clients, but socially and, in the latter days, as dear and personal friends.

Death has a way of bringing us to the reality that life is short, and time is precious. It brought me up against the certainty that each day should count for something, and the people who passed through our lives should be appreciated for the parts they have played in making us better people. We treasured the time we had with Sandy, and we were thankful to have those wonderful memories to carry with us forever. But it also brought me to the reality that several years ago, when I was fighting cancer, I promised myself I would 'make today count.' Now, here on the rock, time was slipping away for me—Highborne was stealing my days without me ever knowing they were gone.

The early winter also brought Karen and Doug back to Highborne. They were the usual transient residents of Norman's Cay pond, coming in each November and staying three or four months before they moved on. They were a strange couple: Karen was a psychiatrist who had left her husband and her practice to sail away permanently with Doug. Who was Doug? I surely don't know, but he must have been someone special to draw a doctor away from her practice and her family. We first met this couple at a birthday party for Ralph during our first year at the cay, and we got to know them better since they visited the store regularly for supplies—especially rum. They were also friends with Don and Leslie, and that is probably the reason we saw them quite a bit.

However, this winter when they arrived, I began to notice that Karen was making subtle overtures to Peter now and again. These flirtations *were* subtle. I couldn't put my finger on it, but it was a feeling I couldn't shake: little touches on the arm, sitting close to him at every opportunity, even massaging his toes during dinner on *Waypoint* one evening. As time went on, when we were with them socially, I found my confidence deteriorating, and, for the first time in our marriage, I began to get pangs of jealousy. The first couple of times I noticed these advances, I tried to brush off the feelings as my silly imagination. But, as the weeks went by, I fell into a funk about it. I tried to talk to Peter, but he just scoffed off the idea. Naturally. What guy wouldn't love to have some cute chick be flirtatious? I wanted to talk to Leslie, just to get another opinion, but that was out of the question; Karen was her good friend. I was, once again, stuck on Highborne, alone with what I perceived as a problem.

At around the same time, my father was having a hip replacement in Florida and I thought this might be a good excuse to take my leave from the 'Karen situation' for a couple of weeks. It would be the first time Peter and I had been separated since moving to Highborne. It occurred to me that this might be a mistake—leaving Peter to enjoy Karen's antics. On the other hand, I thought that leaving Highborne to help my father might provide a distraction for me—straighten up my head, and make Peter realize how Karen's antics were upsetting me. As I boarded Rosie's sea plane on my way to Tampa, I can't ever remember feeling quite that frightened about the status of our marriage.

I have no idea what transpired while I was gone. I kept busy caring for my Dad in Tampa and pushed Highborne back into the far reaches of my mind. I didn't call, either.

Finally, on the fifth day, the message light was blinking on my hotel phone; it was Peter. When I returned the call, he sounded happy to talk to me and asked when I was coming home. I took a deep breath. "I dunno. Are Karen and Doug still there?" No tact whatsoever.

"They're gone," he replied.

"How come?" I asked, scarcely allowing myself to believe what I heard.

"They decided to move on," he answered. There was an awkward silence.

"Dad's better. Why don't I call you tomorrow." With that, we hung up, and I sat on the bed and cried.

It was at that moment, through my tears, I began to realize the job had begun to encroach on my happiness. With the sale of the island, Sandy's death and the issue with Karen, I would be watching the 'happiness' scales carefully from now on.

I needed to return to Highborne and to Peter. But, before I went home, I wanted to take a day or two to reassess myself, my marriage and where my life was headed, and I wanted to be sure when I got back to the island, I would never feel that low again.

❧

By mid-January, the marina was filling up with boats again. Business had started to pick up as the larger yachts made Highborne a sure destination. Peter had established several long-term contracts with owners, and this was excellent for business, since the cay could now count on a more permanent income from the marina. Increased revenues did not, however, always increase the bottom line on the P&L report. More boats meant the big generators had to crank out more electricity, and this resulted in increased fuel usage. The fuel costs, themselves, were escalating as well, so it was difficult to show increased profits when the P&L took all of these things into consideration. But, somehow we were managing to show an increase every year.

The main dock during the slow season.

Peter and I continued to push ourselves to improve business, improve the ambiance of the cay, and improve the infrastructure. We designed colorful welcome sheets and maps of the walking trails as hand-outs after yachts registered in. The watermaker we had purchased last year was a cash cow, not to mention the fact that now everyone on the island had wonderful water to drink. Never would we have to worry about a lack of rain again. Peter had done a marvelous job of beautifying the marina with shrubs and flowers, and Ritchie had built a low and exceptionally pretty natural stone wall that now formed part of the path from Cheap Charlie's to the fish cleaning station at the end of the pier. I had refurnished Harborside (on a very tight budget) and the boys had done a nice job painting the interior of the house. Leslie had greatly expanded the store inventory. We tried to improve the interior of the store with new shelving and better stock placement so that once inside, a customer would have a nice buying experience. Peter and I were pleased with the way things were going on the cay—with one exception: drugs.

Over the past few years, the drug cartels had discovered our country and our people, and marijuana and cocaine had become a scourge. With so many islands and small cays in the Bahamas' archipelago, the drug enforcement units were finding it almost impossible to keep control of the illegal drug trade that now ran through the Bahamas. Many of our Bahamian people, especially in the outer islands and away from the big cities, were ripe for a quick dollar. One drug pick up from a passing plane coming through from Columbia could reap thousands of dollars for a Bahamian with a small boat. If he was willing to collect the packages that dropped into the sea from the plane's cargo, and take them to the dealers for cutting and distribution, he would be paid handsomely. Most grass-roots Bahamians had never seen this kind of money, and greed took precedence over common sense and decency. It was a tragedy of the times as we began to lose an entire generation of Bahamians to the drug trade.

In our own area, Norman's Cay had been, from the late 70's into the mid-80's, a major player in the drug scene. One of the main traffickers causing havoc during that time with his blatant drug business was Joe Leader, a Columbian who had taken up residence at Norman's Cay. With a paved air strip on Norman's Cay, and Bahamian officials who were paid to look the other way, the island was an ideal location, away from the mainstream, where drugs could be easily transshipped through the Bahamas and then on to other parts of the world.

Luckily, by the time we took the job at Highborne Cay in '92, the D.E.A. had been called in to help curtail the drug trade through the Bahamas, and Norman's Cay was now under the scrutiny of a special detail of the Bahamas Police Force. Several police officers were placed there as an outpost in the late '80's to live in two little houses next to the air strip and protect the island and its runway from further drug activity. The U.S. had put great pressure on the Bahamas to clean up its act, and this was finally happening. Leader and several of his henchmen had been arrested, and the island, including the precious air strip, was now under the protection of a newly-elected Bahamas government.

After the two robberies in the early part of our tenure, Peter and I had become fanatical about crime prevention, with the drug trade as the biggest challenge. Boats would come in for fuel, and, as Peter pumped their gas tanks full, he would casually observe these vessels, making a mental note of people's faces or the cargo they were carrying. If a go-fast boat arrived for fuel, there might be big plastic barrels in the cuddy cabin, or Peter might see a tarpaulin covering something in the salon or cockpit. He was no longer just thinking 'burglary suspects' but also 'drug traffickers'.

After our first year at the cay and with the two robberies behind us, we decided to make firsthand contact with the U.S. Drug Enforcement Agency's Nassau-based operation. The D.E.A. was the only organization we trusted. It was a general opinion of many civilians during the 80's and 90's that some members of our Bahamas Police Force and some Defense Force personnel were, during this period, 'on the take' from the local drug dealers, and even possibly from the cartels in Central and South America where these drugs were originating. So, if we were going to be informants, we wanted to be sure we were informing the proper people who would act on the tips we supplied and, more importantly, keep our names confidential for our own protection. I made inquiries at the U.S. Embassy in Nassau as to who was the head coordinator of the D.E.A. for the Bahamas operations. I was pleased to learn this person was a woman, and I made a conscious effort to contact her personally. I introduced myself and give her some background of the island, its operations, and that Peter and I felt we were in a good position to provide information to help the D.E.A. in their fight against drugs.

This was a big step we had considered for several months. We knew we might be putting ourselves in danger. It was a known fact that drug dealers don't like people getting in the way of their business or their territory. They want persons who will help them, or at least look the other way.

But, the experience of two robberies had somehow changed us. Those two encounters had made us much stronger individuals. We now had a vigilante outlook. I told the D.E.A. chief we'd be willing to go that extra mile to help them, but in turn, we needed their assurance that they, too, would go the extra mile for us in the event that we needed their assistance.

The Chief was true to her word. She told me that Peter would report directly to her. She gave us her home and work telephone numbers as well as a cell number so we could reach her at any time, day or night. From that time forward, as strange boats came through the marina for fuel or supplies, Peter would be vigilant. One call to the Chief would result in a D.E.A. chopper being dispatched to our area, and often persons and vessels would be apprehended on the high seas after they left the marina, or they'd be arrested as they entered Nassau's harbor.

However, this was dangerous work. Several times the Chief called to thank us for our efforts, as drug interdiction had taken place on several large hauls as a direct result of our reports. The D.E.A. knew we were their friends. I sincerely hoped the feelings were mutual.

However, after occasionally thwarting a large haul, there was always the thought that crept into my mind: Peter's and my life could be in jeopardy at any time here on the island. I knew that anyone could come to the island, just as the burglars had done many months ago, and murder both of us in our home. The murderer would go unpunished because of the Law of the Land out here—that is, *there is no law.* To dwell on this aspect was not good, and I always tried not to get carried away with those feelings.

One particular day, I drove up to Highborne Hill to do some interior work on the house, and as I opened the front door, I happened to glance down at Horseshoe Beach. There on the beach, maybe seven hundred yards from the house's high elevation, I could see five or six people with two Boston Whalers pulled up on the beach. I watched for several minutes but could not see what was actually going on. It was broad daylight, and I hesitated to think this was drug activity being carried out, but I knew Peter needed to be informed. These were definitely not guests.

Purposely avoiding the use of the hand-held VHF, I took the golf cart back to the marina. "Peter, something's going on at Horseshoe Beach," I told him excitedly. "I saw two whalers with guys in camouflage clothing on the beach." Without hesitation, he asked Don to take over at the marina.

"Let's go to our house, first," he said as he slipped into the seat beside me. There he picked up his Remington, a pair of binoculars, grabbed some ammo and dropped them in his pockets. "OK, let's go take a look," he said, resting the shotgun across his knees. I drove him up to Highborne Hill where we could still see the activity down at Horseshoe Beach. A view through the binoculars showed everyone in camouflage clothing, and the boats that had been pulled up on the shore were now being re-floated and boarded.

"Do you think they're hiding stuff down there?" I asked, taking the binoculars from Peter in order to see better.

"I dunno, Kate, but I don't like it. At the least, they're trespassing. At the worst, they might be using the island as a drug stash."

We watched another few minutes before returning to the house to call the Chief, who promised to follow up. Peter told her that we, too, would also follow up here. We split up: Pete checked back at the marina but there was no sign of these two boats. I returned to Highborne Hill, but the boats and people were now out of sight. It wasn't long, however, before the thump-thump-thump of the chopper was heard. The Chief was as good as her word.

The idea of strange people on our island again brought back troubling thoughts of the robberies. I had an uneasy feeling for the remainder of the day, and that night I had difficulty falling asleep. The only consolation was that if we needed help from the Chief, support was only a helicopter away.

During February, business was booming as usual, and the heavy workload resumed. Peter and Don were proving they could work well together, and it was a joy to see Peter come home in the evening, happy with the day's work. Leslie and I, too, complimented each other. I would work in the store, and Les would do the 'runs' back and forth to the marina with customers. Then we'd switch, and I'd do the driving and she would mind the store. Having Don and Leslie as our assistants was a life-saver. We all learned to do every job so we could fill in for each other if needed: Leslie or I could each make up the dock plan, pump fuel, tie up boats and greet clients; Don and Pete each could serve people in the store, take guests (or staff) to the guest houses and meet with the staff each morning. I still had the bookkeeping to do in the evenings which often ran late into the night, but for the most part, the burdens of the job became acceptable. I think Peter and I would have quit long ago if Don and Leslie hadn't been there to help us.

Don was invaluable, too, with his mechanical knowledge. He and Isaac worked as a team to keep the generators in top shape, the trucks and other vehicles running, and tackling any other mechanical or electrical issue that arose. Between the two of them, I was confident they could keep us in good hands. The only time I doubted my feelings was one night, during a horrible thunder storm, the electricity went down. This had happened occasionally in the past and was usually a non-event with no reason to get alarmed. I was in the kitchen, washing up the dinner dishes when we lost power. Within a minute, I saw the lights of Isaac's truck pull off from the front of his little house at the bottom of the hill. He was headed to the generator room.

We lit the oil lamps and waited fifteen or twenty minutes. Nothing happened. "I guess I'd better run down there," Peter said, looking glumly out the kitchen window at the rain that came down in sheets beneath the halogen light in the yard. He went to fetch his slicker in the closet.

"Do you want me to call Don?" I asked him as he came back out with one arm already inside the slicker. I handed him a battery-powered VHF to slip on his belt.

"Don doesn't have any electric either," he answered. "He'll be up soon enough." Since the generators powered the entire marina area including all the yachts, everyone there would be out of power, too. Peter bent low, crouching underneath his slicker as he headed for his truck; the lightning forked through the southern sky in a grand display. I ran to unplug the computer and turn on my own hand-held VHF so at least we would have some communication with each other.

The oil lamps that I set about the living room flickered with every gust of wind and were a poor excuse for lighting. The dogs followed me around the house, foot to foot, cringing with each crack of thunder. I finally finished the dishes using a drizzle of water that was left in the pipes, since the water pump, which pulled the water to the house from the cistern, had shut down with the electricity.

An hour passed. Then two. Still the cay was in darkness. I could take the boredom no longer. I donned my rain gear and headed out the door. It was still pouring, and the water had gathered in large pools in the grass where the ground couldn't soak it up fast enough. I took the golf cart and splashed through rivers on the road as I headed towards the power plant. In the dark just ahead of me, I could barely make out the movement from flashlights near the roadway.

By the time I got there, I could see Isaac, Don and Peter were absolutely soaked to the skin. Peter was wielding a pick into the soft ground, and from the headlights of my cart, I could see a trench had been cut from the generator house to the road, a distance of about a hundred feet. Don was using a shovel to move the soil from the trench, and Isaac was carefully following the thick wire that had been dug up and now lay across his wide palms. The lightning and thunder had eased off, but not the rain, and torrents of water poured off their hat brims. Mud covered the overalls and shoes of each man, and in the dark it was hard to tell who was who. "What's happened?" I yelled above the heavy rain and wind as I pulled up.

Isaac looked up at Don and Peter. "We got it!" he replied. They had just found the spot as I drove up. "We gotta replace this whole segment!" he shouted. "Had to find a short in the main line that runs from the power house to that pole over there."

Don interjected, "Yeah, this ol' line had deteriorated so much, that with these heavy rains, it's been arcing underground. She's just plum burnt out."

"I'll go grab another golf cart for more light!" Peter yelled above the storm. They were now working to replace a fifty-foot segment of cable. I walked back to the house, leaving my own golf cart with its lights on for extra light. I was soaked, and the February wind had picked up. I knew I'd better get a pot of coffee on and take it back for them. It would be a long night for the men.

Finally, just a few hours before dawn, the lights blinked and electricity was restored. The yacht owners could finally retire to the comfort of their staterooms once again, the freezers in the store were back to cooling, the water pumps once more spit out water on demand, and we were returned to "situation normal." However, living on the island proved that nothing is ever normal—just SNAFU. I promised to make a giant version of a Chocolate Devil's Delight, my famous pudding cake, to share amongst the men, and we were thankful that Don and Isaac had the knowledge to tear out the cable and put it all back together again, like new. But, it was also frightening to admit that we were so vulnerable—that one burned out wire was able to shut down the whole island at any time. What if, next time, we couldn't fix it? I didn't want to think about that.

❦

The March winds blew for most of the month, and the ocean was rough for many of those days. While giving the weather report one morning, I learned that a Haitian boat, probably on its way from Nassau to Port au Prince, had run hard aground in Ship Channel's south passage. Haitian boats were typically thirty-five or forty-foot wooden vessels, powered by sail only. This one was, however, a small freighter. Because of the strong current that ran through the north and south passages around Ship Channel Cay, the waters could be treacherous in bad weather. Furthermore, the south cut was shallow, and the vessel, traveling at night, had mistakenly chosen the south cut instead of the deeper water of the north cut.

When she hit, she started to break up, and the Captain, crew and passengers abandoned ship. Luckily, all the people on board had been rescued by a passing freighter, the M.V. *Cavalier* (the same vessel that brought Woody to Highborne four years ago). However, the Haitian vessel, itself, was now beyond repair and sat, with all its cargo, in the middle of the channel in about ten feet of water at low tide.

Pete and Don caught the news on the VHF at Cheap Charlie's and wanted to make a run to Ship Channel Cay to see if there was anything they could salvage. Because of the weather, business was slow, so Leslie stationed herself at Cheap Charlie's while the two men took *Bookalukus* for a ride. In about an hour, they returned with five bicycles, some lawn chairs and a gas generator. It was very, very rough so they couldn't do much salvage work; however, there were several cars and trucks on board which could have been ours if we could figure out how to get them to Highborne. Much discussion took place between Isaac, Peter and Don. If they *could* salvage those cars and trucks, each engine would need to be torn down and completely rebuilt, since the salt water would have done major damage. In the end, they collectively decided that by the time they called the M.V. *Victoria* to raise these vehicles to her deck and transport them to Highborne, and then put in the hours to rebuild the engines, the cost in time and money would have been prohibitive. The men pined briefly for their loss. Leslie and I were, however, thankful for the bicycles and the gas generator, and glad that all the people were rescued without loss of life.

Business was now in full swing once again. From February to August, we knew we would be running full at the marina almost every night. Each year that passed showed a substantial increase in business. The marina was now seeing more and more luxury yachts from the United States, and many were over a hundred feet in length. We were delighted that business had been continually increasing, and we were happy the marina continued to be patronized by our regular clientele from Nassau, many of whom were friends we had known before our Highborne days.

Procedures changed for us, however. With the five new owners, there were more reports to prepare and more goal-setting. Even with Don and Leslie helping us full-time, we were once again putting in very long work days, and I continued to do the accounts at night. The best news we had heard through the jungle drums was that our new owners were planning to begin Phase I of their improvements: work for the new docks would begin shortly.

As time moved forward, however, we realized talking about a project and actually doing it were two totally different scenes. Now, the perception was that everything had to go to 'committee' before any final decisions could be made. All the owners were pleasant people, but they were also hard-working businessmen whose other financial interests were often far more important than their new purchase of Highborne Cay. So, if we had a question, it often took a long time to get an answer. That was frustrating.

On the other hand, our new bosses left us to continue the administration of the cay's business and refrained from micro-management of the island. We really appreciated this fact and obviously did our best to please them.

Occasionally, I pulled out the imaginary happy/unhappy weigh-scales and took stock in my job and my life. Peter did the same, and together we made a pact that if either one of us found the scale to be heavier on the 'unhappy' side, we would jointly make a decision.

For now, I kept my thoughts to myself. We had been married a long time. Our years together had taught us about 'give and take,' and I knew it wasn't very long ago when Peter had struggled through his government job while I enjoyed the benefits, salary and prestige of working for a large corporation. Peter had supported and encouraged me through all those years, even though his job was less than ideal. Now, for the first time in many years, he was excited and happy about *his* job. He loved working outside, and he loved meeting people. He was good at his job, administering the island's day-to-day activities and long term goals with skills he had acquired when he managed the family's wholesale food business prior to its sale many years ago. At Highborne, he was once again the boss, and he loved it.

I, on the other hand, was again feeling the pressure of the work and the sense of isolation. I saw my job as a dead-ender. I saw the pay packet as under-appreciation. I was tired of being tired all the time. I began to hate afternoons when Peter would come home and say, "Honey, let's have a manager's cocktail party tonight."

In the beginning, we had started the manager's cocktail parties so we could meet our guests on a more social level and give everyone a chance to mingle over cocktails and hors d'ouvres at our house. It was a grand idea when it was new. Our guests seemed to love it—something different to liven up one of their evenings at the cay, and it gave us a chance to meet our guests on a more social level—to actually mingle with our clients outside the realm of business.

Now, after four years, these cocktail parties had become drudgery for me. I'd have to scurry around and dig up some ingredients for decent hors d'ouvres, get the liquor and mixers organized and prepare myself to accept a group of people into our home, many of whom I didn't know. Often I wished I could just have an early night, to crawl into bed at 8 pm for a needed night's rest. But an 'early night' was the exception, rather than the rule. Vacation was still several long months away. I prayed the scales would equalize once again. For now, they were, again, tipping precariously towards 'unhappy'. Maybe this would pass. Yes, I would keep my thoughts to myself for now.

As spring melded into summer, we continued to work closely with the D.E.A. and OpBat, the two drug enforcement agencies in the country. With the Bahamas' general election several years ago, the new party in government had vowed to rid the islands of the scourge of drugs that had plagued our shores for almost two decades. With the cooperation of the Bahamas Police Force and the Drug Enforcement Agency of the U.S.A., the Bahamas had access to more helicopters and go-fast boats for the apprehension of the drug criminals than ever before. Most civil-minded citizens were pleased about this fact, and so were we, with the exception of one night in the middle of June.

We heard the choppers about eleven p.m. Their thump-thump-thump could be heard from our house long before they arrived. We had recently prepared an area near Coral Point that would be easy for them to set the chopper down without the risk of hitting electric wires or flying debris. They always called ahead of time (by telephone) to let us know they were coming and what they were here for.

This time was different. This night, as the noise of the choppers got closer and closer, nobody called. I left my desk where I was balancing the accounts for a month-end report and walked out into the kitchen near the VHF to a window that faced the southern exposure to the island. Although it was dark, I could see the black shadows of two choppers in tandem. Neither headed towards the landing area at the southern end; instead, there was a sudden burst of bright light underneath their fuse-lage as they lit up the space below and began their descent to what appeared to be the dock beach.

Peter had fallen asleep in his chair in front of the TV, but with the sound of the choppers overhead, he was now fully awake and walked up behind me. "Where the hell're they going?" he asked, looking out the window from behind my shoulder. We both stared as the big lights gave indication that the choppers were landing at the marina.

"Holy crap!" I exclaimed. "What do we do now?" Without further comment, I turned to the telephone, picked up the receiver and dialed the drug unit's number. Something was going down, and we were out of the loop.

As I waited for a voice to answer, Peter grabbed his keys and left for the marina to investigate.

"DEA, Special Agent Hoyle. How can I help?"

"Hi, this is Kate at Highborne Cay, Exuma. Can you tell me what's going on? Two choppers just landed at our dock beach and we weren't informed. Can you tell me anything about this?"

"Ma'm, this is a routine search following up on a tip."

"A tip? A tip? What do you mean?" I must have sounded annoyed.

"Ma'm," he said, "The men need to inspect the marina area."

I took a breath. "Listen, we work really closely with your agency. We've helped you in several drug busts and have kept close surveillance on the island on your behalf." I took another breath. "May I speak to your director?"

"Ma'm, I'll have him call you as soon as he comes in the morning." Him? Him? What happened to our great lady Chief?

"Sir," I began, "we always worked closely with Carol Lunsford. She'll vouch for us, I am sure."

"Ma'm, Miss Lunsford's no longer here. She was transferred to Washington two weeks ago."

Damn. That was the end of that. Something had happened, and we were definitely out of the loop on this one.

The night was warm and sticky as I went to the golf cart. I thought about all our guests at the marina being wakened at this late hour. What I failed to comprehend (until I arrived at the marina) was that when the choppers landed on the beach, their blades had blown up a ton of sand, and shot it through the air, onto the decks of the multi-million dollar yachts that sat at dockside. Their sleek finishes had been literally sand-blasted, not to mention the mess on their decks and on the dock. By the time I arrived, our guests were hopping mad.

The D.E.A. agents in their camouflage suits scoured the bushes near the beach and behind Cheap Charlie's. They were obviously looking for something as they searched the area. As I hopped out of the golf cart, I could see Peter near the chopper, in the midst of a heavy conversation with the commanding officer. A few words drifted above the sound of the idle chopper blades: 'cooperate fully', 'sand-blasting these yachts', 'southern landing area'. From what I could glean from this, Peter let the officer know that we would cooperate fully with their search, but never again were they to land near the yachts. The whole scene was over in less than an hour, but the military tactics had made everyone very uneasy. Both Peter and I were embarrassed and upset that our guests had been so inconvenienced.

Two nights later the unit was back. This time, however, they landed at the southern clearing, and Peter took the bus down to meet them. We, again, had no idea what was going on. This time they brought two dogs, both straining at their collars to get to work. Peter remained at the marina with the unit, and the work was much quieter this time, since the chopper wasn't sitting on the beach with its blades thumping. However, it was disconcerting to our guests to see the D.E.A. for a second time within a few days.

Peter returned home, and this time *he* made the call to the D.E.A. After explaining our past work with their organization, he asked the officer in charge to give some insight into the landings over the past two nights.

The officer was reluctant but finally relented. "Mr. Albury, we received a tip a few days ago, and we have to follow up on tips."

Peter thought for a moment. "Well, sir," he answered, "Highborne has a great deal of unprotected coastline which we are trying to monitor, but I seriously doubt anyone would stash drugs at our marina. There're just too many people around for that to happen." He suggested to the officer several other islands that had similar types of areas and promised to give the matter some further thought.

About a week later, I was 'copying the mail' while working in the store and heard that a big stash of drugs had been found at a well-known location twenty miles down-island. The area of the island did, in fact, have the shape of a 'Y' like Highborne's marina area, and the stash of drugs had been found underneath a dinghy that had been overturned and resting near the beach.

I wondered at the time if we would ever win the war on drugs. With seven hundred islands in the Bahamas, and the drug trade well entrenched in a society of greed, I doubted if our little country could ever be clean again.

We were now just two months from September, a time that marked another anniversary of our job. I continued to hope I could keep myself together when our vacation, once again, would provide some needed rest and a change of scenery. I finally began to admit to myself that I had a case of rock fever, again. I felt trapped on Highborne with a workload that continued to cause stress; I hadn't been off the rock in almost four months, and I was discouraged with the lack of communication from the owners regarding an increase in salary that we had asked for some months ago.

To make matters worse, I went to feed Woody one morning and found him hobbling lame. The culprit was a roofing nail in the bottom of his hind hoof. Guilt overwhelmed me. I had been so busy the past week, I had neglected to groom Woody and check his feet, something that should be done each day. I was devastated. The nail in his foot could have been there for several days! How could I have been so remiss?

By the time he came up lame, the injury signaled immediate attention. Luckily, over the years, I had become very proficient with horses. I could administer injections, shoe a horse, and do basic veterinary work. Out here, this was a necessity. So, I gathered up all the necessary equipment: pliers, iodine, Epsom salts and hot water to immediately soak the foot, and bandages and gauze for the final dressing. It took about half an hour from start to finish that morning. However, I knew about puncture wounds in the hoof: It wouldn't be long before the infection drove deep into the sensitive areas of the hoof where it would travel, seeking to abscess at the top of the hoof. I prepared myself for the arduous task of soaking the foot each morning and evening for the next two or three weeks in Epsom Salts and water, coaxing the infection to drain. Each soak would mean a fresh set of bandages.

For half an hour at daybreak and again before dinner, I trudged to the stable for this duty. The soaking help keep the hoof soft and, in turn, helped with the pain. Woody was a trooper and quietly set his foot inside a bucket of warm water and Epsom salts for his twice-daily soak. In time, with the constant soaking, the infection popped out above the hoof. Once that happened, I knew things would be all right. The pressure from the infection had now been released, and the pain ceased almost instantaneously. Now all that remained was to keep the flesh wound clean and open with continued soaking for another week or so.

This was the first major catastrophe with Woody, and I vowed to make this the last. I scoured the machine shop with Isaac; I needed that big magnet I had used several years ago when I first made ready Woody's area. Rigging the magnet with a tow line, I dragged it back and forth across the ground. Click, click. The iron nails underneath the soil flew into the strong magnetic field. As the nails and bits of metal attached to the magnet, I had no idea of how lucky Woody had been. Shoeing my horse was one thing; having to nurse him back to health from a nail wound was another. I shuddered to think of all the problems Woody and I could have had, but were now sticking securely to the magnet. It had been a long haul to get him sound again. I said a little prayer of thanks that one errant nail had caused many others to be found, reducing the risk of further injury. But I also realized that the work I was putting into the horse far outweighed the benefits of the riding. Woody had become a true labor of love.

Towards the end of summer, my restlessness was starting to show. As hard as I tried, I just couldn't keep my feelings concealed from Peter. I was grouchy and complaining. Even Leslie noticed. But, it was a busy season, and whining didn't slow things down. So, I tried to put my nose to the grindstone and dig in for the duration until vacation could give me a respite. Les and I kept our routine of early morning walks, which helped my psyche. It gave me a chance to talk out my frustrations and get some proper exercise before each day began in earnest.

One afternoon in late August, Leslie and I were working at Cheap Charlie's when a phone call came from Indigo Island. This gorgeous piece of real estate was owned by a family in Britain. The island, somewhat smaller than Highborne, was located about twenty-six miles south of us, but was even more beautiful with high coral cliffs, a long white sandy beach, and a little harbor that had been carved out of the rocks to make a quiet berth for several of the owner's boats. There was exceptional beauty in the surrounding waters as well; the deep channels with fast currents around a myriad of nearby shoals displayed every shade of blue and turquoise that could be in an artist's palette. Anyone visiting Indigo Island could understand its popularity with the rich and famous.

Tom and Susan had used a very successful promotional program that advertised the island as 'all inclusive and very secluded,' and this idea had attracted many famous people including sheiks, a president, a prime minister and a number of people from Hollywood, all of whom were familiar names. Tom treated each rental as a confidential business arrangement, never revealing until later who the guest or guests actually were. This arrangement of leasing a whole tropical island appealed to many high profile people who were looking for a quiet week of relaxation without the worry of the media or other interested persons. Movie stars were repeat customers; political figures from abroad flew in aboard their private helicopters with their security personnel doggedly following them, as if Neptune, himself, presented a risk.

For each rental, Susan hired and flew in (via Rosie's sea plane) a private cook, a butler and several housekeepers from a reliable employment agency in Nassau. Tom and Susan acted as the host and hostess, and they were good at it. They were able to rent the island in this manner for about ten to twelve weeks out of the year. It was high stress work, but it had paid off.

On several occasions we had Tom and Susan for lunch, and they reciprocated. We enjoyed their company, and I often wished they weren't a 45-minute boat ride away.

On that particular afternoon, the phone call from Susan caught me off guard. After the usual pleasantries, she dropped her bombshell. "Kate, you may remember I told you that Tom and I are thinking about moving on. We've got some plans to move further south, and our boss would really like to meet you and Peter." I was shocked. I did not remember such a conversation, and I was stunned.

"Uh…" My voice trailed off; I didn't know what to say. I had absolutely no idea Tom and Susan were planning to leave, especially after purchasing a beautiful piece of property on a nearby island.

Susan jumped right back in. "I know it's short notice, but do you think you and Peter could come for lunch tomorrow, say around noon, and meet Mr. McSweeney?" She continued, "He'd really like to talk to you both."

I finally found my tongue. "I'm sure we can do that, Susan. Let me check with Don and Leslie to make sure we're covered, and I'll get back to you soon." I could hardly believe my ears. We were being head-hunted, out here in the middle of nowhere!

The next morning I fidgeted. I couldn't concentrate. We were leaving at eleven o'clock, but it seemed like eleven o'clock would never come. I curled my hair, put on some eye make up (which took much longer than expected), and was in and out of several outfits before I settled on a nice white pair of Bermuda shorts and a turquoise-print blouse. I grabbed a pretty straw hat from the closet and headed down to the marina where Peter was already waiting in *Bookalukus*.

It was a beautiful, calm day as the sun sparkled on the water. I always enjoyed an outing with *Bookus*, but this was especially exciting—to be asked to come for an interview! I was ecstatic, albeit, somewhat nervous.

Tom and Susan met us at the dock. Standing next to them stood the two housekeepers and the butler. Everyone was dressed in shirts and skirts of matching red-and-pink flowered fabric, and it was an impressive sight. I made a mental note that possibly their boss required this, and Highborne might do well to do the same.

While Tom helped Peter tie up *Bookus*, Susan asked me if I'd like to see the main house before going down to the beach cabana for lunch with Mr. McSweeney. "We've done lots of renovations since you were here last," she chatted, as we walked up the path to the house. I took note of the manicured gardens, a small swimming pool and the beautiful Bougainvillea in its vibrant shades of pinks and purples that wound its way up an arbor. Compared to Highborne, this was a real class act.

The house was cool as we entered. A tray with four martini glasses sat on the coffee table. Brightly-colored towels were artistically stuffed into a big straw basket near the hallway, awaiting a trip to the beach nearby. The furnishings were fresh and tropical, and I quickly noticed the whole house had been transformed since my last visit. Susan had done an incredible job. Her excellent taste in decorating was evident in every corner of each room. (I secretly thought how nice it would be to decorate our *own* guest houses without the restrictions of a tight budget.)

She led me down a long hallway, stopping at each bedroom to show me the tastefully furnished rooms in a tropical decor. "What I really want you to see," she said as she opened the last door, "is the owner's suite. I've worked hard to make it really special."

I stepped over the threshold and looked in, suddenly shocked to see people lying all over the bed. Jumping back into the hall, I tried quickly to pull the door closed. "Geezus, Susan," I whispered, "there's people in that room!!" I was embarrassed that we'd disturbed some guests.

"It's ok, Kate. They're expecting you." A sly smile crossed her face. When I re-opened the door, I caught my breath. My best friend from high school in New York, my two closest friends from Nassau and my wonderful sister-in-law, all with their husbands, were lying across the bed, laughing and crying "Surprise!" I stood there, stunned, my brain still trying to process this strange event. Peter, now behind me, whispered "Surprise...Happy Birthday, honey."

I finally got the scoop. Peter had been working on my surprise 50th birthday for almost a year. How I didn't catch him I'll never know. He had organized the event, flown everyone in from their various hometowns, and rented Indigo Island for the weekend. He had planned the meals, ordered the liquor, hired a one-man band and flew him to the island to play after dinner one evening. He had even packed my suitcase and my camera and quietly placed it in the boat so I'd have some clothes to wear for the weekend! It had been an incredible plan to pull off.

It didn't take long before I started to worry about the expense. On our meager salary, this was over the top. But, Peter assured me he and Tom and come to an arrangement, and I was instructed to forget the finances, at least for the weekend, and enjoy myself.

I did. Everyone ate caviar, rack of lamb, baked Alaska, smoked salmon, and filet mignon. The Rum Punches and Bloody Marys flowed as we partied through the weekend. We laughed, got drunk, and generally had a marvelous time. At the end of our stay, everyone packed up and piled into *Bookalukus* as we headed for Norman's Cay airstrip. Another charter plane was waiting there to take our guests back to Nassau for connections to their flights home.

When the birthday bash was over, I had an opportunity to reflect on the tremendous amount of work that had gone into that party weekend. Peter had looked after every minute detail, including champagne and donuts for everyone on the charter plane. He had orchestrated the entire event without giving away his secret. I was in awe. This man, this love of my life, had given me a party of a lifetime, and had shared his efforts and his savings so that others could enjoy a weekend on Indigo Island. For that one weekend, we and our guests were all the 'rich and famous', thanks to Peter. His nickname stuck: Peter the Great.

The beginning of September marked the end of our fourth year on the island. I found it hard to believe. However, 'Rock fever' was taking over, and we needed to get away. We hoped with our month's holiday we could rejuvenate ourselves with different surroundings—surroundings as simple as a shopping mall, a couple of movies (in a real movie theater) and a few meals at a nice restaurant. Such things had become a luxury for us, and we looked forward to seeing the autumn leaves of New York once again.

THE FIFTH YEAR

This time, it seemed more difficult after our return from holiday to return refreshed. I knew we would have to rally—to jump into our fifth year with vitality and energy. But this time, it was real drudgery to come back. The scales were tipping towards 'unhappy' yet again, and I couldn't shake the feeling. The isolation, the lack of conveniences, the long hours of the hospitality industry all pushed to the forefront of my thoughts. No raise had been forthcoming. No communication had come from the owners. The store's old building continued to fall apart, money was tight. I realized I had only a few weeks to pull myself together before the season started once again.

I finally mustered the courage to confront Peter about this and surprisingly, I found he, too, was feeling negative and down-hearted. Together, we decided that we'd give Highborne Cay several more months; then we'd seriously re-assess our situation. Until that time, we'd buck up and move forward.

Peter had a temporary change of heart, however, when he heard the news that the owners were finally moving ahead with a new marina. He learned this fact, not from them, but from a team of 'experts' who suddenly appeared at the Norman's Cay airstrip one day to do a feasibility study on the present docks and possibilities for further expansion. They had flown into Norman's on a charter plane, and one of the local residents there had called on the radio to say these unexpected visitors needed a pick-up.

This was our first major sign that things were about to change dramatically. Several more months would pass before another group would slide in under the radar with a set of plans showing the proposed marina with a dredged harbor, a turning basin and forty individual slips, plus several long piers which could accommodate vessels up to two hundred feet in length. Peter sidled up to the men as they gathered near the dock for a site meeting, and he tried to glean as much information as he could from their discussions. There were also plans afoot to move the big fuel storage tanks that sat on a hill not far from Cheap Charlie's. New power pedestals would be installed, giving the docks hundred-amp service to the larger vessels requiring more power. Included in the discussion (but not shown on any plans) was the fact that the 'store' in its present location would be demolished and a new store would be built within walking distance from the marina.

We had been at Highborne over four years, and it would have been nice if someone had asked for some input, even if only that. To ease Peter's wounded feelings about being left out of this loop, I tried to impress upon him the fact that we didn't need the burden of helping to build a new marina. We were hired as managers, not planners. However, Peter found little consolation in this spiel.

Our intuition told us this was going to be a very disruptive year to come. However, our primary concern would still be to our guests, insuring that their stay at Highborne continued to be a special experience.

One of the really amusing activities on the island was to take a jaunt to 'the spring.' Of course by the fourth year, we'd cut some wonderful walking trails for our guests, and the cay's beaches were still as pristine as ever, but 'the Spring' always brought a smile to the face of every person who had been here previously and explored that Seventh Wonder of the island.

The spring was shown on the printed map of trails which was always given to newcomers, along with a welcome sheet about the cay. People would ask if they could actually swim in the spring and our answer was always, "Don't forget your towel." They would hike up the road, searching for the markers that would point them to their destination. Following the not-so-well-marked signs, they would continue down a fairly precarious and hilly incline as if on a scavenger hunt. When they finally reached the base of the hill and followed the arrows into a dense path of vegetation, they would finally reach the spring, a big bed spring that hung precariously from a nearby branch. Most of the guests who had fallen for this pastime, especially those who had been convinced by other guests to make the hike, returned to the marina, laughing at themselves for being so gullible. Once in a great while someone was not amused; but, for those who were, we always laughed along with them.

However, about three weeks after our return from holiday, we were not laughing when Ted, one of the younger staff members, rolled the old Farmall tractor down that steep hill to the spring. It was an act of laziness, not to mention dangerous.

At the spring, as well as in various other locations around the island, we always kept trash containers strategically positioned so that no one would be tempted to throw any type of trash into the bush or surrounding areas. We relied on our guests to help keep the island clean. On that day, Ted's duty was to empty all these trash containers into the small trailer that he pulled behind the tractor.

The old tractor was a mess.

The spring was the only location he couldn't reach with the tractor; this part of the job required actually walking down the hill, removing the plastic liner from the trash bin, and then walking it back up to the trailer. Simple enough. (In hindsight, I wondered why I assumed 'simple' tasks were not always simple to island folk.) On that particular day, Ted had decided the old tractor could make the haul down the precarious slope if he backed her down with the trailer leading the way. The old lady struggled against the slope; Ted soon lost total control as her brakes began to fail and the whole apparatus jack-knifed and rolled over several times down the rocky incline. Ted somehow got free of his driver's seat on the first roll and landed in a pile of rocks where he watched his charge tumble down the hill and land in a heap in the vegetation with the trailer in tow. By the time he had limped back to Cheap Charlie's, he was a mess, both physically and mentally. "Er....Mr. Peter....er....the tractor got kinda messed up," was all Ted could say as he met Peter at Cheap Charlie's. He winced as he stood on one leg and rested the other.

"Ted, what the hell happened?" Peter showed little sympathy in his first response. Ted stood there, his shirt torn, a bad bruise beginning to show above one eye, and his left ankle had started to swell. He was one frightened dude. I am not sure if he was scared that he almost lost his life, or scared what Peter might do when he found out what really happened.

I took Ted back to his house for some clothes and then flew him to Nassau with Rosie to be checked out at the hospital. Meanwhile, Peter and Isaac headed to the spring to assess the damages. Viewing the mess from the top of the hill wasn't nearly as bad as viewing it at close proximity. They shook their heads as they stood looking at the old tractor; this was going to be a difficult repair. Parts were hard to find on such an old machine. Assessing the damage, Isaac commented that he had lived on the cay most of his life, and the old Farmall had been here long before he had arrived! The cay carried no insurance on such a loss, so there was no choice but to try to make the necessary repairs.

That afternoon, every man on the cay was called into action to right the ancient machine and assist in towing her back to the mechanic shop for further assessment. That old tractor was a tough piece of equipment. She had amazingly survived the fall without breaking up altogether. However, the radiator was damaged and needed to be shipped to Nassau for re-coring. The water pump, too, had been severely smashed, but nobody in the entire Bahamas could fix that part. It had to be sent to Florida. That meant we had to wait for Bill Marshall's next visit. He would be the person to fly the water pump back to Homestead, have it repaired and then ultimately return the pump on one of his subsequent trips. It was becoming obvious that much time would pass before this tractor would be fit for work again.

There was also the business of two new tractor tires that had blown in the accident. These had to be specially ordered, arrive at the supplier's, and then wait for the next mailboat delivery to bring them to the cay. When they finally arrived several months later, it took four men to lift each tire off the mailboat's deck.

The men knew repairing this tractor was not going to be an easy fix. However, no one guessed that it would take almost six months before she ever left the machine shop.

In retrospect, the accident could have been much worse. Ted only suffered minor cuts and bruises and a sprained ankle. I shuddered when I thought what could have happened had he been thrown the other way, under the tumbling machinery. When he returned to the cay a few days later, he told me, "Miss, when dat tractor start tumbling, I was so scared I felt like a black cat on Halloween!"

"Yeah?" I replied with a smirk on my face. "Well, you used up one of your nine lives; you better be darned careful with the rest of 'em."

When the tractor was finally on the road again in May, *The Gunner* had been docked at the marina for the past week. Günter, always the artist, asked Isaac to bring the old tractor to the dock for her inaugural run. As she chugged down the hill towards Cheap Charlie's, everyone in the vicinity stepped out into the road and applauded.

Günter gives the tractor a new life.

For the next two hours, Günter worked with his pallet of paints and brushes and when finally completed, he called all of us over to view his work. There, on the side of the engine cover, were the words, "Born Again." Next to this, Günter had depicted a big egg with the top cracked open, and many nuts and bolts popping out of the eggshell. Very appropriate. The old tractor had been given a new life.

The Christmas/New Years holiday was usually a stressful time for me on the cay. The marina was always chockablock with multi-million dollar yachts from the States, plus our regular visitors from Nassau who always booked months in advance for dock space. My job included, among the usual things, organizing the New Year's Eve party that was held at the marina every year. I found this really difficult, especially the first year. Planning the food and drink for well over a hundred clients seemed to be a monumental task out here on the cay. But as the years passed, the job became easier, and I began to actually enjoy the camaraderie. People on the various yachts were asked to bring a dish, and once I got a balance of appetizers, main dishes, side dishes and desserts, the rest was easy.

Highborne always provided the liquor and mixers, and there was a complimentary open bar all the way through the evening. Peter, Isaac and Don always took care of that aspect of the party, including the ice, beer and glasses. After Leslie had joined our little band of workers, we had more than enough people to get the job done right.

The only stress was Fred, our newest employee and a sporadic alcoholic. Peter assigned Isaac to the job of monitoring that situation. (I remembered last Easter when we'd done an Easter egg hunt using miniature liquor bottles as the 'eggs'. We had hidden the bottles all around the dock area the night before, but the next day, when it was time for the hunt, all the 'eggs' had disappeared, and Fred was as drunk as a skunk!)

This particular New Year's Eve, our fifth on the cay, we wanted to do something really special. Peter had the idea that maybe we could bring Willie Wilson, the one-man-band who had played for my 50th, to our New Year's Eve party, thereby making it even more festive with live music. The cay's budget couldn't afford his rate, so we humbled ourselves and passed a cup around to the various boats docked at the marina to help defray the costs. The last boat that departed Nassau for Highborne on New Year's Eve very kindly gave Willie a free ride with all of his equipment.

What a hit that party was! Everyone ate and drank to their hearts' content. The serving tables had a feast of stewed fish, steamed conch, curried goat and the usual sliced roast beef, ham, and turkey, and all the side dishes to go along with everything. Another table held the fabulous desserts and sweets.

When dinner was done, Willie started his music production. People gathered around to hear his synthesizers and electronic equipment that really sounded like a five-piece band. We had cleared a space in front of Cheap Charlie's where people could boogie all night to calypso, rock, soft shoe and the oldie goldies. The staff was always invited to the New Year's Eve party, but this year in particular, they reveled in the music.

I believe this was the first New Year's Eve party I ever really enjoyed while we were on the cay. I had plenty of help, I indulged in a few drinks, and I danced the night away with anyone who was fool enough to take me on.

Around midnight, we did the Junkanoo, an old Bahamian custom. In Nassau and some of the family islands, there was always a festival parade in the wee hours of the morning that followed New Year's Eve. Every year, groups, who made brightly-colored costumes out of cardboard, finely cut crape paper, some feathers, sparkles and glue, marched up and down the streets to the beat of goat-skin drums, horns and cow bells. The sound of ka-lik, ka-lik came from the cow bells as they were shaken up and down in each participant's hands. The skillful pounding of the goat-skin drums added a raw and unusual beat. Junkanoo was always a very happy celebration of the holiday, and groups were judged for their costume and their music using cow bells, horns and drums.

At Highborne, we mimicked such Junkanoo celebrations. Over the years, I had been collecting horns and cowbells for our guests to join in Highborne's own Junkanoo parade as it went up and down the docks. Isaac had a goat-skin drum, and he was a skillful drummer. His beat led our Junkanoo parade up and down the marina until his hands were blistered and raw. A friend in Nassau had obtained some used Junkanoo costumes for us from last year's celebration, and these added a splash of color to an already-inebriated crowd.

As the beat went on, somewhere in the back of my mind that night, there niggled an idea, however brief, that this might be the last Junkanoo for me at Highborne. Maybe it was the rum-and-cokes that allowed this thought to stealthily creep into my mind. After all, it was New Year's Eve and I was free to think as I pleased.

Through most of February, I had my first health issue since arriving at the cay over four years ago. Getting sick or injured when medical help is inconveniently many miles away often ends up being a crisis.

Don and Les had taken a few days of their vacation to cruise the Southern Exumas, and Pete and I were trying to hold the fort with a packed marina and full guest houses. I had a minor toothache for a couple of days that I was desperately trying to ignore. I took Advil to calm the pain and marched through several more days until Don and Les returned before I finally decided to fly into Nassau to see a dentist.

By the time I left the island, the pain had become serious. The dentist diagnosed a badly infected tooth, but he encouraged me to take antibiotics to get rid of the infection and save the tooth by doing a routine root canal treatment several weeks later. I agreed and filled a prescription at the local pharmacy before returning to Highborne to let the infection subside. However, within twenty-four hours of my return to the cay, that tooth blew up. I was in agony the entire night. Another trip to Nassau was mandatory.

Jerry Hughes, one of our good friends at Norman's Cay, had a little Cessna 172 that he routinely flew back and forth to Nassau. When he learned that I was in dire need of another visit to the dentist, he kindly volunteered to fly me in to Nassau the next morning. I elected to have the tooth extracted, but by this time, the infection was rampant and the dentist had to perform oral surgery to help clean up the surrounding tissue.

My Dad was living in Nassau at the time, and I bunked in at his house for the next two days. I couldn't believe how one little tooth (which had now been extracted) could have given me such a hassle over the past four weeks! But the big question in my mind now was: If I had not been living on the island—if I had been closer to my dentist—would I still have that tooth?

Unfortunately, that was not the major crisis of the year. Several months later, Don was working with Isaac to hook the fuel trailer to the tractor. The fuel trailer was an old converted boat trailer with a large three-hundred-gallon fiberglass container that was welded on top. Since there were no fuel lines running directly from the main diesel tanks at the dock to the generators in the machine shop, one of Isaac's jobs each day was to take the trailer to the marina, fill it with fuel at Cheap Charlie's, and return to the generators to fill up for the day.

On that day in May, the trailer hitch wouldn't unlock. Don and Isaac were hard at work outside the generator house, trying to jimmy this hitch off the tow bar of the tractor. The front of the trailer, now heavy with fuel, rested gingerly on a supporting jack, as the two men tugged and pulled at the hitch. Without warning, the supporting jack at the front of the trailer suddenly gave way, and the full force of the trailer, frame and all, came crashing down onto Don's right foot. Don was screaming, as he and Isaac now used every ounce of energy they had to lift the hitch off Don's foot. With Don swearing like a trooper, Isaac lifted him into his truck and came barreling down to Cheap Charlie's.

"Jesus, what happened?" asked Peter as he helped Isaac lift Don out of the truck and into a chair. "It's bad, man," Isaac said as he shook his head.

Leslie came running from *Waypoint*. She worked to get the shoe off while Don screamed in pain. "Please Les," he begged. "Leave the sock on!"

We could all get an idea of the damage by looking at Don's foot, now still in the blood-soaked sock. The profile of the big toe, the ball of his right foot, and an area just behind all the other toes was evident; the foot had been crushed. With his white knuckles gripping the chair, Don sat at Cheap Charlie's, waiting to be flown to Nassau on Rosie's emergency flight. His quiet groans were enough to tell us how bad the pain was.

I called ahead to the hospital in Nassau to alert them of the accident and have an ambulance waiting for him at Rosie's boat ramp. From there, he went directly into surgery to repair the foot. He stayed overnight in the hospital and returned to Highborne with Leslie the next day.

Leslie worked hard to keep Don quiet and settled the week following his return, to give his foot a good chance to heal. However, despite the best care on the island, the toe turned gangrenous, and Leslie had to take Don back to Nassau once again to have additional surgery—this time to amputate the big toe and part of his foot. It was a hard pill to swallow. Everyone on the cay was upset when they heard this news. Especially Isaac. It again brought to mind that our jobs could be 'high risk.' Working around fuels, heavy equipment and large boats can be a hazardous business.

Leslie remained in Nassau with Don for several more days until he recuperated enough to return to the cay; But even then, he was laid up for another week, with doctor's orders to stay quiet for six weeks.

Keeping Don 'quiet' was a work in progress. To prevent him from going stark-raving mad aboard *Waypoint*, we tried to find small jobs he could do from a chair in Cheap Charlie's. Leslie, Peter and I picked up the slack in the workload as best we could.

Slowly, over the next two months, Don improved. He was such a trooper during those painful weeks, but he was tough. Soon he was hobbling around with his bandaged foot, insisting that he was doing o.k. The pain was still intense, but he took his pain meds and pressed on through the healing process.

Part of Don's foot was gone. The same question came to mind: If he was in Nassau and not out here at Highborne, would the doctors have been able to save that toe? Were the precious hours it took to get him to Nassau critical to the results he obtained? Was the fact that he was too far away from professional wound care critical to his healing? These questions remained unanswered.

For the past two years, I managed to squeeze out of my tight schedule another four hours per week to meet a request that was made back in the spring of 1995. Ted approached me in the store one day. He was nervous and stood there cracking his knuckles. "Miss Kate, I wanna ask you sometin' real personal," he began, as he looked down at his shoes. Whatever he was going to ask had to be a grave question, the way he swayed first on one leg, then the other, never making eye contact. I waited patiently while he collected his nerve to ask, while at the same time, I wondered what could be this important. Finally, he blurted out, "I want you to learn me how to read." He wouldn't make eye contact. "What you t'ink, Miss Kate? I'd study real hard." I wondered if I looked as surprised as I felt.

"I know I can do it, Miss Kate. I know it." He spoke with sincerity.

I thought about the idea of teaching Ted. It would definitely be a challenge. "Ted, you know this is going to take a great deal of time for both of us. Can you sacrifice some of your free time to do this?" He nodded. "Are you willing to work hard, Ted?"

"Oh yes, m'am. I'll make you real proud!"

"I'll see if I can get some information in order to teach you properly," I said. "No sense in hum-drumming around. We might as well do it the *right* way, with the proper books and all. I'll make a couple of calls and see what we can do to get started."

Ted emphasized his main concern: "This would have to be our secret, Miss Katie. This would be 'tween you and me, O.K.? I sure don't wanna get no ribbin' from the rest of da staff."

"OK," I replied, "but, I'll *have* to tell Mr. Peter, as you and I'll need several hours of time off each week so we can get the job done."

"Gosh, Miss Katie," he said, now looking directly at me with a big wide grin that showed all his front teeth, "I never thought you'd say yes!"

So, for the next two years, every Tuesday and Friday, Ted would come to the house from 8 am to 10 am to sit in the office with me so I could give him instruction.

I loved teaching. Several years before coming to Highborne, I had coached the Bahamas Equestrian Team to a victory in Jamaica, and again in Virginia when the team travelled abroad to compete. I also taught riding to local children on the show circuit in Nassau.

In order to give Ted proper instruction and the best chance of success, I called on *Project Read,* a group in Nassau sponsored by one of the Rotary Clubs who provided all the material for the lessons as well as an instructor's manual. If I followed the instructions, it would be easy, I thought.

However, as I got into the program with Ted, I found my time was now stretched even thinner. I had budgeted four hours of instruction each week, but I had failed to consider all the extra work needed to develop a lesson plan for each class. I knew we both had to be committed: Ted to his homework, and me to the lesson plans. It was hard work for both of us, but I knew something Ted hadn't yet realized: literacy would open many doors. It was a chance of a lifetime for Ted, and I felt a personal responsibility to make everything work.

By early spring of '97, Ted was making wonderful progress and working at a solid third grade level. He was proving to be a good student and took his responsibilities seriously. Even if a busy day consumed all his energy, he somehow managed to save enough time for evening homework.

I'd been able to secure a variety of reading material from Nassau, and Ted pressed forward, eager to learn. I knew, however, that it would be a long and arduous process, and I hoped that, after all our hard work, he would not give up. I now had a great deal of my own precious time invested in his education, and I wanted nothing more than to see his dream fulfilled.

❧

Several months after Don's foot had healed, Marlin Marine, a Nassau-based marine store, organized a very large fishing tournament which was being widely promoted throughout the Bahamas. This was to be their first annual tournament. There were big prizes offered, including a nineteen-foot Boston Whaler, complete with a 115-hp. engine to the overall winner. Marlin Marine organizers were expecting a large participation of anglers, and the tournament chairman telephoned Highborne Cay to see if we'd be willing to be a weigh station during the two-day tournament. Work on the harbor hadn't yet commenced, and Peter thought this would be a great way to increase business, since we were expecting a big drop in revenue as soon as the dredging for the new docks began. As a further incentive, he decided to offer special dockage rates and host an anglers' welcome cocktail party on the Friday before the start of the tournament.

Within a week after Marlin Marine began to publicize the tournament, our dock plan for that weekend quickly filled up. It was going to be a successful and fun two days.

The boats began arriving around mid-day on Friday. By Friday night, we were so full that vessels coming in without reservations had to raft alongside other vessels who had secured their berths early in the afternoon.

Friday afternoon, Jack Sands, a good client of the cay, came looking for Peter. Jack knew the tournament rules called for four anglers per boat, and he was short by two people on his boat, *Charade*.

"Peter, two of my anglers backed out at the last minute. Would you and Don like to fish my boat with Betty and me?" Peter was ecstatic! He and Don were both good fishermen, but they never dreamed of fishing in the tournament. They were both like kids on Christmas Eve!

Both men could hardly wait for the next morning to arrive. They also realized, however, that with four people fishing, they'd need help in the stern. So, during the welcome party, Peter pulled Jack aside. "Should we consider getting a professional mate to help us?"

"Good idea, Pete. Got anybody in mind?"

Peter thought a minute. "Dudley's pretty good with the lines." Dudley, a boat captain whose yacht was at Highborne the majority of the time, had been a friend of Peter's since our arrival back in '92. Dudley wasn't pretty good; he was the best. He could rig a bait and tie a leader as fast as any pro, and his gaffing skills were outstanding. "If *Charade* has Dudley in the stern, we'll have a fair chance of doing well in the tournament," Peter added.

Jack nodded in agreement. "Let's get all the help we can!" he laughed, pouring himself another Scotch while Peter went off in search of his friend.

Leslie and I both knew having the men away from Highborne for two days with an over-filled marina wasn't going to be easy. But, we realized this was a great opportunity for the guys to fish on a really decent vessel, have a good mate to help in the stern, and have a chance to win excellent prizes as an added incentive. The two men had so little diversion working on the cay. This would be a great opportunity for them to have some fun.

The next morning at dawn, about thirty fishing machines roared out of the harbor at seven a.m. sharp. In the early morning light, it was downright thrilling to see each boat jockeying for position in a run for the best spot on the ocean! The weather was sunny, but the wind was blowing about twenty to twenty-five knots out of the east, so I knew we'd probably see some boats returning earlier than usual. Fishing wouldn't be easy in the rough seas, especially for the smaller vessels. Backing down on a big fish in rough ocean often resulted in a sea of foam splashing over the transom. On the other hand, rough seas could be an advantage to the fishermen; if they could handle the motion of the ocean, there was a good chance they might hook a billfish. When it was rough, the blue marlin, white marlin and sailfish paid particular attention to the bait as it skipped across the tops of the waves, looking realistic and enticing.

Each vessel carried a camera to photograph each and every billfish caught, since the rules of the tournament stated that all billfish (blues, whites and sails) were to be released. The photograph was final proof of the catch. This procedure was becoming the norm in most fishing tournaments as conservation had became a top priority for these beautiful, hard-fighting fish.

Some boats even 'tagged' their billfish catches. To tag a fish, the fish would be hooked and reeled in towards the stern of the boat. Once near the boat, the mate would use a tagging stick and small barb to insert an i.d. tag under the dorsal fin. The fishing line would then be quickly cut at the base of the hook, and the fish would be free to fight another day. If the fish was caught in the future, the tag would give information about where it had been caught previously, and researchers would then be able to track such things as migration and life span.

In the Marlin Marine Tournament, all other edible fish including Wahoo, dolphin and mackerel could be caught and brought back to the weigh station at Highborne. This was known as the 'on the dock' catch. Each vessel's limit was five of a species. These fish were excellent to eat. None would be wasted.

At lunchtime, I took a break and went back to the house for lunch. Eating my sandwich, I picked up the mike of the big radio and put out a call to *Charade*. Jack answered the call.

"Hi Jack! How's it going? Pretty rough out there?"

"Doin' ok, Kate. Nobody's sick so far!" Jack chuckled. "Anybody give up yet?"

I smiled. "Yep. A couple of boats came back a half hour ago."

"Yeah? Well, we're doing pretty o.k." He wouldn't give away a thing. No fishing boat in any tournament wants to give away their position or their catch if they're doing well. It was the same with *Charade*. I assumed they had a few in the boat, although I knew they were having a tough time in the high seas. *Charade* was a forty-eight foot Ocean Yacht and capable of taking the rough water, but even some of the larger yachts had quit and returned to port.

By the afternoon, the wind was howling. The call went out over the VHF for "lines up!" and all vessels had thirty minutes to return to Highborne. One by one they came streaming into the harbor. As they returned to their slips, the fishermen and their captains all looked tired from the day's fishing. They had banged around in five- or six-foot seas for the past eight hours.

I walked down the dock as Dudley on *Charade* threw the lines to tie up. Don looked up. He, too, looked weary. Fishing in rough seas is always a challenge. But once he caught my eye, he winked and smiled. "Hell of a day," he said quietly, as the grin spread over his face.

A large beach towel covered a stack of fish on the floor of the cockpit—fish that were larger and longer than the standard five-foot fish box. Peter threw back the towel to reveal the outstanding catch. "We hit the jackpot." He looked up at me from the transom of the boat. "And, guess what? The best part I can't even show you! We had to release 'em," he said, puffing up like a braggart.

"You're kidding…" I said with wide eyes.

"Me, too," added Don. "I hooked into a nice sailfish," he paused, "and, check out this big ol' Wahoo to weigh in." I looked at the big fish, now resting on the floor of the cockpit. "Guess he'll tip the scales at over fifty pounds."

I was stunned. What a catch! Dudley was grinning from ear to ear. "Pretty good day. These fellas made me work my ass off!" he laughed. "But, there's still another day's fishing ahead, and anything can happen."

The second day, at least seven of the fishing yachts declined to fight the rough waters. They'd had enough the day before. *Charade*, however, pulled out of the harbor with everyone else, ready to take on another day on the high seas.

This time everyone was quiet on the radio, an indication that the fishing was hot. Sure enough, at the end of the day, the boats came in loaded with dolphin, kingfish, Wahoo and mackerel. As the fish were weighed in, the on-the-dock scores were posted on the tally board at the fish-cleaning station. Don's fifty-pound Wahoo still stood as the heaviest fish of the tournament. He was a happy man.

I was shocked, however, when the release scores were posted. There, in large black letters at the top of the list, was PETER ALBURY. Aside from yesterday's catch, he had caught another billfish that second day, giving him a 'grand slam' (a blue marlin, white marlin and a sailfish) for the two days of fishing and enough points to win the whole damned tournament! I could hardly believe it.

As icing on the cake, when each of the boats' points had been tallied, Jack's *Charade* had become top boat with the most combined points. There was a great deal of black-slapping and hand-shaking that afternoon, not to mention the rum punches. With a total of seventy boats in the entire tournament, the team had done well. In addition, Peter knew his stern-man had been the best. The Boston Whaler would be Peter's, but Dudley would get a healthy share of the cash when Peter's prize was eventually sold.

Charade's whole team, Jack, Betty, Don, Peter and Dudley, would remember this tournament for a long time to come. Nobody could have asked for more.

By late spring, the marina work had finally started. The dredging equipment arrived in April at our busiest time of the year. We couldn't understand the owners' planning, and business began to fall off as the crane and bucket started to dig out the harbor and make a breakwater. The sailboat moorings were lifted out and taken away, so most of our sailboat friends left for cleaner waters and quieter places. As the water in the harbor became muddied, much of the sea life that lived there, including the rays and a turtle, left for other habitats. The noise from the dredging took away from the peacefulness of the area, and we watched from Cheap Charlie's as our customers passed us by and cruised to other harbors.

The sand from the dredging began to pile up in eight- to ten-foot mounds in places where there had been no sand before. Soon the dredging equipment began to carve out a deep turning basin. We went about our chores as usual, trying hard not to blame ourselves for the loss of business, and tried to improve the falling income by luring boats to our docks with special rates. But, things weren't going well. The crystal clear waters of Highborne Cay's harbor were now milky with the silt that was being stirred up by the dredging equipment. This sediment never settled; it remained suspended, moving to and fro with the motion of the water.

Life On A Rock

To make matters worse, the mailboat had been giving us a hassle lately about stopping in with supplies. On one trip, they forgot to unload ten cases of goods when she made a scheduled stop at the cay, and the Captain promised to call me when he could stop in again to drop these off. He never called, his boat phone was out of order, and Peter, who had gone to Nassau for a doctor's appointment, had tried unsuccessfully to reach him while he was there.

About two weeks later, a large yacht, *Santee*, was docked at the long pier. In the wee hours of the morning, the mailboat arrived at the marina, blowing her horn for dock space, (now occupied by *Santee)* to unload the ten cases of goods and one other item: Isaac's wife, Becky. She was returning from a trip to Nassau and needed to get to shore.

Because our house was a half mile from the marina, we knew nothing of the fiasco until the next morning. The mailboat captain had not called or contacted us in any way to inform us of this unscheduled stop. Peter and I were embarrassed to learn that Mike, the captain of the *Santee*, had left his bunk at 2:30 am to take his dinghy out to the mailboat that sat in the harbor blowing its horn. Mike had picked up Becky but did not have the space in his little dinghy for the ten cases of dry goods. The mailboat captain started yelling obscenities at Mike for not wanting to take our freight into shore.

When I heard about this, I decided it was time to investigate alternative methods of getting goods to Highborne. There *had* to be someone else who would like our business! The mailboat incident was just another example of an almost insurmountable problem that could cause a crisis at any time–and my brain had reached its limit.

Not long after that, I heard some sip-sip that several of the residents of Norman's Cay were unhappy with the service they had been receiving lately at Highborne. I could fully understand this. We were not the happy-go-lucky people we had been over the past few years. We were continually stressed with the construction, the lack of business and the poor communication with the new owners. Some of the construction workers were now living on the island, so all the guest houses were full of workmen, not paying guests. There were a number of weeks during the construction when I didn't think we'd even make the Friday payroll.

The north side the main dock was closed to boats as the barge and crane worked ten-hour days to set pilings and planks. Often the work would come to a complete standstill as the dredging crew awaited further instructions from the engineers.

Peter and I both knew we were losing out on the business of the 'high season' because of the construction. We crunched some numbers and had to admit there would be no profit on the books of the cay this year. It appeared that all the public relations and client services for which we had become well-known over the past four and a half years was now for naught. There was no way a raise or a bonus would be forthcoming without profits.

Just when I was becoming despondent over the situation, Peter got a phone call from a large condominium community in Nassau. They were head-hunting for a property manager, and Peter's name had apparently been submitted as a possible candidate. The interview was all very preliminary, but the option was now out in the open and we had a real chance to honestly evaluate our positions and consider whether we'd be interested in leaving Highborne.

When I began to ponder on such an event, I had such mixed emotions. I knew we had to stay impartial as we considered our options. We were really entrenched here at Highborne. To leave would be a major upheaval—probably as bad as when we moved from Nassau five years ago. But, Peter and I were getting older. The work was becoming almost too physical for us—unloading mail boats, pulling fuel pump hoses, lifting bundles of shingles and fifty-pound bales of flour. Another consideration was that new jobs for people our age didn't come along very often. Whatever happened, we knew we would have to be very objective in making our decision.

With Peter's interview, the floodgates had opened for me. Now that the possibility of leaving Highborne was real, this was a good time to give my imaginary weigh scales another test. Weighing towards the 'unhappy,' I summed up my thoughts in realistic terms: I was really tired. I was tired of the mosquitoes; tired of the long, hot days in the sun. I was tired of trying to solve insolvable problems; tired of the lifting and tugging; tired of having to smile all day; tired of having to use my evenings to do the damned paperwork–check-writing, Government paperwork, payrolls, cash balancing, inventory lists, you-name-it-I-do-it stuff. I could finally admit to myself that I was tired of staff issues, mailboat issues, and construction issues. With such a big load, the scales were, without doubt, weighing heavily on the 'unhappy' side. Yet, I knew the challenge of this job had kept me hooked…. hooked on Highborne Cay versus anywhere else in the world. I really loved to wake up in the morning to the sounds of the ocean, to have breakfast on the porch overlooking the island, and not have to drive through stoplights and heavy traffic. I liked having my own boat, fishing for dinner, having the most beautiful beach only a short walk from my front door, and of course, the opportunity of working at the most diverse and challenging job in the whole world! So where was middle ground? I realized

I'd have to take each day as it came, trust in God, and know that our direction would eventually be made clear.

As we moved into the summer of '97, I began to fully comprehend how confusing the cay was becoming. Workmen were staying in all of the guest houses. Carpenters were busy planking the docks, electricians were here to help install the new generators that had been ordered, masons were breaking down and re-building the old generator room to make more space for the new equipment. (I dreaded the day those huge generators would arrive; somehow they would have to be moved from the dock area to the generator room, and I thanked God I didn't have to solve THAT problem.) New electricity poles were delivered by barge and would soon be installed along the roadway as an upgrade to the island's electric supply. The dredging barge continually broke down, often in the middle of the harbor, a feat which managed to inconvenience the few boats who still tried to navigate into the marina.

In all the confusion, I found I had trouble sleeping again. My mind always seemed to take advantage of the night, when the house was quiet, when the phones stopped, the VHF radio was silent, and when my mind could think freely, whether to think about my own life or to solve problems for Highborne Cay. A sleeping pill would have been the answer, but that could become an easy habit out here on the rock; I did not want to succumb to it. Sometimes it would be two or three a.m. before my mind turned off enough to rest.

I prayed daily that our situation would improve. Communication with the new owners was still poor, and we never knew of construction issues until they happened. Even though he said very little, I could tell Peter was becoming discontented.

It was a tough time for the staff, as well. The construction crews were now our 'clients.' Guest houses still needed cleaning, green grocer duties still needed attention, shelves still needed stocking and pumping fuel was still in our job portfolio. And, of course, the mailboat continued to be my nemesis once a month. We continued with our usual responsibilities, but we were now running at a loss.

We tried to make 'business as usual' our prime goal, except that basically, the staff now catered to the workmen who had replaced the majority of our marina guests. The old capitalistic instinct of making profits for our owners was slowly being chipped away. Our incentives were basically disappearing. Most of our clients weren't here anymore, and we missed their company. Our clients had been the best in the world. Would things ever return to normal? What WAS normal? I had almost forgotten.

I was making up a financial report for the owners one evening when the phone rang. "How's everybody at Highborne?" Frannie asked, when I said hello. Frannie and her husband, Monty, lived and worked in Nassau and were excellent clients of the cay, as well as good friends. Their business was scuba diving, and Highborne had become a perfect spot for them to bring clients.

"We're good," I answered. "When are you guys coming to Highborne? I could use a couple of new bar shoes for Woody." Monty, in his past life, had been a blacksmith, but a serious war injury while on duty in Viet Nam had permanently sidelined that career. However, Monty was my mentor when it came to shoeing a horse. Before I came to the cay five years ago, he had taken the time to teach me the trade.

"Well," Frannie replied, "we're supposed to come down week after next, but we're gonna have to drop an anchor at Allen's Cay this time." I understood what she meant. Our harbor had become so cloudy, and Allen's Cay was still pristine and beautiful—a much better experience for her divers. "But, listen, what I called you about is this: My friend, Linda, here in Nassau, is looking for a quiet horse."

She paused for a second or two so things could sink in. "Wha'do you think? Would you be willing to send Woody back to Nassau? This nice lady, Linda, rides at my stable. She'd take really good care of him, and he'd still be yours. Maybe it could be a lease arrangement." She paused, waiting for me to say something. The silence hung heavy. "It's just an idea I had," she continued, "knowing how hard it's been for you to take care of him out there on the cay."

I was taken off guard at the first sentence, but as she spoke, the initial idea began to make sense. I had seen Woody suffer with the mosquitoes, the poor quality of hay, too little exercise and the fact that I, personally, had to shoe him every five weeks. Often I was at the stable giving him a brush in the dark because I hadn't found the time to do it earlier in the day. Yet, as much as I loved this wonderful horse and did not want to part with him, the idea could possibly benefit both the horse and me, especially now that the option of leaving was on the table.

Linda arrived by seaplane at the end of the following week. I liked her immediately. She was quiet, yet direct. She asked many questions about Woody and we talked at length. I told her his age (twenty-six) and all the medications he required. I showed her the special shoes he wore, and I explained about the degenerative disease that was in his front feet. Linda had traveled from Nassau just to talk to me and ride Woody. I felt I owed it to her to be honest. I gave her all the negatives, all the positives, and let the conversation take its course.

Woody had come to the cay on my whim. He had struggled with the heat, the bugs and a lack of attention when the cay was busy throughout the season. Like Peter and me, he had been required to adapt to the circumstances of out island living. His run-in shed was a long way from proper stabling. Now he had a chance to return to real civilization: quality hay, regular exercise, a fancy stall with plenty of bedding, and professional shoeing. I loved Woody too much to deny him these finer things. But, I secretly wondered if I could get along on the island without my horse. He was about the only constant thing I had here. He was about the only thing that kept me sane.

When she had ridden about twenty minutes, Linda happily admitted that she loved the horse, and I finally had to confess that I thought she actually would give him a better home that he had here with me on Highborne Cay. She wasn't a great rider, but my old friend took good care of her, and I could tell she would reciprocate. My heart ached as I made the decision that he could go to Linda, back to Nassau. Linda agreed on an informal lease so that I could retain ownership.

Over the past two hours, I had come to like this lady and her quiet way with my horse. I was concerned about her lack of experience, but I was impressed with her kindness and knew if anyone could make the relationship with Woody work, she would. I knew getting the old horse back to Nassau would be a real challenge, but the first hurdle was behind us.

For the next few days, I caught myself spending much more time at Woody's paddock than I should. It was as if I was trying to make it all up to him. I began to put aside precious spare time to brush his coat to a fine sheen. I trimmed his mane and clipped the stray hairs on his chin. I oiled his feet. And, in return, he would quietly rest his big head across my arm. As I lovingly stroked the errant hairs on his wide forehead, I wondered how I would ever be able to break this bond. I prayed that I had made the right decision.

July was upon us. The heat and the bugs were always our enemies in the summer. Peter and Don were hard at work on a repair to the water maker. I had taken a break about lunchtime to grab a cold drink and make some VHF calls. I loved working the radio in the kitchen, as the view from the window that looked south over the island was spectacular. The tops of the trees were virtually all the same height, so from my perspective, the vegetation that spread out below looked like a soft, green blanket over Highborne. As I talked, however, I was unexpectedly distracted. In the far distance, I saw a large cloud of black smoke rising in the air. I immediately thought of our friends, Bethany and Jerry Hughes who owned one of the few houses on Norman's Cay. Memories flashed across my mind; Bethany had organized a party for us soon after our arrival, and Jerry had volunteered to fly me to Nassau with my bad tooth. They were always willing to help whenever they could. I signed off my working channel, returned to the hailing channel and called Bethany.

She answered, sounding out of breath and upset.

"Beth, I can see a big black cloud down your way. Is it coming from Norman's?"

"I don't know, Kate. I heard a loud crash and went to look, myself." She sounded stressed. "Jerry took the car to the airstrip this morning so I can't go and check. I can't see from my house, either. Jerry flew to town this morning, and he's due back shortly." Her voice cracked.

"Why don't you call Ralph on the VHF, Bethany. Maybe he can ride to the air strip to check things out. I'll stand by the radio and copy the mail." I followed Bethany on the radio as she called Ralph. Ralph told her his car was broken down, but he agreed to take his bike and cycle the five miles to the airport to investigate.

Now I was starting to worry. The big black cloud began to stretch to the heavens, rising higher and wider by the minute. I was at least eight miles away from the Norman's Cay airstrip, and even this far away I could easily see the smoke. Not more than a couple of minutes went by when Peter called me on the VHF. He, too, had been following the conversations on the VHF and could see the black smoke from Cheap Charlie's. Soon everyone at the marina was on the alert and peering southwards.

"Should we go there?" I asked Peter over the VHF. "Maybe there's a house fire. Maybe there's something we could do." I felt so helpless, waiting there by the big radio at the house, but I had promised Bethany I would stand by. If she needed help, we could organize and deploy people as needed.

It seemed like an eternity before I heard Ralph call Bethany. He was on his hand-held VHF this time and was transmitting from the airstrip. His voice was hesitant. "Uh…There's been a bad plane crash, Beth. I don't know whose plane it is. It's…uh…" There was a long pause while Ralph tried to decide if he should continue. "It's burned beyond recognition."

"Oh my God…" whispered Bethany. "Two planes went out of here this morning: Jerry's and Dale's! Also, several charter flights were due in this afternoon…" She was on the verge of hysteria, now.

"Beth, this is Kate. I'll call Nassau Flight Control by telephone and see if they can tell us who's filed a flight plan or who's still in the air. Stand by." Bethany had no phone.

I immediately dropped the mike and picked up the phone. A nice lady answered at Nassau Flight Control, but I seemed to have trouble staying calm, myself. I couldn't catch my breath, and the words sporadically escaped as I tried to tell her what happened. "Miss, there's been a plane crash....at Norman's Cay, Exuma.....and.....could you give me.......give me the names of any persons who......who filed flight plans....today from Nassau to Norman's Cay?" I paused and tried to settle myself. With apprehension, I added, "We aren't sure...whose plane it is." There was a sinking feeling in my stomach and a slight tremor in my hand as I held the receiver.

"Just a moment, please," she answered, and I heard a shuffle of papers that I could only imagine were piled on her desktop. "Yes," she said, "I see there were two flight plans filed with us." I took a breath and waited. "Jerry Hughes filed to leave Nassau at thirteen-hundred hours; Dale Harshberger filed at thirteen-thirty..."

The nice lady started interrogating me about the crash, but I dropped the phone as I heard Ralph calling from his hand-held VHF. "Highborne Cay, Highborne Cay. Come in!"

Without even switching to our working channel, I answered, "Ralph, this is Highborne. Go ahead."

Ralph paused for only a second. "Kate, it's Jerry's plane." Ralph had been waiting at the air strip, trying to assess the situation when Dale had flown in and landed his plane safely. He had been about thirty minutes behind Jerry. It *was* Jerry's plane that had crashed and exploded, sending the dense black cloud of smoke skyward and visible for many miles in all directions. It was Jerry and his plane that now lay in a crumpled, smoldering pile of metal on the east side of the runway. "I'm headed to Bethany's house," he said with emotion and signed off.

We learned later from several vessels that were anchored in waters not far from the runway that Jerry had tried unsuccessfully to abort the landing and had lost control, hitting the tree tops of several casuarina trees. His little Cessna 172 had exploded on impact, leaving nothing but a fiery ball that had melted in a molten mass of metal.

Before departing for Norman's Cay, I sat for a few minutes on the porch, trying to gather my thoughts. Jerry, our friend, was gone. Jerry....the guy who was going to teach me how to fly some day....

Jerry had only been at Highborne a couple of days before. He and I had talked so much about my idea of learning to fly, and I told him that if we left Highborne and returned to Nassau, I was going to study for my pilot's license. He was my inspiration. He cherished his little Cessna 172 and encouraged me to go with that aircraft. "It would be the best starter plane for you, Kate."

How he loved to fly! He used to go into Nassau once or twice a week for Bethany's supplies and to do errands. He was so enjoying his retirement! He had renovated his little island house on Norman's Cay and was just beginning to enjoy life. Several times he had helped me get to Nassau in an emergency. I recall how he used to load his plane with cases of sodas, liquor and paint—heavy stuff—flammable stuff. I also remember him telling me the story of how the air traffic controllers in Nassau always kept track of him along his route. He'd say his call letters, "November 8-4-6-5-3," followed by "destination Norman's Cay—heavy." He bragged about the word 'heavy' at the end of his sentence; it always meant that his plane was, in all probability, overloaded.

I sighed. We would close Cheap Charlie's for the day and head to Norman's Cay. Bethany would need all the support she could get.

The toughest part for me was the funeral. Dale had a six-seater aircraft and volunteered to fly anyone to Nassau who wished to go to the funeral several days later. I was Highborne's representative. That morning, I had taken *MFWIC* to Dale's dock at Norman's Cay and tied her there. I walked the path to the air strip where Dale's plane was waiting. As I stepped out onto the air strip, I saw the mangled mass of metal on the edge of the runway that once was Jerry's little Cessna. I felt sick. Where was my courage now? It was buried under my grief. Turning away, I slowly walked to Dale's plane, never looking back. That day, I really didn't feel like flying. In fact, I was so upset that once I was in Nassau, I found it necessary, after the funeral, to hitch a ride by boat to return to the cay. And, it was a long time thereafter that I recalled the vision of the mangled N84653 aircraft that had once carried my friend, Jerry.

As July rolled into August, Peter's job offer was still in negotiation. There had been no communication from the owners regarding a pay raise, and I continued to pray for answers. I asked God for his advice by making it so plain and clear that it would be obvious what our future path should be.

The answer finally came by way of a phone call. I was shocked when the president of an investment firm called to see if I would like to return to Nassau. He laid out the job offer, including the benefits and bonuses. I listened, not quite believing what I was hearing. I was now over fifty, and job offers were scarce for people my age.

I told Peter about the phone call over dinner. With the possibility of Peter's prospective job offer coming to fruition as well, a clear path now appeared.

"There's no question, Kate." He said this with conviction. "I think you should take the job. Maybe it's time for us to move on. Frankly, I am as tired as you are. I love Highborne, but the job has really become drudgery."

He was right, of course, but we sat there, trying to weigh ALL the facts. Just the thought of returning to the terrible traffic congestion and the high crime rate were issues that we'd now have to face. We'd have to leave the island solace for a metropolitan life again. He reminded me how hard it had been for me to move to the cay; it would be harder to return to Nassau. My memory served me well.

We talked and drank coffee into the wee hours of the morning, finally climbing into bed around 2 am after wrestling with a tough decision. We had given five years of our lives to the cay—a contribution of our total energy. We had made substantial improvements on the island and had seen the client base grow continuously each year. We had set up more efficient systems and a means of checks-and-balances. Profits for the past four years had been up, and we knew in our hearts that we had labored well for both Mary and our new owners.

In doing this, we had been able to sample island life for more than five years. We had learned to do without numerous things which we used to call necessities, and we had found we could improvise with many things to make our lives a little more 'normal.' Island folks had taught us about their customs and idiosyncrasies, and we discovered much about ourselves in the meantime. It had been a great ride. But, it was time to close up shop, to move on to the next challenge. We hoped that two months' notice would be fair to our owners. For the first night in months, I slept well.

The next day, Peter and I walked over to *Waypoint;* Don and Leslie were enjoying their island breakfast of fried fish and grits. As we sat down in the salon, they must have guessed something big was about to be revealed; why else would we be disturbing their breakfast? Peter talked about my job offer and his and revealed the decision we had made the night before. Don and Les were noticeably shaken.

"Why?" was all Leslie could say.

"Five years in enough," Peter replied. "We should've paced ourselves better, I guess, but we're pretty burned out."

"Yeah," I added, "we should've picked up the 'island pace' by now, but we never got that picture." Breakfast was forgotten as they rose to give us both hugs. There was no concealing the tears. With all we had been through together over the past several years, we had melded into a good team. Even more than that, we had become special friends.

"You guys will do just fine," Peter said, winking at Les and giving Don a handshake. "I've taught you all I know, and you still don't know anything!" We all laughed at Peter, but each of us, deep inside, knew that this would mean a big change for all of us. Our team would be dissolved in a couple of months. It was a bittersweet moment.

THE FINALE

The next two months passed quickly. There was much to do. Boxes lined the hallway of our house as I started packing up. We were lucky in several respects. Firstly, Woody had gone to Linda in Nassau a month earlier, so he would not be adding to the confusion. (Shipping him out is a story for another time!) Secondly, our house in Nassau had not sold, and it was presently empty, awaiting our return. But, I was still in a funk about leaving. I couldn't put my finger on my feelings, but I knew that I would miss my morning walks on the beach, fishing for breakfast or even doing the green-grocer thing in the store.

A month before we were due to leave, Don and Leslie organized a big surprise party. The first Monday in August is a British bank holiday, and that was the weekend they chose to invite all our close friends and clients to a Highborne Cay bash in our honor. Ralph and our other island friends, and most of the staff were there, too. How could I ever forget Highborne Cay? For the past five years, this had been my life on a rock.

The morning of our final departure, *Bookalukus* looked like a Chinese junk with three dogs, a cat, a parrot, Peter and me, all stuffed in between the twenty-three boxes of our goods that were returning to Nassau. Packed securely up front in the cuddy cabin was the computer, the TV and the stereo, along with the two guns that had saved our lives. There was a filing cabinet full of personal papers and Pete's recliner that I had bought him for Christmas one year. We were chockablock full, and memories came flooding back to my arrival five years ago.

As we motored out of the harbor for the last time, I was compelled to look back and ponder on the changing face of Highborne. The new docks were almost finished, and the shiny new generators for the power plant had arrived. Highborne's ambiance was being altered from what it had been five years ago when we first arrived. I concluded change was not bad—just different. The stand of Casuarinas was still there, lining the dock beach and swaying in the breeze, this time bidding farewell.

I was filled with many emotions and reflections. I knew part of me would be left behind. The sadness of leaving this lovely place weighed heavily on my heart—this island paradise, frequented by many, but known by few. I was sad to leave the East Beach where I galloped Woody on sunny days at low tide. I was sad to leave the view from my house, looking south over the island towards Long Cay and Norman's. I had completely and utterly given five years of my life to this place without ever asking anything in return but a kind word and some encouragement. This island took me to the depths of my very soul. It taught me that I could do whatever was necessary to get the job done: nurse, policewoman, veterinarian, rescue worker, weather lady, whatever.

Now, as Peter put his compass heading on a northwest course to Nassau, I know that I wouldn't have traded those five years for all the tea in China. It was at that very moment I thought of Robert Frost's poem, "The Road Not Taken." Over the past five years, we had come along a route that few had been privileged to take, mainly because it takes conviction and individuality to comfortably walk the less-traveled road. In our case, it meant giving up the usual for the challenge of the unusual....and to find a different path than the norm. Our life on the rock had been a walk not taken by many others, and as I reached over for Peter's hand that now guided *Bookus* in a new direction, I realized we had taken a good path. I was honored to have been chosen to be there in that place in time.

K. Alison Albury is a born Bahamian, having lived and worked in Nassau most of her life. She was educated in the United States and earned a Bachelor's Degree in Business from Webber College. Upon returning to Nassau, she became an executive assistant and worked with several prestigious corporations during her career. She brings her organization and precision to the pages of her true book about life on a small island in the Central Bahamas where, accompanied by her husband, Peter, she spent a sabbatical of five years from the corporate world.

2129158

Made in the USA